C0-AVO-272

The Heritage of American Catholicism

A TWENTY-EIGHT-VOLUME SERIES DOCUMENTING THE HISTORY
OF AMERICA'S LARGEST RELIGIOUS DENOMINATION

EDITED BY

Timothy Walch

ASSOCIATE EDITOR
U.S. Catholic Historian

A Garland Series

"Highly Respectable and Accomplished Ladies:"

CATHOLIC WOMEN RELIGIOUS IN AMERICA
1790-1850

BARBARA MISNER, S.C.S.C.

Garland Publishing, Inc.
New York & London
1988

BX
4220
.U6
M57
1988

COPYRIGHT © 1988 BY BARBARA MISNER, S. C. S. C.
ALL RIGHTS RESERVED

LIBRARY OF CONGRESS CATALOGING-IN-PUBLICATION DATA

Misner, Barbara, 1931-
  Highly respectable and accomplished ladies.
  (The Heritage of American Catholicism)
  Originally presented as the author's thesis (Ph. D.-- Catholic University of America, 1981) under title: A comparative social study of the members and apostolates of the first eight permanent communities of women religious within the original boundaries of the United States, 1790-1850.
  Bibliography: p.
  1. Monasticism and religious orders for women--United States--History--18th century.
  2. Monasticism and religious orders for women--United States--History--19th century.
  3. Nuns--United States. 4. United States--Church history--18th century.
  5. United States--Church history--19th century. I. Title. II. Series.
BX4220. U6M57 1988   271'.9'0073   88-6006
ISBN 0-8240-4096-1 (alk. paper)

DESIGN BY MARY BETH BRENNAN

PRINTED ON ACID-FREE, 250-YEAR-LIFE PAPER.
MANUFACTURED IN THE UNITED STATES OF AMERICA

TABLE OF CONTENTS

PREFACE

TO THE GARLAND EDITION

Bicentennial, women's movement, pluralism--these are a few of
the words common to Church historians as the 1980's draw to a close.
They are ideas of particular interest to historians who are studying
women religious in the American community. While this study was
begun at the time of the Bicentennial of the United States, it may
now serve as background for the celebration of the bicentennial of
women religious in the United States.

The Ursuline Nuns were in New Orleans long before the thirteen
colonies declared their independence, but there were no women religious in the United States before the arrival of the Carmelites in
1790. Nine years later (1799) the small community that was known as
Visitation Nuns after 1816, was established in Georgetown and opened
their "Young Ladies Academy." The six remaining communities in this
study were the Sisters of Charity, Emmitsburg, Maryland (1809); the
Sisters of Loretto, the Sisters of Charity of Nazareth (1812), and
the Dominican Sisters of St. Catharine (1822) in Kentucky; the Oblate
Sisters of Providence, Baltimore (1829); and the Sisters of Charity
of Our Lady of Mercy, Charleston, South Carolina (1829). The Carmelites were the only religious in this group to come to the United
States from Europe as professed religious. Three of the four women
who made the initial establishment, however, were from the Matthews
family of southern Maryland. The other seven communities were

established by women who were either born in this country, or who had

lived here long enough to understand and appreciate the unique qualities

of the new nation and its people. During the period in which these

communities were founded several other groups of women religious from

Europe attempted to establish convents and schools but failed to make

permanent establishments. The evidence would seem to indicate that

their failure resulted from a lack of understanding of the situation

in the United States.[1]

By 1830, these first eight communities, which were truly

American, had proven that religious life could be both an attractive

way of life for many women and an effective Christian service in this

new nation. There was little talk of a women's movement, but it was

there, at least in a seminal state. The word, pluralism, is also

missing; but the readiness of the sisters to serve Protestants as well

as Catholics testifies to their acceptance of the concept. The sisters

in these eight communities proved, moreover, that it was possible to

support themselves and their institutions without an income from sub-

stantial dowries and foundations from government sources and wealthy

patrons.

In 1962, when Cardinal Suenens published The Nun in the World,

the rivulets of change that had been forming suddenly became a

thundering river and very few American women religious were left

untouched. During the years that followed, discussions, meetings, and

publications became our regular fare so that when the Fathers of Vati-

---

[1]Sister Mary Christina, S.U.C.S., "Some Non-Permanent Foundations of Religious Orders and Congregations of Women in the United
States (1739-1850)," Historical Records and Studies, Vol. XXXI,
New York: The United States Catholic Historical Society, 1940,
pp. 7-118.

can II told us that our renewal comprised "both a constant return to
the sources of the whole of the Christian life and to the primitive
inspiration of the institutes, and their adaptation to the changed
conditions of our time,"[2] most of us thought we were ready. But
were we? Did we know our sources and our primitive inspiration?
Did we, as American women religious, know our common sources? We
had heard many times during the sixties that American Sisters had
some unique qualities. Yet there was no history of women religious
in the United States. Do we really have unique characteristics, or
is this just an example of national pride? If we do have unique
characteristics, why do we have them? Are these characteristics of
value in our world today? Without historical studies of women religious in the United States we will remain without answers. As I considered this situation, the general topic of a study seemed very
clear, but how could I keep it within manageable boundaries? My
initial research led me to the interesting fact that before 1830, no
organized community of immigrant women religious succeeded in making
a permanent foundation within those boundaries of the United States
which were determined by the Treaty of Paris in 1783. It seemed wise,
moreover, to limit this study to those communities which were founded
within the area where the Anglo-American culture predominated. For
in spite of the important contributions of other cultures to our
present make-up as a nation, the Anglo-American culture has retained
its dominance.

 This study could only be a beginning. Its aim was to determine
who the women were who entered these communities, as much as possible

---

[2]*Perfectae Caritatis*, Art. 2.

about their background, and whether there was any clear relationship between who they were and their choice of community. The possible sources of related material were too extensive to be consulted in their entirety. It was impossible to read every extant record of the period; therefore, I relied principally on archival sources. My focus was primarily on the total membership, rather than the leadership, and the manner in which these communities lived their lives and carried on their apostolate in the American environment. Aspects of the communities' development such as institutional development and spirituality were considered only as they affected the work of the sisters and their relationship with the total community or as they indicated possible causes for the different development of the several communities.

A major portion of this study centers around the available data concerning the young women who entered these eight communities between the date of their founding and 1850. These data range from a name on the community register to the detailed biographies of Saint Elizabeth Seton. For my purposes I was principally interested in the date of birth, entrance, death or exit; the place of birth; family status; the degree of education the woman had when she entered; whether or not she was a convert; the type of work she did in the community; and the cause of her death. Needless to say, much of this information was not available, but there was enough to give an indication of strengths and weaknesses. Moreover, there is probably more information about these women than can be found about any other group of women of a similar size (1,441) during the early nineteenth century in the United States. This information about individual sisters was utilized in a computer program which made it possible to see some interesting trends.

When I began the research in the fall of 1976, I also began searching for comparable studies that might be used for the purpose of comparison. Professors from Catholic University who were familiar with European or American history of the same period or the history of women religious at any period were consulted, as were Professors Timothy L. Smith and Robert Forster of Johns Hopkins University. No one knew of comparable studies, but they did offer helpful advice for background and other possible sources of information. Since that time the number of good histories of individual communities of women religious has been steadily increasing. At this time I am unaware of any published, comparative history of American women religious based primarily on archival sources. Several persons have contacted me about studies that are in process and it is hoped that these studies will soon be available. The field is vast and many archives have rich sources. One need only look to recent histories of the American Catholic Church to realize that the authors had very few monographs about women religious from which to draw their information. The result is that the recognition of the contribution of women religious to the life of the Church in the United States is not in proportion to the work they have done.

Many people have shown a real interest in the history of women religious. They may have known sisters as teachers, nurses, or heard missionaries relate their experiences. Sisters were there; they belonged there, but the past was hidden, and usually unquestioned. In recent years many people have become more aware of the role of women

religious in the life of the Church because sisters are not always in

the places they had come to expect them to be.

Professional scholars and women religious in many communities--

not just the eight communities considered in this study--have en-

couraged me to pursue this comparative history of early American

women religious. The major superiors in all eight communities were

most generous and gracious in granting me permission to use their

archives. The administrators, the archivists, indeed all the sisters,

not only opened their archives to me, but their homes and themselves

as well. I learned much about the spirit and traditions of these com-

munities from the many sisters who generously gave me unstintingly

of their time during the days I spent working in their particular com-

munity archives. If I have misinterpreted documents, it is my respon-

sibility, not that of the sisters who were always ready to help in any

way they could.

None of the communities seemed to worry about weaknesses that

I might uncover in my research. In fact, weaknesses that did come to

light served to make the total story more remarkable. These were

women who experienced the realities of life and often the difficulties

apparently outweighed the satisfaction. Strong human emotions and

deep faith provided these women with the strength necessary to move

forward in spite of increasing calls for their service, the changing

social scene as immigration increased, and the expanding territory of

the United States as the frontier was pushed westward. The foundation

they laid has been firm. Not all the specific works they began in the

first half of the nineteenth century are still dependent on women religious at the close of the twentieth century. Once again, however, there is a need for women religious who will be ready to meet changing needs and move into fields of work that would otherwise be neglected.

The information that I gathered from my research in the varied archives and libraries presented me with a problem. I am concerned about persons, not numbers, but I had far too many data to collate by hand or, even worse, to just work with impressions and what appeared as significant examples. Dr. Richard T. O'Neill of the Computer Center of Xavier University (Cincinnati), with the help of two students-- Kathleen Adam and Thomas Fefele--shared their time and expertise to plan the computer program and teach me to punch cards. Xavier University ran the program and I was presented with a mass of interesting data. After having studied it carefully I attended the workshop, "We Count Women," at Newberry Library, 5-7 July 1979. I concluded that there is probably a great deal more that a statistician could deduce from the data I had. Nevertheless, the information I had culled from my data in conjunction with the archival sources seemed to be the best way for me to answer my basic questions in such a way that the "primitive inspiration" for American women religious might have some vitality and meaning today.

I wish to express my gratitude to Fathers Robert Trisco and Kevin Seasoltz, O.S.B. and Doctor Edward C. Carter II for their advice and encouragement during the years when I researched and wrote the dissertation. My thanks are due to my own religious community for making this work possible, and to Mrs. Jean Barrett and Mrs. Mary Fischvogt who hastened the completion of the dissertation with their typing. I especially wish to thank the archivists who took time to review the work as I prepared it for publication. Sister Constance Fitz Gerald pointed out to me that cloistered communities such as the Carmelites have limitations on the number of members they may have in one monastery. This limitation may determine the number of applicants they may accept during a given time period. Sister Florence Wolff very kindly checked all the references to the Archives of the Sisters of Loretto and gave me the citations as they are now. And Sister Aloysia Dugan shared with me the more accurate information concerning Sister Mary Ann McAleer that she found in her work in the Emmitsburg Archives of the Daughters of Charity. Finally, I am grateful, as well, to all those who lent or helped me locate books, offered advice and encouragement, or bore patiently with me during the course of this work and in the intervening years.

Barbara Misner, S.C.S.C.

Milwaukee, Wisconsin
24 August 1987

LIST OF TABLES AND GRAPHS

LIST OF APPENDICES

INTRODUCTION

1790 - 1850

The United States in 1790, although the borders had been ex-
tended from the thirteen original states to the Mississippi River on

the west, the Great Lakes on the north, and Florida on the South, was

still essentially a coastal nation. Settlers had begun moving beyond

the Appalachians, but the settlements were small and tended to con-

centrate near the principal waterways. The leadership within the

country came mainly from New England or what Bridenbaugh terms the

Chesapeake Society. Leadership within the Catholic community was also

drawn from the old Catholic families who had originally settled in

southern Maryland and were part of this Chesapeake society. When

John Carroll was appointed the first bishop of the Catholic Church in

the United States, he sought additional help. After some negotiations

he accepted the offer of the Sulpician superior in France to send priests

to the United States. The French Revolution also caused other priests

to flee to the United States about the same time. These priests played

an important part in the early development of the Church in the United

States and were prominent in the formation and early development of

several of the first permanent communities of women religious.

John Carroll, as superior of the American mission, had sent his

first report to Rome in 1785. He reported about 15,800 Catholics in

Maryland, 7,000 in Pennsylvania, and not more than 200 in Virginia who

were visited four or five times a year by a priest. He also wrote that

1

he had been told there were about 1,500 Catholics in New York. These
Catholics had recently made their own arrangements and brought a Franciscan priest from Ireland to serve them. Carroll had heard that there
were many Catholics between the Mississippi River and the Atlantic
coast, that is, the area formerly part of Canada and ceded to the United
States by Britain in the peace treaty. Some of this area had been under
the jurisdiction of the Bishop of Quebec. To serve these Catholics
there were nineteen priests in Maryland and five in Pennsylvania. Two
priests were over seventy years of age and three were close to seventy;
there were others in bad health.[1] The Catholic Church in 1785 was small
and unorganized, but the Catholic communities that existed in Maryland
and Pennsylvania and the few communicants who were scattered elsewhere
were not only free to practice their faith openly, but as Americans they
were also caught up in the excitement of founding a nation. Part of the
excitement, almost inconceivable in the late twentieth century, was that
there seemed to be no limits to either the land or its resources.

Before the middle of the nineteenth century startling discoveries
would begin changing the way people lived and worked and, therefore, the
way people viewed their world would begin to change. The United States
was firmly established on such constitutional principles as the "consent
of the governed" and the freedom enunciated in the Bill of Rights. But
new developments were not limited to governmental forms; for example,
the steam engine was perfected and the telegraph was invented. What
changes resulted from just these two technological developments! By

---

[1]Cf. John Tracy Ellis, ed., "The First American Report to Propa-
ganda on Catholicism in the United States, March 1, 1785," Documents of
American Catholic History (Milwaukee: The Bruce Publishing Company, 1962
Second edition), pp. 148-149.

3

1850 ships were no longer dependent solely on favorable winds and at least on the principal overland routes steam boats or steam engines were making long journeys easier and more rapid. The steam engine also began transforming industry. The telegraph made rapid communication possible. When such developments were combined with freedom and the availability of vast tracts of land, what was to stop the bold, imaginative person from moving forward?

Catholics, like other Americans, had their share of bold, imaginative--and restless--people. The western lands of Kentucky were hardly opened up before settlers began to move in from the more settled areas along the eastern coast. While there were individual Catholics earlier, the earliest Catholic settlement dated from 1785, the same year John Carroll had sent his report to Rome. All the earliest Catholic settlers were from Maryland and most of them were descendants of the original Catholic settlers in Maryland.[2] It was not possible at this time for John Carroll to fulfill the requests for priests sent by settlers in the western lands. The first priest, Father Whelan, arrived in Kentucky in 1787, but left again in 1790.[3] Other priests followed but only a few remained more than several years. Those who stayed were unable to establish parishes and become resident pastors. When Bishop Benedict Joseph Flaget arrived in Kentucky as its first bishop, June 1811, he was accompanied by four seminarians and his confrere, Father John Baptist Mary David. There were six priests serving the entire Kentucky area at that time.[4] The only other diocese west of the Appalachians was New Orleans and there was no resident bishop there when Flaget came to Kentucky.

3

[2] Ben. J. Webb, The Centenary of Catholicity in Kentucky (Louisville: Charles A. Rogers, 1884), pp. 24ff.

[3] Cf. Ibid., pp. 32-33.   [4] Ibid., pp. 224-225; 340.

Bishop Flaget, like many of the priests who came to serve the Catholics in the west had been born, reared, and educated in pre-revolutionary France. The institutions that supported the Church and through which the Church functioned in France were lacking on the frontier. Not only were schools, seminaries, convents and the like missing, but there were not even parishes--nor many church buildings for that matter. Even more, the majority of Catholics who were living in Kentucky had never experienced such institutions. Their faith, for the most part, was strong. They wanted a priest who would say Mass and provide some instruction as well as administer the sacraments. There were very few Catholics, however, who had much understanding of their faith. Neither had the colonial experience prepared them to support the clergy and the works they would initiate. It must have seemed like an impossible task, yet when Flaget died in 1850, the Church was well established and its institutions were well known and producing an educated laity as well as outstanding leaders among the clergy and religious. When the American bishops assembled in the First Plenary Council of Baltimore in 1852, more than twenty bishops who came from the territory west of the Appalachian Mountains signed the Pastoral Letter. What had happened during the approximately sixty years between the time of the first Catholic settlements and Bishop Flaget's death?

Large urban centers and industrial towns were becoming characteristic of the northern Atlantic coastal area. The United States was attracting more and more immigrants. When famine struck Ireland and then Germany in the 1840's, more and more people looked to the United States as the land of plenty. A series of revolutions also rocked Europe between 1790 and 1850. Refugees from the turmoil or subsequent reaction to democratic ideas looked to the United States as a land where freedom reigned and democracy was really practiced, not just talked about. Within the United States the congestion of the cities or worn-out eastern farm land was leading many to consider the move westward an attractive, even if risky, alternative. As frontiersmen settled the Indian "problem" to their own advantage and technology began transforming not only the old urban centers but also the means of transportation, many people from both the "Old World" and the thirteen original states joined the westward movement.

As industrialization and the westward movement were gaining momentum the United States was experiencing other changes. Capitalism began to move toward its dominant position in American life. The ideal of the small farmer and independent craftsman or merchant remained to color the rhetoric, but the market proved its influence as Americans experienced periodic depressions. The largest number of immigrants from Europe formed the foundation of the growing transportation systems and nascent industries. Few immigrants became farmers and the South attracted very few. The differences between North and South became more distinct as the nineteenth century progressed. By 1850 "Slave State" versus "Free State" was becoming a volatile issue among Catholics as well as other Americans.

The Catholic Church, in spite of all its long history and traditions, found itself as a new member of the social and institutional structure of the nation. The American Catholic community was a veritably unorganized branch of a highly organized Church in 1790. The initial leaders had an acquaintance with the various structures within the organization, but the vast majority of American Catholics lacked

this acquaintance. If they knew anything about it at all, the knowledge
had come to them through someone else or through reading imported literature. Immigrants, already acquainted with the organization of the
Church in their homelands, swelled the ranks of the Catholic Church
in the United States, but most of them were unprepared to aid in establishing such an organization in the United States. This was not a society in which people were rooted to a specific geographic location for
generations. There always seemed to be a new frontier and never had
the Church faced the necessity of serving in a pluralistic society of
this magnitude.

The first great waves of immigrants were largely destitute and
unskilled Irish, most of whom were Catholic. The needs were great and
the Church was forced to adapt and change some of its outward appearances.
By 1850 the only other nationality to immigrate in sizable numbers was
the German. These people had the added problem of a foreign language.
Recent history offered the leadership of the Church no precedent for
dealing with such problems. Furthermore, the influx of foreigners
threatened the settled character of the port cities and the jobs of
many Americans who had come in from marginal farm land. The foreigners
were willing to work for lower wages. This threat, coupled with strange
or different practices and traditional anti-papism, led to growing
Nativism. The Church had not only the needs of the immigrants to
care for, but also a public relations problem it was unprepared to
meet. Some among the clergy and hierarchy were ready to attack Nativism
with apologetics, but the institutions, especially the schools and
later orphan homes and hospitals of the sisters, probably did much
more to win the esteem and respect of important segments of the general
population.

The statistics for the Catholic Church as found in the Metropolitan Almanac for 1850 (published in 1849) reveal a Church that John
Carroll and his contemporaries probably would not have recognized.
John Carroll had reported a Catholic population of about 24,500 plus
an unknown number beyond the Appalachians in 1785. The 1850 Almanac
gives figures for 30 dioceses with a total Catholic population of
at least 1,233,350 (several dioceses had no population statistics given)
and 1,081 priests to serve these people. The dioceses by 1850 were
found in the area west of the Mississippi River and even as far away as
Oregon City, as well as the older parts of the country.[5] McAvoy speaks
of the "Formation of the Catholic Minority" which began during this
period. The nucleus of this minority had been the Anglo-American Catholics. The present study confirms his basic thesis. There is no doubt
that much of the important leadership before 1850 had come from this
nucleus or were closely allied with it.[6]

Women Religious, 1790-1850

One of the families who played an important part in the early
years of the "formation of the Catholic minority" was the Matthews
family. Sometime after the close of the Revolutionary War, Father Ignatius Matthews encouraged his sister, the Carmelite nun Mother Bernardina,
to return to America from Belgium to establish a Carmelite monastery.

---

[5]Cf. The Metropolitan Catholic Almanac and Laity's Directory,
1850 (Baltimore: Fielding Lucas, Jr., 1849; Washington, D.C.: Microfilm
edition, Catholic University of America Press, n.d.), pp. 231-235.

[6]Cf. Thomas T. McAvoy, C.S.C., A History of the Catholic Church
in the United States (Notre Dame & London: University of Notre Dame Press,
1969), Chapter VI, pp. 123-162. See also: John Tracy Ellis, American
Catholicism, Second Edition, Revised (Chicago: The University of Chicago
Press, 1969. The Chicago History of American Civilization, Daniel J.
Boorstin, editor), Chapter II, pp. 41-83.

He wrote: "Peace is declared and Religion is free."[7] Mother Bernardina
and her two nieces, Sisters Mary Aloysia and Mary Eleanore Matthews,
together with an English woman, Mother Clare Joseph Dickenson, arrived
in Port Tobacco, Maryland, along with Father Charles Neale (see below,
Chapter I) in 1790. Catholicism was not unknown in southern Maryland,
but in many areas of the United States it was known only as it was presented in much of the Protestant literature of the day. Many, if not
all, the evils seen in what Americans perceived as less enlightened
areas of Europe and the New World were attributed to Papism. Among
the most misunderstood and calumniated groups of Roman Catholics were
women religious. When the Awful Disclosures of Maria Monk first appeared
in 1836, it was not the first publication of its kind, but it certainly
became the most famous. There is no doubt that people believed the
tales of illicit affairs and cruelty portrayed in such works. While
the masses of common people were the ones most affected by the publications and lectures which spread the inhuman tales, the leadership of
the movement included men such as Lyman Beecher and Samuel F. B. Morse
whose names are familiar to many even today.[8]

In order to survive, women religious had to deal with the reality
of such prejudice. Wherever they had schools or hospitals they also
served non-Catholics. In most cases, the support they gained from their
pupils or patients, their families, and others who recognized the good
that was being done by the sisters was sufficient to overcome the threat
of violence. In Charlestown, Massachusetts, it was not. There, despite

---

[7]ACM-B. Death Book. Mother Bernardina Matthews.

[8]Ray Allen Billington, The Protestant Crusade, 1800-1860: A
Study of the Origins of American Nativism (New York: The Macmillan
Company, 1938), pp. 98-108; 125-127.

the respect of the well-to-do Boston families who sent their daughters

to Mount Benedict to be educated by the Ursulines, the lower classes of

people were imbued with superstition and the hatred of anything Catholic

that had been part of their Puritan/Congregational heritage for genera-

tions. Since most of the non-Catholic students at Mount Benedict were

from Unitarian families there was no one who could bridge the gap between

the sisters at the convent and the enraged mob. The convent was burned,

11 August 1834, and eventually the Ursulines had to give up all hope of

rebuilding and leave Massachusetts--anti-Catholic prejudice was too

strong. At the same time, however, the Sisters of Charity had the direc-

tion of an orphanage in Boston which was left unharmed. If the day-la-

borers who were so enraged that they burned the Charlestown convent had

heard of the work of the Sisters of Charity, they had probably forgotten

it since they were not living among the Irish; the orphanage posed no

threat such as the apparent alliance between the influential Unitarians

and the dreaded Catholic nuns with their fine school.[9] This incident

was certainly the most violent to affect the life and work of women re-

ligious before 1850, but every section of the United States was prone

to such prejudice. The Sisters of Charity wrote of their fear during

the riots in Philadelphia. The volatile situation which resulted from

Sister Isabella's "escape" from the Baltimore Carmel affected not only

the Carmelites, but the Sisters of Charity and the Oblate Sisters of

Providence as well.[10]

---

[9]Cf. Ibid., pp. 68-73.

[10]Cf. ASJCH. Letters, II:20-22, "Foundations," Three letters of
Sister Mary Gonzaga to Mother Etienne Hall. St. Joseph's Asylum, Philadelphia 8, 12, 17 May 1839. ACM-B. "Transcriptions by Sister Stanislaus," 1839, pp. 34-37. AOSP. "French Diary," p. 57; July 1834 (This

With such prejudice to deal with, how could any group hope to

flourish outside the few Catholic enclaves that existed in places such

as Maryland, Pennsylvania and Kentucky? And if they did get a start,

could they have any hope of expanding? There is no evidence in the

early records that there was ever a conscious consideration of such

questions when the communities were founded. Archbishop Whitfield re-

quired the Carmelites to open a school when they moved to Baltimore, be-

cause the prejudice then existing in Baltimore would preclude begging,

but that was about forty years after the community was founded in

America.[11] In the case of the Oblate Sisters of Providence, both the

Archbishop and Father Joubert considered the problem of racial prejudice,

but they considered it as a problem within the Catholic community rather

than one that resulted from religious pluralism.[12] It seems evident

that in the case of the eight communities under consideration in this

study both the women who founded the communities and the priests and

bishops who aided them simply saw a need and set about to fill it. By

the time each community was formed, everyone who was directly involved

----

date is almost certainly a mistake. See pages 47-48 below.)

Sister Isabella Neale, who had attended the Visitation Academy, was professed as a Carmelite nun two years after her mother, Sister Barbara Neale, was professed. She began to show signs of mental illness sometime after her mother's death in 1825. Finally, in 1839, she left the cloister when no one was watching and asked for help. There was almost a riot as nativists capitalized on the incident, but the mayor acted quickly and firmly. The Sisters of Charity took Sister Isabella to the Maryland Hospital and she remained under their care until her death in 1864. While no riots developed, mobs continued to threaten the sisters for several days.

[11]Cf. p. 18, below.

[12]Cf. AOSP. Sr. Theresa Catherine Willigman, "A few facts relating to the Oblate Sisters of Providence of Balt., Md.," p. 17.

was well aware of existing anti-Catholic prejudice and had learned how to deal with pluralism, at least in the immediate area. They acquired experience over the course of the years and in the fulfillment of their tasks. And, probably more important, in the course of their daily lives and labor the sisters touched many people who came to know them as real women who found joy and satisfaction in their work. Moreover, the work was done thoroughly and competently. There must have been many non-Catholics in nineteenth century America who, having experienced the dedication and concern of the sisters as teachers or nurses, would have been ready to echo Marcelle Bernstein in 1976, when she wrote:

> Why should any woman choose to live the life of a nun?
> . . . it is, I am reluctantly convinced, incomprehensible.
> It is a mystery of the human spirit that cannot be
> completely explained or understood.[13]

---

[13]Marcelle Bernstein, The Nuns (Philadelphia and New York: J. B. Lippincott Company, 1976), p. 16

CHAPTER I

NEW INSTITUTIONS FOR A NEW NATION

The Development of the Communities

The Catholic Church, like other institutions of the colonial period, began to exhibit different facets as it adapted to new conditions. Catholicism in Maryland was as old as the colony itself, but except for a brief initial period the Catholics had not been able publicly to acknowledge their faith. The oldest churches were in Pennsylvania where public worship by Catholics was tolerated. But if Catholic church buildings were practically unknown in the British colonies, there was even less experience with the organizations and structures within the Church that European Catholics had known for centuries. Convents and monasteries along with schools and institutions to serve the poor, the sick, or any class of needy persons were almost totally lacking. The Jesuits had ministered to the Catholics from the inception of the Maryland colony, but they had had to provide for themselves by managing their own plantations and their several attempts to provide Catholic boys with at least an elementary education were all halted by the enforcement of penal legislation.

The opportunities of the new continent, however, made it possible for many Catholics to provide well for themselves and their families and many were educated abroad. When the opportunity to speak openly was presented there were Catholics who were both able and ready

12

to assume leadership in both Church and state. By 1790, as Bishop Carroll was beginning to organize the Catholic Church in the United States, the revolutions on the European continent were forcing some priests to flee. Many of the priests who came to the United States at this time were well-educated Frenchmen. Nonetheless, in this initial period, the Church was to have a unique Anglo-American character.

Joachim Wach in his study, Sociology of Religion, outlines the stages in the development of "founded religions." While a religious community is not a new religion there is a parallel between the model he gives for the development of a "founded religion" and that of a religious community. The model contains three major steps: 1) the circle of the disciples, 2) the brotherhood, and 3) the ecclesiastical body or institution. The first stage requires one or more charismatic leaders who draw persons with similar goals and ideals to join them. The brotherhood, or in this study the sisterhood, develops after the first major crisis, the death of the founder. At this stage the emphasis is placed on the ideals and message of the founder. Gradually the oral tradition must be systematized and standardized. This process begins during the period of the sisterhood but continues and evolves into a doctrinal statement on the third level.[1] Periodically all religions face protest which may be "dissent in the field of doctrine, criticism of the cultic expression, and objection to the nature or development of the organizational structure."[2] The general outline of

---

[1]Cf. Joachim Wach, Sociology of Religion, 11th Impression, (Chicago: University of Chicago Press, 1944; Phoenix Books, 1967), pp. 130-145.

[2]Ibid., p. 166.

these steps can be seen in each of the eight religious communities under consideration in this dissertation.

The following sketches of the formation and development of the first eight permanent communities of women religious within the original boundaries of the United States, that is, within the area of the United States where the culture was predominantly Anglo-American, will give some idea of these stages. While none of them escaped at least one threat to their existence as religious communities, there was still, in 1850, an air of flexibility in most of the groups that indicated that even though they had reached the third stage, that of an institution, on paper, it had not been totally actualized among the members.

Carmelites[3]

John Carroll who, in 1789, had been named as the first Bishop of the United States, sailed to England for his consecration. In 1790 three women of the Matthews family of Charles County, Maryland and an English woman, Mother Clare Joseph Dickinson--all members of the English Carmelite convents in Belgium--left behind an impending threat to their continued existence by followers of the French Revolution and came to establish a Carmel at Port Tobacco, Maryland. Such a life would have been an impossibility here just a few years before. Now, despite Bishop Carroll's preference for an active order,[4] he welcomed them, though he did secure permission for them to teach school.[5] The Carmelite nuns

---

[3]The historical sketch of each of the eight religious communities considered in this study is based on the research done in the archives of each community and published works. Information about the principal sources can be found in the "Bibliographical Essay."

[4]Thomas O'Brien Hanley, S.J., ed., The John Carroll Papers. 3 vols. (Notre Dame: University of Notre Dame Press, 1976), I:312.

[5]Ibid., II:84-85.

were not teachers and they did not choose to use this permission. It was almost ten years before other women felt called by God to live a common life dedicated to the service of God and His Church through the instruction of children.

As the French Revolution spread and the needs of American Catholics became more apparent several groups of women religious came from France. Later communities came from other countries as well, but none of these succeeded in making a permanent foundation east of the Mississippi River prior to 1830.[6] The conditions in the new nation, even when not complicated by a language barrier, seem to have required adjustments in life-style and the concepts of the role and needs of the women religious that were beyond the capabilities of these women and their superiors. Nevertheless, seven other communities were founded by 1829. Women in America not only could live religious life, but many found that it satisfied their own personal desires for a life of dedication at the same time as it met needs within the growing Catholic community.

If there is one word that best indicates what the impulse was behind the foundation of the early communities of women religious it is "utility."[7] The very lack of an obvious usefulness of the Carmelite foundation is an occasion for pointing this out. The letters of John Carroll leave no doubt about the place he envisioned for women religious in the American Church. In 1800 he wrote to his friends Charles and Robert Plowden in England:

_____

[6]Sister Mary Christina Sullivan, S.U.S.C., "Some Non-Permanent Foundations of Religious Orders and Congregations of Women in the United States (1739-1850)," Historical Records and Studies, Vol. XXXI (New York: The United States Catholic Historical Society, 1940), pp. 7-118.

[7]John Carroll Papers, II:88.

. . . Those of the same order from Hoogestraet (Carmelites) have multiplied themselves considerably, and give much edification by their retirement, and total seclusion from the world, and I doubt not of the efficacy of their prayers in drawing down blessings on us all: but their utility to the public goes no farther. They will not concern themselves in the business of female education, tho the late Pope, soon after their arrival, recommended it earnestly to them by a letter sent to me by Cardl. Antonelli, in consequence of the Popes own directions to him. [8]

The letter to Bernadine Matthews from Bishop Carroll, 1 March 1793, informed her of the above mentioned permission. Carroll wrote:

The Cardinal prefect of the Propaganda having laid my letter befor his Holiness, informs me, that it gave them incredible joy to find that you were come hither to diffuse the knowledge and practice of religious perfection, and adds, that, considering the great scarcity of labourers, and the defects of education in these States, you might sacrifice that part of your institution to the promotion of a greater good [italics mine]: . . . [9]

The pragmatism, so often seen as a major factor in American policies, was not at all foreign to the leadership of the early American Church.

As noted above the Carmelites' foundation was not made in response to a social need within the Catholic community, but this is not their only claim to uniqueness. Another unique feature is that they were the only permanent foundation before 1830, in which the foundresses came from abroad as professed religious with some years experience in the life and traditions of a well-established community. Since three of the four foundresses were native Americans and the priest (Father Charles Neale) who was primarily responsible for the negotiations necessary for the transfer of the nuns from Belgium to the United States was also a native American there seems to be no reason for not considering them as an American foundation. Moreover, the Carmelites are the only group to

---

[8] Ibid., II:319.

[9] Ibid., II:84-85. For other references to this permission see also: I:312; II:32, 88, 94; III:6, 157.

have made a major move so far as the location of the principal house was concerned.

The original register of vows for the Carmelite nuns is introduced by a short account of their coming to the United States in which it simply says they came "at the request of several in Maryland." After Mother Bernardina Matthews' death there was a separate entry in the "Death Book" that expanded on this:

> It is principally to the zeal of the Rev. Mother Matthews that we are indebted for our foundation of Carmelites in America. This dear Mother had left her country in Charles Co. Md. to cross the ocean in order to become a Carmelite nun, there being no religious in the United States [sic]--She went to Hoogstratt, and became a very edifying member of that community. . . . Her 2 nieces Sr. M. Eleanora and Sr. Aloysia Matthews came with her. They had long desired to be Carmelites, but could not cross the ocean on account of our Revolutionary War but as soon as the war ended they went to Hookstratt and joined their aunt in doing all they could to procure the blessing of a new foundation in their own country. Rev. Mr. Matthews had written to his sister saying "Now is your time to found in this country for Peace is declared and Religion is free." . . . 10

In response to this request, the three Matthews women and Mother Clare Joseph Dickenson, accompanied by Father Charles Neale, set sail for Maryland. Father Neale was not only their first spiritual director but also an outstanding benefactor. Their first residence was "at the mansion house of his Father," but after a few months Mr. Baker Brooke offered them his home. Some of the land was purchased by an exchange with part of the Neale land in addition to a cash settlement of "twelve hundred & seventy seven pounds three dollars." Claims were made on this land almost from the beginning and after the death of both Mr. Baker Brooke and Father Charles Neale lawsuits dragged on until finally Archbishop Maréchal asked Roger B. Taney if he would undertake the cause of the

---

10ACM-B. "Death Book." Cf. United States Catholic Miscellany (Charleston, S.C.), 2, 12 January 1849.

Sisters. Taney brought the case to a favorable conclusion; but, despite the Court order, the sisters never received any reimbursement for their costs. This, coupled with difficulties arising from having to depend on overseers for the farming after Father Neale's death, depleted the sisters' resources and necessitated the move from Charles County to Baltimore in 1831.

It was at that time that the Carmelite Nuns submitted to "practical requirements" and assigned three nuns to teach school. Archbishop Whitfield had considered this a requirement for their transfer to Baltimore. Nativism was becoming a force to be reckoned with; begging for subsistence by a group of Catholic nuns would have been cause for even more ill will.[11] The sisters' official records give only the opening of the school in 1831 and its closing in 1851. The sisters met the practica[l] need, and met it well, but they did so reluctantly. More information about the school can be found in such public sources as Catholic Directories than in the records of the community. Theirs was a life of prayer and solitude and they meant to keep it that way.

Visitation

The second permanent community was typical of the early communities in so far as the immediate cause of its formation was the need to provide education for girls. Three women, Mrs. Sharpe, Alice Lalor and Mrs. Marie McDermott, had known Father Leonard Neale in Philadelphia and had sought his direction. When Bishop Carroll called Leonard Neale to become his co-adjutor and also president of George Town College, Neale

---

[11]Cf. ACM-B. Archbishop Whitfield to Mother Angela Mudd. 6 July 1830. See also: Charles Warren Currier, Carmel in America: A Centennial History of the Discalced Carmelites in the United States (Baltimore: John Murphy & Co., 1890), pp. 183-185.

found three French Poor Clares in Georgetown struggling for their existence by maintaining a school they were not prepared to conduct. Their
way of life, added to their inability to speak English, made the undertaking very difficult.[12] Father Neale then asked the three women to
come from Philadelphia to help. All three of these women had been born
in Ireland, but had come from families who had the means and the desire
to see that their daughters had more than just a basic education. We
know very little about Mrs. Sharpe except that she was the best teacher
and after her death in 1802, the quality of the school diminished for
some years.

Once these three "Pious Ladies" arrived in Georgetown (1799)
they began to live the regular life of religious but without any standard Rule. Apparently they soon decided that they desired to be distinct
from the Poor Clares in order to pursue an apostolate of teaching. It
is not quite clear whether they started their own school or simply took
over the school begun by the Poor Clares, but there does not seem to
have been any friction between them. In 1804, Mother de la Marche died
and the two remaining Poor Clares decided to return to France. There
seemed to be a greater possibility of living a life according to their
Rule in France where religious were beginning to return to their convents.
Leonard Neale, who had been consecrated as Carroll's co-adjutor bishop in
1800, now purchased the property owned by the Poor Clares and four additional Threlkeld lots adjoining the property already held by the Pious
Ladies.[13]

---

[12]Cf. John Carroll Papers, II:94.

[13]A "Map of GEORGETOWN in the District of Columbia by William
Bussard, 1830" on which it is written, "Traced from an Original Engra-
ving loaned by Wm. Forsyth City Surveyor, Washington, D.C. -- July,
1803," is in the collection at the National Archives. It clearly shows

Property alone, however, has never been sufficient to guarantee

the permanence of a religious institution. These Pious Ladies, whose

numbers were slowly increasing, had no official recognition as religious.

Whether the original idea of following the Visitation Rule was the re-

sult of an earlier vision of Bishop Neale's or the familiarity of the

Order to those priests who had studied in Europe,[14] it is certain that

this particular Order was suggested by Bishop Neale and that after a

French copy of the Rule was found among the books left by the Poor Clares

the desire to be Visitandines became ever stronger. The sisters soon

began a novitiate under the direction of Bishop Neale. Archbishop Car-

roll wanted the sisters to be canonically recognized for he saw this as

an essential step to stability which would in turn bring more prominence

to their school. He, like Bishop Edward Fenwick of Cincinnati at a later

date, seemed to see no real difference in communities of women religious

so long as they could be given ecclesiastical approval and would embrace

education as their chief apostolate. The women, however, did see a dif-

ference, and were determined to be Visitandines even if they must wait

years to do so. In the meantime they would live the life of Visitation

Nuns and do their best as teachers.

No diaries or convent annals are extant to tell the story in

their own words but the story can be pieced together through some offi-

cial ecclesiastical correspondence, the tradition of the Georgetown

---

the square of property bounded by Fayette, Third, Lingan and Fourth
Streets as the "Convent." The changes made in the map of 1803 by Mr.
Bussard in 1830 are clearly marked over the 1803 lines. There are no
such changes in the convent property. The sisters did acquire more
property later, but at this early date they already had a considerable
amount of property for a new and struggling institution.

[14]Eleanore C. Sullivan, Georgetown Visitation Since 1799
(Privately printed, 1975), pp. 50-51.

Visitation Convent, a few contemporary secondary sources, and the very

fact of its continued existence and growth between the foundation in

1799 and its formal recognition and approval by the Pope in 1816. It

was the Papal approval which made it possible for the sisters to take

Solemn Vows after 1816.

Bishop Carroll's concern for the regularizing of the community

is clear from his letters. He wrote to Thomas Betagh in Ireland, 14

July 1805, that his co-adjutor, Bishop Neale had

> formed under the conduct of four or five pious Ladies, a female
> academy at George Town, and has acquired for them a handsome
> property of lots & houses. These ladies, long trained to all
> the exercises of an interior and religious life, are exceedingly
> anxious to bind themselves more closely to God by entering into
> an approved religious order, whose institute embraces the edu-
> cation of young persons of their own sex, poor and sick.

He continues that he has heard Thomas Betagh has such a community under

his care and that both he and Bishop Neale wish that he would

> if possible engage two of those Ladies, fully approved by you,
> to leave their country & Sisters, & friends, to establish here
> a house of their order. One of them ought to be fit to become
> immediately the Superior & Mistress of novices, and the other
> to preside in the female academy-- The two principal ladies
> of this institution are natives of Ireland & both women of
> exemplary and even perfect lives-- I know not whether one of
> them, whose name is Lawler (Ally Lawler) be not known to you.[15]

The community under Father Betagh's direction was very probably

Ursuline, the community most often referred to by Bishop Carroll in his

early attempts to establish women religious. In 1807 Carroll wrote to

Bishop Neale:

> I receive no encouragement yet from Ireland for your good
> Ladies-- This is much to be regretted; for the morality and
> religious education of girls would be much safer under the
> inspection of Mrs. McDermott, Ally Lawler &c, than in our board-

---

[15]John Carroll Papers, II:483-484.

ing schools; but they require assistance for giving the elegant accomplishments, without which their school can never be popular.

He continued to encourage Neale to follow a possible lead for trying to get some Ursulines and spoke of a young woman desiring to enter religious life. "She is much better qualified for a convent, such as you propose, than for the Carmelites-- Yet if you have no prospect of success, I must gratify her longing desire by solliciting her admission at Mt. Carmel."[16] At that time it never seemed to have occurred to Bishop Carroll to encourage the formation of a new institution in which the ladies, with the help of a priest familiar with traditional religious life, would adapt an approved Rule to their own needs. Within a few years, however, he would encourage Elizabeth Seton to make such a move. It may be that the insistence on the importance of experienced religious was the reason for the determination of the Pious Ladies in Georgetown insisting that they would be Visitandines regardless of how long they must wait. In the end, these ladies did become formally recognized by the Church without European direction. That came only some years later and the accounts leave the modern historian with the impression that it was more necessary to satisfy the ecclesiastics' need for propriety than to add to the sisters' essential understanding of the Visitandine way of life.

Twice during March 1808, Bishop Carroll wrote to Neale about his problems concerning the sisters. Essentially his problem was that he doubted his own right to allow vows to be taken in an approved order without the approval of the highest superior within that order. As he closed his letter of 27 March he concluded:

---

[16]Ibid., III:6-7.

Reflecting farther on the subject of establishing a Convent of the Visitation, it seems to me that much of the difficulty may be gotten over by the ladies making the same vows (tho only simple) as are prescribed by the rules of the Order, after passing thro' such a novitiate, as the rule directs; to which may be added the vow ingrediendi religionem [of entering religion], . . . I mention the vow ingrediendi religionem hypothetically, that is, if approved by you, after due consideration: for you know, that tho, I think, we both possess the power of dispensing from it, yet it requires more urgent motives, than a dispensation from or commutation of other simple vows, . . . [17]

This is one of the earliest indications that among many of the clergy only solemn vows entitled a woman to be called a religious (see Chapter III, pp. 100-102).

Once Elizabeth Seton determined to begin a community whose immediate purpose would be to provide educational opportunities to girls Bishop Carroll suggested that the ladies in Georgetown combine forces with her. The sisters declined to go along with this suggestion.[18] The two communities were to develop along very different lines within the near future, and because of the insistence of the ladies in Georgetown that they wished to be Visitandines they would not be officially recognized until seven years after the sisters in Emmitsburg.

Archbishop Neale's letter to the Superior at Annecy, which he dated 6 March 1817, gives the best general account of the development of this community from 1799 to 1816. In speaking of the years immediately preceding 1816, he wrote:

. . . The number of pious ladies increasing, and postulants pressing in on all sides to procure admission, I found it

---

[17] John Carroll Papers, III:48; 49-50.

[18] Cf. George Parsons Lathrop and Rose Hawthorne Lathrop, A Story of Courage: Annals of the Georgetown Convent of the Visitation of the Blessed Virgin Mary from the Manuscript Records (Boston: Houghton, Mifflin and Company, 1894), pp. 168-169.

necessary to establish Superiors for the regulating and conducting of the Community, in which I conformed myself to the
system followed in the Order of the Visitation. . . . they
made the three vows of Obedience, Chastity, and Poverty, for
a year, and then promised that at the expiration of the year,
they would again bind themselves by the same vows, and would
annually do the same until their Community should be admitted
by our Holy Church, as legally united to the Order of the
Visitation of Our Blessed Lady, . . . [19]

After Carroll's death Neale "was obliged as Archbishop of Baltimore to

carry on a correspondence with the Holy See." In this capacity he

realized he could request the Holy See to grant him the power to receive

the solemn vows of the sisters with "all Privileges, Indults, and Grants

enjoyed by the Order of the Visitation of the Blessed Lady, instituted

by St. Francis de Sales." This power was granted and the Solemn Pro-

fession of Miss Lalor, Mrs. McDermott and Miss Harriet Brent took place

on 28 December 1816. Three more made their Profession on 23 January,

and thirteen on 29 January 1817.[20] At that time Archbishop Neale wrote

to the Reverend Mother at Carmel: "The Community is large 33 in number

& others expected."[21] Thus finally, after seventeen years, the George-

town Convent was officially recognized as a Visitation Convent. It

would be another eight or nine years before the academy would be recog-

nized as an outstanding school, one that would provide the "elegant

accomplishments" as Carroll expressed it. But the possibilities for

the stability and the ecclesiastical support that was necessary to

achieve this goal were now present.

---

[19]AGVC. Archbishop Neale to the Superior at Annecy (France),
6 March 1817. Sullivan gives the date of the first temporary vows as
1814 (p. 52).

[20]Ibid.

[21]ACM-B. Leonard Neale to the Superior at Mt. Carmel,
21 December 1816.

It was 1829 before any personal contact was made between the Visitation Nuns in Europe and the Community in Georgetown. That year, Father Michael Wheeler, the spiritual director of the Georgetown Visitation Convent, was able to obtain two French nuns and one Swiss nun to come to the United States. After their arrival Mother Juliana Matthews resigned her position as Superior in favor of Sister Madeleine d'Arreger. Within two years a new addition, the monastery, was added to the buildings and Mother Madeleine was making preparations for establishing a second Visitation Monastery. In September 1831, two of the three nuns returned to France. This contact with the Visitation Nuns in France which had been considered essential for over a quarter of a century was a short-lived reality. The Convent records indicate that Sister Agatha Langlois, who had been appointed mistress of novices in 1830, became ill and was obliged to return to France. Sister Marie Regis Mordant returned to France with her.[22] The realization of a personal contact of the American Visitation Nuns with the old communities in Europe and initiating the establishment of new foundations, which certainly would have come shortly in any case, are the most apparent results of the presence of the three nuns. The spirit and regular life of the American Visitandines do not seem to have needed more. In a wonderful example of a friendly letter filled with news items of interest to Bishop Fenwick in Cincinnati, Father William Matthews of Washington, D.C. wrote: "We have sent back to France two of the Nuns whom Mr. Wheeler conducted from france--they are now on their way to N York, whence they will sail on

---

[22]Cf. Sullivan, pp.81-82.

the first of next month -"[23] One can almost hear his satisfaction with
this turn of events. No record of his thought was found related to the
departure of Mother Madeleine d'Arreger with the first group of sisters
to leave for Mobile, Alabama late in 1832, at the invitation of Bishop
Portier.

By the mid-1820's the Visitation Academy was acquiring for itself a wide reputation as an excellent school. From the time of his
arrival in 1818, Father Clorivière did much to improve the quality of
education by teaching the sisters themselves, seeing to the erection of
new buildings, and even advertising. Still, it was several years before
results would be seen and as late as 1823, the threat of dissolution
loomed on the horizon. The economic distress that began to affect the
country in 1818 resulted in the renewal of straitened circumstances for
the community. Archbishop Maréchal made arrangements for them to live,
at least for a time, in Ursuline convents in Quebec and help them with
their schools. At this critical time Mr. Lasalla, a New York merchant,
arranged for his three daughters and his youngest sister to attend the
Academy in Georgetown and paid all the fees in advance. With this help
and the services of an accomplished teacher, Sister Mary Augustine
(Mrs. Jerusha Barber), the school had much to commend it to many families. The school continued to develop and upgrade its curriculum with
the help of subsequent spiritual directors and talented young women who
joined the community.

Two additional works also gained the attention of outsiders,
especially the growing number of humanitarians. The sisters gave help

---

[23]UNDA. Archdiocese of Cincinnati Collection. Fr. W(illiam)
Matthews, Washington, D.C. to Bishop Fenwick, Cincinnati, 25 September
1831.

to Maria Becraft in her direction of a school for colored girls which
she opened on Fayette Street opposite the convent. According to the
Commissioner of Education they continued to extend their help until "a
depraved public sentiment upon the subject of educating the colored
people had compelled them to a more rigid line of demarcation between
the races."[24] This indirect educational work was short-lived, but the
second work was not. From the beginning the sisters had a school for
the poor girls of the neighborhood. They, like all the other teaching
communities, supported the school for the poor girls by the careful use
of the fees from the Academy. While it did much to foster admiration
and good will among outsiders and was fully approved by local Church
authorities it required rescripts from Rome to allow the sisters assigned to this work to leave the enclosure. (That is, they left the
monastic portion of the convent property, but not the property itself.)

Throughout these years a large proportion of the women who entered the Georgetown Visitation Convent were former students. A few
outstanding converts also became the outstanding teachers in the early
years since they came from families who had been able to provide their
daughters with "elegant accomplishments." The community grew at a surprising rate between 1830 and 1850, especially when one realizes that
they were actually engaged only in the Academy and Benevolent School,
both located at the Georgetown Convent. The number of new Visitation
monasteries and schools that were founded directly from the Georgetown
convent or by members of several convents in the mid-nineteenth cen-

[24]U.S. Department of Education, Special Report of the Commissioner of Education on the Condition and Improvement of Public Schools
in the District of Columbia, Submitted to the Senate, June, 1868, and
to the House with Additions, June 13, 1870 (Washington, D.C.: Government
Printing Office, 1871), p. 205.

tury is an important testimony not only to the importance of their work
but also to the quality of their own lives and the education they provided.

Sisters of Charity - Emmitsburg

The third community, in order of founding, is that of the Sisters
of Charity of Saint Joseph, whose central house was located at Emmitsburg, Maryland. (The present sisters at Emmitsburg are known as Daughter
of Charity and St. Joseph's is but one of the American provincial houses.
The foundress, Mother Elizabeth Ann Seton, has the distinction of being
the first native of the United States to be canonized a saint in the
Roman Catholic Church. The account of her life as a member of a prominent New York family, wife, mother, widow and convert, is readily available. Here we are more concerned about the effects of her leadership on
the many women who were inspired by her and who, by 1850, had brought
her desire to give loving service to those in need to almost every area
of the United States where there were large population centers.

When the young widow came to Baltimore in 1808, she was already
an experienced teacher, but her deepest concern was to rear her five
children in reasonable security and in a place where the Catholicism she
had so recently adopted would not be a constant source of enmity and
criticism. The need for schools for the Catholic children was great.
Help and encouragement came to her from various sources within the
Catholic community of Baltimore. The idea of forming a community of
women religious evolved as the need for schools became more apparent and
other women came to share her life and work. The Sulpician priests became Mother Seton's principal guides while a convert clerical student,

Samuel Cooper, provided the means for establishing the permanent center at Emmitsburg. In the summer of 1809, Elizabeth Seton and her small
community moved to Emmitsburg. The candidates for admission came steadily—surely an encouraging sign—but also requiring the sisters to increase their facilities.

Between 1809 and 1814, the sisters concentrated on teaching the
young girls in the Emmitsburg area and those who were sent from more
distant areas to attend St. Joseph Academy, a boarding school. In 1814,
at the request of Father Michael Hurley of Philadelphia, the first sisters left Emmitsburg to take care of St. Joseph Orphanage in that city.
Mother Seton sent her closest associate, Sister Rose White, as the superior. Sisters Susan Clossy and Teresa Conroy completed this first mission.
Before Mother Seton died in 1821, the sisters also began to work in the
Domestic Department and Infirmary of Mount Saint Mary College in Emmitsburg, and St. Patrick Orphan Asylum in New York. In a broad sense, the
outlines of their future had already been made. Between 1821 and 1850,
they would continue to grow and would begin new works as quickly as sisters could be provided. By 1850, missions of the Sisters of Charity
from Emmitsburg could be found from New England to the Gulf of Mexico,
and from the East Coast to the western bank of the Mississippi. They
were engaged in teaching, nursing, and the care of orphans. While the
first great need was to establish schools, orphan asylums soon became
important. The recurrent epidemics and the growing number of impoverished immigrants left many children without families to care for them.
The fear that Protestants would provide help and thus gain influence
over the education of children who had no one else to care for them
led to the organization of asylums. Many of these were organized by

the laity and initially, at least, governed by a board of "managers."
As the need grew and sisters became available the care of orphans was
turned over to the sisters. The Sisters of Charity, by mid-century,
could be found doing this work in many large centers of population
throughout the United States. It was the Sisters of Charity who set
the precedent for American religious to work in both parish and "city"
institutions as well as conducting a variety of institutions which
were the property and responsibility of the particular community of
women religious.

It was the work with orphans that was to become the focal point
of much of the tension between a number of bishops and the superiors in
Emmitsburg. At first the sisters cared for boys as well as girls in
some institutions. The need was great and there were so few persons
able to meet the need. In time the Church in the United States grew
not only in actual numbers, but also in the development of a variety of
religious communities and societies, which seemed able to meet those
needs. The number of orphans increased more rapidly than buildings were
erected and conditions often became unsuitable for large numbers of
children of both sexes. The superiors at Emmitsburg began withdrawing
sisters from the care of boys and asked the bishops to make other arrangements. Some bishops considered this practice quite proper and, in
spite of real difficulties, complied with the new order. Other bishops
found this an occasion, because of the difficulties and problems involved,
to insist upon their authority. Bishop Hughes of New York, was the most
forceful and the first to make this a test case. Who had the final
authority to say what work a sister would do and where she would be
assigned? Was it the bishop of the diocese to which the sister had been

sent, or the superiors of the Central House who had initially provided

for the sister and sent her to a given mission? The conflict came

into the open in 1845 and continued throughout the next year. The

Emmitsburg records speak of the "New York Secession, 1846."[25]

The sisters who chose to remain in New York formed the nucleus

of the Sisters of Charity of New York. Other communities were also

aware of the implications of the final outcome of this dispute. The

basic tension between episcopal authority and the authority of reli-

gious superiors, especially superiors of communities who work in more

than one diocese, has been a constant in the history of women religious

to our own day.

The third major area of work undertaken by the Sisters of

Charity was nursing. They nursed the sick of their own community

and took charge of the infirmary at Mount Saint Mary College. Very

possibly they also nursed sick neighbors in their homes when it was

needed since references to such activity in later documents are re-

corded very matter-of-factly. Nursing in a more formal, institutional

setting, had not been initiated. Archbishop Carroll, in a letter

of 11 September 1811, to Mother Seton wrote:

> A century at least will pass before the exigencies & habits
> of this Country will require & hardly admit of the charitable
> exercises towards the sick, sufficient to employ any number of
> the [sis]ters out of our largest cities; and therefore they
> must consider the business of education as a laborious, chari-
> table & permanent object of their religious duty.[26]

---

[25]Cf. [Daughters of Charity], Mother Etienne Hall (Emmitsburg,
Maryland: St. Joseph's), Chapter II, pp. 18ff.

[26]John Carroll Papers, III:157

Twelve years later, after the deaths of both the Archbishop and Mother Seton, the sisters began their hospital work at the Baltimore Infirmary. By 1850, they were working in at least five hospitals across the country, including Mount Hope Retreat which they organized and managed as a hospital for the mentally ill. They had worked in several other hospitals for short periods, but conditions were not favorable to their remaining. Nonetheless, by 1850, they were well established and recognized as capable nurses.

During the various cholera and typhoid epidemics the community responded to the needs of the suffering in emergency quarters. The selfless and efficient work of the sisters won the esteem of the public authorities as well as the sick and their families. The accolades given to the sisters were in striking contrast to what was to be found in contemporary nativist literature. While there were some victims among the sisters, the number was small compared to the number who nursed the sick and the conditions under which they worked.

There was no clear-cut professional training for any field of labor at this period. Teaching came closest to having what a twentieth century American would consider a professional training. It was not unusual for a sister from Emmitsburg to be changed from one field of work to another, and sometimes this happened several times during her life. Moreover, the change might also mean a journey of hundreds of miles to a different climate and culture. In 1850 the community was vastly different, in some respects, from the small number who gathered around Elizabeth Seton in the first years after she moved from Baltimore to "the Valley" (Emmitsburg) in 1809.

Sisters of Loretto

Just three years after Elizabeth Seton began the formation of her community in Emmitsburg, Maryland, two new communities were formed within the diocese of Bardstown, Kentucky. The first community is commonly known as the Sisters of Loretto but was officially designated by variants of "The Friends of Mary at the Foot of the Cross." The founder, Father Charles Nerinckx, had been a zealous missionary in Kentucky before Bishop Flaget arrived in 1811. He recognized the great need to provide an education for the children growing up in the area, but the means were not available. Mary Rhodes also came to Kentucky in 1811. Apparently she had come only to visit her brother and his family and her younger sister, Ann, who had come with her brother some years before. Once she arrived she was made acutely aware of what the pioneer children were missing since there were no schools available. Many of the parents of these children had immigrated from Maryland, where they had had the advantages of at least an elementary education as well as instruction in their Faith. They were not unmindful of the lack of education but frontier conditions made it impossible for them to remedy the lack. The few priests also found it very difficult to prepare children for the reception of the sacraments. Illiteracy, compounded with the vast territories to be served by a single priest, seemed overwhelming. Mary Rhodes was educated; according to community tradition she had attended the Visitation Academy in Georgetown.[27] At first, she simply

---

[27]Any records Loretto may have had would have been destroyed in the fire that destroyed the Motherhouse in 1858. At the Visitation Academy in Georgetown there are no lists of students for the early years. Since it was the only convent school in the East between 1799 and 1809, the tradition is not to be entirely disregarded.

asked Father Nerinckx for permission to teach her niece and a few neighbor children the catechism and give them a basic education. That such an education was valued by many is proven by the fact that soon more children applied than she could care for at her brother's home. A nearby, rough, neglected cabin was fixed up as well as possible and a "school" was opened. Soon Christina Stuart joined her and gradually the idea of a religious community dedicated to teaching evolved. On 25 April 1812, Mary Rhodes, Christina Stuart and Ann Havern were received as novices in the log church of Saint Charles by Father Nerinckx.

The need to provide education for the young girls was once more the catalyst which led to the formation of a new community. The care of orphans also became a concern for the sisters. Unlike other communities, the Sisters of Loretto neither founded nor staffed orphan asylums. The orphans were cared for in their other schools, most of which provided boarding facilities. Between 1818 and 1848, they conducted Gethsemani school at the site of the present Trappist Monastery. The motherhouse records note that this particular school "mothered so many orphans it has sometimes been designated as an orphanage."[28] By the 1820's the sisters were moving in the direction of preparation for, and development of, an Academy that would prepare young ladies for the more cultured life in the higher levels of society. Contemporary writings as well as the annals and other accounts written at a later period contain contradictory evidence concerning Father Nerinckx's view of this development. It would seem that Father Nerinckx must have encouraged this development since he remained in charge of the community until he left for

[28] ASL. RGs VIII - 4.

Missouri, just a few months before his death in August 1824.[29]   By 1828,

the "Female School of Loretto" published its Prospectus in the United

States Catholic Miscellany.[30]   No music was yet being offered, but

other advanced subjects for female education are in the course of study.

By the 1830's public examinations were being held and Henry Clay gave

the address on one such day.[31]   And in the 1840's art and music at the

Academy were so well taught that the Sisters of the Holy Cross sent

some of their members there to perfect their talents.[32]

As early as 1823, the sisters made their first foundation out-

side of Kentucky, at Bethlehem, Perry County, Missouri, at the request

of Father Joseph Rosati, C.M. Within a short period they were not only

teaching, but accepting candidates in Missouri. As new Catholic settle-

ments developed in the West the sisters branched out to meet the needs.

For a time the sisters in Missouri and the area to the west were quite

autonomous. In 1828, Bishop Flaget told Bishop Rosati it would be best

for Kentucky to have no responsibility for those under his care—only

spiritual ties would remain.[33]   According to the Annals, Bethlehem in

Missouri had increased by 1834 through new receptions and some arrivals

---

[29]Cf. "Historical Studies and Notes: Letters from Bishop Benedict
Joseph Flaget to Bishop Joseph Rosati, St. Louis, Mo.," Social Justice
Review (November 1969), 62:242. Also the "Annals" as compiled by Sr.
Theodosia Kelly, ALM, p. 11 of the typescript copy.

[30]USCM. (12 January 1828), p. 216.

[31]ASL. RGsp XXXIV - 1.

[32]Brother Bede, C.F.X., A Study of the Past and Present Applications of Educational Psychology in the Catholic Schools of the Diocese of
Louisville, Master's Dissertation, University of Louisville, 1923, Revised,
1926 (Baltimore: St. Mary's Industrial School Press, 1926), p. 47. He
refers to the Catholic Educational Review (September 1911).

[33]Social Justice Review (December 1969), 62:279.

from Loretto in Kentucky.[34] Uncertainty about the Rules, particularly Part II concerning the government of the society, kept the situation somewhat fluid for many years. Individual sisters found this lack of certainty difficult; however, it was the very absence of clear legislation regarding the government of the community that made it possible for the sisters in Missouri and Kentucky to recognize one central administration a few years later when improved means of travel and communication along with the need for an adequate teacher-training institution made such centralization desirable.

The Loretto Sisters, before 1850, also engaged in two other pioneering works. The first was a Deaf and Dumb Asylum at Loretto. Althoug the school lasted only about three years (1840 to about 1843) it is important as an initial attempt to care for the physically handicapped. Bishop Flaget was interested in this work and had his niece, Eulalia Flaget, and another young woman trained in sign language and the method o teaching the deaf at La Chartreuse, France.[35] No other information about the school or the reason for its closing seems to have survived. The second pioneering apostolate opened a field of work which had a longer life span. In 1847 the Sisters of Loretto were asked to open a school for girls at the Mission for the Osage Indians in Kansas, where the Jesuits were already working. Both the national government's Superintendent for Indian Affairs in St. Louis, and the Osage Sub-Agent wrote very favorable reports concerning the work of the sisters in their annual report of 1850 to the Commissioner of Indian Affairs.[36] This school remained open until 1895, when the building was destroyed by fire.

---

[34]ASL. Memoirs - Sr. Theodosia Kelly.   [35]ASL. RGsp XXXIV-12

[36]National Archives, Serial 587, Executive Documents Printed by

The Sisters of Loretto did not become involved in small parish schools during this period. The schools they staffed served larger areas and were almost always boarding schools. The practice seems to have been to send colonies of about ten sisters when a new mission was opened. In 1850 there were four missions in Kentucky in addition to the Academy at the Motherhouse and six missions in the West.

Sisters of Charity - Nazareth

In November 1812, the first two members (Elizabeth Wells and Teresa Carrico) of the group who founded the Sisters of Charity of Nazareth placed themselves under the direction of Father David.[37] They, too, hoped to aid in the education of girls. Unlike the communities previously founded, none of the original members had sufficient education to immediately begin teaching, but Father David was able to prepare them within a few years.[38] In the meantime they lived in a house at St. Thomas and did whatever work they could to help the bishop, priests, and seminarians who also lived there. By 1816, the sisters already had an enrollment of more than thirty pupils at St. Thomas and the quarters were becoming overcrowded. In 1819 property in Bardstown was purchased and a school was opened under the direction of Sister Harriet Gardiner. It seemed advisable for the sisters to leave St. Thomas in 1822 because of difficulties

Order of the Senate of the United States during the Second Session of the Thirty-First Congress, begun and held At the City of Washington, December 2, 1850. In 5 volumes. Vol. 1 containing Document No. 1 (Washington: Printed at the Union Office, 1851), pp. 66-71.

[37] Catherine Spalding, the first superior and the one honored as foundress of the community, entered in January 1813, but received the habit with the other two on 7 April 1814.

[38] ASCN. "Annals" by Mother Catherine and others, DLB IV:16.

connected with the deed to the property. They purchased a farm just a short distance from Bardstown and named it Nazareth. Here they opened an Academy and established their Motherhouse.

The Community, from the beginning, followed the rules and constitutions of the Sisters of Charity as written by St. Vincent de Paul. Father David had been the Father Superior at Emmitsburg for a time, and it was Bishop Flaget who had procured and brought to the United States these same rules. The first plan was to have sisters come from Emmitsburg, so that Nazareth would be considered a branch of that community. Bishop Flaget and Father David, however, desired to retain full authority concerning the sisters in Kentucky. This was unacceptable to the administration in Emmitsburg. A copy of the rules and constitutions, as it had been adapted for use in Emmitsburg, was sent to Kentucky. In later years Bishop Flaget again considered a union between Emmitsburg and Nazareth, and the two with France. The Sisters of Charity of Nazareth made it very clear to him that they would consider this an unsettling move, and one that would be unfaithful to the wishes of Bishop David and their original spirit.[39]

As new members swelled the ranks, new works were waiting to be undertaken. The Sisters of Charity, like the Loretto Sisters, were concerned about orphans. Orphans were cared for, whenever possible, in their schools, but a specific orphanage was founded in Louisville, Kentucky in 1832. Mother Catherine saw the number of children left homeless after the cholera epidemic and determined to do whatever she could. By the late 1840's, Louisville, too, was receiving its share of destitute Irish

---

[39]Cf. ASCN., OLB, I:43. Sr. Catherine Spalding, et al., to Bishop Flaget (6 July 1841).

immigrants. The orphanage, which had never lacked for applicants, was

often the only hope for the children of immigrants whose parents died

shortly after their arrival. The Infirmary which had been founded in

1836 in connection with the orphanage also had additional demands placed

on it. The Motherhouse Archives contain an interesting series of letters

to Mother Catherine from H. H. Gray, the editor of the Prin[cipal?]

Current, St. Louis, Missouri, between March and May 1845. They concern

his wife whom he had placed at the Infirmary for treatment of a mental

disease. There is no indication of how the original arrangements were

made, and it is the first indication of the care of the mentally ill. In

his first letter Mr. Gray wrote: "Trusting that experience in similar

cases will suggest to you the most effectual course to be pursued to

usual speedy recovery, . . . "[40] It seems strange, if there had never

been mental patients at St. Joseph's Infirmary before that a man in St.

Louis, where the Mullanphy Hospital had been opened by the sisters from

Emmitsburg in 1828, would send his wife all the way to Louisville, Ken-

tucky. In any case, the incident indicates the sisters' willingness to

provide care for anyone in need. Lack of facilities seems to have been

the only real deterrent to acceptance. References to the orphanage in-

dicate that this was often a very real problem there. Mother Catherine

did not fear to beg for the orphans, but space and supplies both re-

mained a problem in spite of the generosity of many.

The Nazareth Motherhouse also sent sisters beyond the state of

Kentucky before 1850. Sisters were sent to Vincennes, Indiana in 1824,

while that state was still under the care of Bishop Flaget. They were

withdrawn in 1834, but sent back in 1835. They were again withdrawn in

[40]ASCN. DLB, I:130-131; 134-137.

1838. The decision was made in March, but the sisters were to stay until August, so the Bishop of Vincennes, Simon Bruté, could arrange with
the superiors in Emmitsburg to send sisters. They were also sent to
White River, Indiana in 1832, but conditions there did not make it practical for them to remain even one entire year. Here, as in so many cases
involving most of the communities, the great need for sisters did not
warrant maintaining sisters in an area at great expense when the number
to be helped was small.[41]

In 1842, sisters were sent to Nashville, Tennessee, at the urgent
request of Bishop Richard P. Miles. The first work was a school for
young girls. The sisters began their work in a rented house with the intention of buying property at a later date. The following year Bishop
Miles found a house for sale that he concluded met all the requirements
of the superiors. In the same letter (6 October 1843) in which he
thanked Mother Catherine for agreeing to help the Church in Nashville pay
for a house for the sisters, he told her he had authorized Mr. Stephen-
son to purchase a house for $11,050.00 to be paid in three annual in-
stallments without interest.[42]

In April 1848, a hospital was established in what had been the
old cathedral. Orphan girls were also cared for there. In May, the
cholera epidemic struck Nashville, and the sisters cared for many of
the victims. But difficulties between the bishop and the superiors at
the Motherhouse were beginning to develop. Some sisters apparently
traced the difficulties back to the break between some of the Sisters
of Charity in New York from the Motherhouse at Emmitsburg. An implica-

[41]ASCN. Account prepared for centenary of Vincennes.

[42]ASCN. OLB, III:35.

tion found in the archival records, as well as in other writings of the time, was that once Bishop Hughes proved it was possible for a bishop to maintain control of a sufficient number of sisters to proceed with the work without the help of the central house other bishops decided to try the same. In this case Nazareth recalled the sisters only in 1851. The few who chose to remain were the nucleus of the community that later moved to Kansas and became known as the Sisters of Charity of Leavenworth.[43]

Dominican Sisters - St. Catharine, Kentucky

The final community in the Kentucky triad was founded ten years after the first two. On 28 February 1822, Father Wilson, O.P., spoke particularly to the young women in the congregation at St. Rose Church (Washington County, Kentucky). It was a moving "vocation talk"; nine young women offered themselves for the work of Christian education and the religious life as a result of it.[44] Four members of this group, Maria Sansbury, Mary Carrico, Sevily Tarleton, and Judy McMan, received the religious habit in St. Rose Church on Easter Sunday, 7 April 1822. The community was given a very brief constitution based on the Rule of St. Augustine and the Constitutions of the Dominican Order. They were professed as tertiaries, but with the expressed purpose of becoming Second Order Dominicans when conditions would permit. The constitutions are unique in that they contain more about the ascetical life than apostolic work even though educational needs seem to have been a primary

---

[43]ASCN. "Sketches of Branch Houses Now Closed."

[44]AOPStC. Profession Book, 1822-1919, pp. 3-4. "Brief History" written in 1846. One name, Molley Johnson, is found only in this account. There is no record of her profession or work.

purpose in their coming together. Fathers Wilson and Miles were said to have begun instructing the young women immediately in the necessary subjects to prepare them for teaching. St. Magdalen School (later known as St. Catharine) was opened in 1823 on land near St. Rose that was secured for them by Sister Angela Sansbury.

The sisters experienced a period of great difficulty and poverty about 1830. Father Wilson had died and Father Miles had been called to Ohio by Edward Fenwick who was both Bishop of Cincinnati and Commissary General of the Order of St. Dominic in the United States. The new superior at St. Rose was Father Muños, a Spanish Dominican who opposed the sisters from the beginning. The debt, incurred when Father Miles was in charge of the sisters and was in his name, had become the source of a dispute. It was suggested that the sisters sell the property, disband, and go home. Bishop Fenwick offered the alternative of a few going to Somerset, Ohio where the Dominican priests had established themselves. A few of them did go, among them Sister Angela Sansbury, the first prioress in Kentucky. Bishop Fenwick also suggested, and asked permission of the Master General, that the sisters change to a black garb like the Sisters of Charity and work as such in Cincinnati.[45] This latter the sisters refused, just as they refused to disband. Within a short time Father Stephen Montgomery, a native of Kentucky, was sent back to St. Rose as superior. He not only understood the sisters' position, but assured creditors that the sisters would repay the debt.

By 1833, the debt was repaid and improvements were made at St. Magdalen's Academy to bring it up to the standards of the time. About

---

[45] AOPStC. Cf. translation made from the original letter of Bishop Fenwick to the Master General, Rome, 10 October 1829.

the same time a school for boys under twelve years of age was opened.
The records are not specific about the years it was in existence. Most
of the information that has survived was written in later years by one
who had been a student there and from the recollections of older sisters.
What has survived shows no indication that the teaching or care of young
boys (some of them boarded at the school) was an exception to be tolerated only because of unusual circumstances. The priests had a school
for older boys and the sisters were primarily concerned about the education of young girls. It was a problem of space and available personnel
rather than a question of principle that led to the closing of the school
several years later.

During the years preceding 1850, the community remained rather
small in Kentucky, but the Academy of St. Magdalen gained in importance.
It was chartered in 1835, and the first formal graduation was in 1845.
The closing days of each school year with examinations, displays, and programs were important enough in the latter half of the 1840's that the
bishop and a few priests came from a distance. Some Jesuits even came
from Cincinnati.

In 1846, the sisters decided it was time they had a real church.
They had no money, but began digging the foundation themselves and begging for funds as well as help with the actual construction. Their en-
thusiasm was so contagious that by 1848, they had a fine Gothic church.[46]
It is of interest that the church was modelled after plans of the churches
connected with monasteries of Dominican Nuns in Europe so that it had a
choir grill separating the sisters from the rest of the church.[47]

---

[46]AOPStC. The building was destroyed by fire in 1904, but a few
pictures remain as testimony.

[47]AOPStC. "The Story of the Little Chapel," Sr. Margaret Hamilton.

Also in 1848, the sisters wrote a petition to Pope Pius IX.

After stating their involvement in education and the advantages for the

Church in the United States which resulted from this work, they stated

their request:

> In our profession we add a clause, to embrace the Rule of
> St. Augustine and the Constitutions of the Order of Preachers as
> Sisters of the Second Order of St. Dominic, whenever we may
> judge it proper to do so.
> After deliberation, it has seemed to us that the present
> time is favorable to this end. But on account of the parti-
> cular circumstances in which we are placed, it is impossible
> either to sustain the choir or to be enclosed. We cannot re-
> cite the Divine Office, because the number of those who are
> capable of teaching being so small, it would consume more time
> than they could possibly devote to it. Nor can we be enclosed
> because our convents are not built in a suitable manner, and we
> have not sufficient revenues to change their present form. Again,
> were we enclosed, we should lose our pupils, Catholics as well as
> Protestants, and would thus be deprived of the means of support.
> Wherefore, submitting these considerations to the wisdom of your
> Holiness we join in one common prayer for a dispensation of be-
> ing enclosed and allowing us to recite the Office of the Blessed
> Virgin Mary, instead of the Divine Office, and to grant us the
> favor of making the solemn profession as Nuns of the Second Order
> of Our Holy Father St. Dominick.[48]

There seems to be no record of a response to this petition; the sisters

never took solemn vows but continued to live and work as Sisters of the

Third Order of St. Dominic.

The only work other than education which involved the sisters

during this period was their care of the sick during the cholera epidemic

of 1832. Bishop Flaget wrote to the Society for the Propagation of the

Faith that these Dominican Sisters had as much right to be recognized

as the other two communities. Of great interest in our contemporary

world is his account:

> There being only 10 or 11 sisters in their community in Ken-
> tucky they had recourse to holy ingenuity in order to multiply
> their forces, . . . They induced women of mature age and

---

[48]AOPStC. Copy of the Petition to Pope Pius IX, 1848.

known virtue to associate themselves with their works of
charity. For many weeks they might be seen at all hours of
the day and night in those houses where the sick were most
numerous and misery at its height. Not one of them or their
companions died; but all of them were exhausted and worn out
beyond the power of words to describe. Without special pro-
tection of Divine Providence it would have been impossible
for them so long to continue such toils of mercy and compassion.[49]

In 1851 the Sisters had the Act of Incorporation changed. Instead of
the "Literary Society of St. Magdalen" it would "be known and called by
the name of St. Catharine of Sienna."[50] Accounts written after 1850
often interchange the names. There was no change in the place or type
of education offered by the institution.

Oblate Sisters of Providence

As the 1820's drew to a close there was a sizable colony of free
black people in the city of Baltimore. Many of these people were French-
speaking people from the West Indies. Some among them still had sufficient wealth to live comfortably for they had been members of the planter
class and had fled at the time of the slave revolts. Other black people
from the West Indies were craftsmen of one kind or another and so were
able to live in reasonable comfort, but there were also many black families who only succeeded in subsisting from day to day. The financial
status of the family, however, had little effect on the educational opportunities of the children. Schools were not open to them. The date
at which Miss Elizabeth Lange began teaching black children is uncertain.

---

[49]AOPStC. Writings of Sr. Margaret Hamilton, re: General Superiors. Also found in: Victor F. O'Daniel, O.P., The Father of the Church
in Tennessee, or the Life, Times, and Character of the Right Reverend
Richard Pius Miles, O.P., the First Bishop of Nashville (Washington, D.C.:
The Dominicana, 1926), pp. 238-239.

[50]St. Catharine Convent, Office of the President, "Act of Incorporation."

It is only certain that she and several companions had been doing it for
some time by 1828, when Father Joubert, S.S. was introduced to them.
The need for education--a good in itself, but also an important prerequisite for a successful catechetical program for the young--was again
the immediate cause for the formation of a new community of women religious.

According to the French Diary begun by Father Joubert, Elizabeth Lange, Marie Magdaleine Balas and Rosine Boegue began their novitiate on June 13, 1828, but continued their teaching. Father Joubert
wrote the Constitutions for these women and presented them to Archbishop
Whitfield in June 1829. Four sisters made their first profession on 2
July 1829. (The fourth member was Marie Therese Duchemin.)[51] Because
these sisters were black women their development was even more difficult
at times than that of the other communities. When one considers the time
one must marvel that there were so few difficulties, and that their diff.
culties were so closely paralleled in other communities. The primary aim
of the community was the education of young girls. Father Joubert had
written in the Constitutions, under the heading, "General Observation":

> The object of their institute is one of great importance[;]
> greater, indeed, than might at first appear to those, who
> would only glance at the advantages, which it is calculated
> to impart to a great portion of the human race, and, through
> it, to Society at large. [I]n fact, these girls will either
> become mothers of families, or be introduced as servants, into
> decent houses.[52]

Although he also wrote in the Constitutions that "reading, writing
and the first rules of arithmetic are sufficient" along with sewing,

---

[51]AOSP. "Early French Diary," pp. 1-11.

[52]AOSP. Original Constitutions, "General Observations," #9.

embroidery and washing . . . [and] the first principles of religion,"[53]
it is clear that the teaching of these subjects in both French and English was on a par with other schools of the time. The finest testimony
to their work is to be found in the account of the Commissioner of Education in his report to the Congress which was published in 1871. Repeatedly, when speaking of schools for free black children in the District of Columbia before the Civil War, he attributes the fine teaching
in several schools to the fact that the young woman who conducted a
specific school was educated at the Baltimore Convent.[54]

The Baltimore school, like those of the other teaching communities, was both a boarding and day school. Those who could paid for their
education, but there were also many poor students and orphans to be supported. Father Joubert arranged for the importation of fine fabrics and
the sisters made vestments of all kinds. In 1832, they, too, went to
nurse cholera victims in the city's almshouse. They received a letter of
commendation and thanks for their work from the Trustees of the Poor,[55]
but there is no record of public acknowledgement of their service such
as was given to the Sisters of Charity. Beginning in 1835, through the
remainder of the period under consideration, depending on conditions,
two or more Oblate Sisters directed the domestic work and the infirmary
at Saint Mary Seminary in Baltimore.

According to the French Diary the Oblate Sisters and the Carmelites were threatened by a nativist riot in 1834. Several priests and
other men prepared to protect the sisters and stayed at the convent

---

[53]AOSP. Ibid., #3.

[54]Cf. Special Report, 1871, pp. 211; 216-217.

[55]AOSP. "French Diary," pp. 30-31.

through the night. The Carmelite records say nothing about this threat
to them and the "Sisters of Color" in 1834. They do record a similar
situation in 1839, after Sister Isabella Neale fled the convent in a
state of mental unbalance. It is probable that the date in the French
Diary is incorrect. The last entries were made by Sister Teresa Duchemi
and were possibly done sometime after the event.[56]

Father Joubert died 5 November 1843. This was not only a loss
such as that experienced by many communities at the death of a "Founding
Father"; the Sulpicians were being withdrawn from the work of directing
communities of women by their superior in France, and the new Archbishop
of Baltimore, Samuel Eccleston, was not concerned about the continued
existence of the Oblate Sisters of Providence. There is a strong tradition in the community that Archbishop Eccleston thought the sisters shou
disband and become house servants. Mother Theresa Willigman, the commun
ity's first historian, had been a young girl in the care of the sisters
in 1843. She wrote: "We pass over these sad years. To many it seemed a
if the good work was to be abandoned. The good Father Deluol did all in
his power but no one dared come forward to take up the work."[57] And in
another place she wrote: "Of the sorrow and deep distress of the Sisters
in the years following [Father Joubert's death] we draw a veil."[58] The
year 1847 brought the first real hope to the brave community that had
struggled on in spite of virtual ostracism. A young Redemptorist, Fathe
Thaddeus Anwander, with the consent and encouragement of his superior,
Rev. John N. Neumann, gained the consent of Archbishop Eccleston to take

---

[56]AOSP. "French Diary," p. 57.

[57]AOSP. Sr. Theresa Catherine Willigman, "A few facts relating
to the Oblate Sisters of Providence of Balt. Md.," p. 7.

[58]AOSP. Another (probably later) "edition" of the above, p. 5.

charge of the sisters. His eight years with the Sisters marked a new

beginning. When he left, the number of sisters and students had in-

creased, additions to the Convent/School had been built, and a school

for boys had been opened.[59]

The intervening years had seen the departure of three sisters

for Michigan. Sister Theresa Duchemin, one of the founding members had

also served as superior of the Oblate Sisters. When the future looked

so bleak in 1845, she along with Sisters Ann Constance and Stanislaus,

planned to begin another community in Michigan. Sister Theresa went to

Michigan first. Sister Ann Constance followed her later, as planned,

but Sister Stanislaus was told not to come (she had already severed her

ties with the Oblate Sisters) because she was too dark.[60] The two who

did go to Michigan, founded the Sisters of the Immaculate Heart of Mary.

Sisters of Our Lady of Mercy

Late in 1829, Bishop England returned to Charleston, South Caro-

lina, from the Council of Baltimore after having met four young women who

were ready to aid him with the work in his vast diocese (North and South

Carolina and Georgia). His first concern, like that of many of his fel-

low bishops, was the lack of basic education among the people and the

need for religious instruction of the young and the care of orphans.[61]

The four women—Mary and Honora O'Gorman, their niece Mary Teresa Barry,

[59]AOSP. Mother Theresa C. Willigman, "Short History written as a 'festal bouquet,'" p. 56.

[60]AOSP. Cf. Mother Theresa C. Willigman, "Memories of Sr. Theresa Duchemin," pp. 11-14.

[61]Cf. USCM. "Address of the Right Rev. John England, D.D., Bishop of Charleston, to the Seventh Annual Convention of the Roman Catholic Church of the State of South Carolina, on Monday, November 23rd, 1829." (5 December 1829), p. 177.

and Mary E. Burke--were established in community in Charleston by Bishop

England in December 1829. He gave them the title, Sisters of Our Lady

of Mercy. He did give them some basic rules, but never wrote a Consti-

tution for them as he had promised. He explained his viewpoint in a

letter to his friend, Judge William Gaston of North Carolina:

> The Sisters whom I am endeavoring to establish will not be a
> band of those at Emmitsburg nor dependent on them, as I do
> not wish to make my institutions depend on Superiors over
> whom I have neither control or influence. Hence, I shall try
> what can, within the diocese, be done upon the same principle.
> I have four who cost me very little and do much service.[62]

Clearly, Bishop England expected to be in control. Difficulties arose

because he was unable to do all the work himself. His diocese was vast

and the Catholic population was small. Not only did he find it necessary

to visit Europe seeking funds and recruiting priests and sisters as many

other bishops did, but he was also appointed papal visitor to Haiti.

During England's long absences from Charleston, his Vicars General, those

priests he had assigned as ecclesiastical superiors of the sisters, and

at one time his coadjutor, Bishop Clancy, took an interest in the sisters

and tried to help them. Since they were without specific constitutions

this often led to "confusion and disorder,"[63] and when Bishop England re-

turned he would again change things. One thing was clear--Bishop England

wanted the Sisters of Our Lady of Mercy to confine themselves to service

of the lower classes of people whether white or black. He wished to have

others staff an Academy for the upper classes. An example of this took

place during England's absence during 1836-1837. Bishop Clancy assigned

---

[62]"Letters from Right Rev. John England, D.D. to the Honorable
William Gaston, LL.D.," Records of the American Catholic Historical Society of Philadelphia (1908), XIX:147-148.

[63]Cf. Sister M. Anne Francis Campbell, "Bishop England's Sisterhood, 1829-1929" (Ph.D. dissertation, St. Louis University, 1968), p. 25.

the sisters to take charge of the Cathedral choir and encouraged three
or four sisters to study music in order to teach it. When Bishop England returned he turned the Cathedral choir over to the Ursulines and
forbade the Sisters of Our Lady of Mercy to teach either French or music.
He did concede that he might later rescind the prohibition to teach
music.[64]

As early as 1835, Bishop England had seen to the Incorporation
of both the Ursuline Sisters and the Sisters of Our Lady of Mercy.[65]
He had also opened a school for free colored children. Two seminarians
taught the boys and two sisters taught the girls. The school was successful but was closed due to pressure from some leading citizens of
Charleston. Bishop England agreed to close his school for free colored
children only if the other denominations closed theirs, thus three schools
were closed 10 August 1835. Another school for free colored children
was opened in 1841 and continued to 1848.[66] Almost from the beginning
the sisters had done the domestic work for Bishop England's seminary. In
1836, they nursed the sick during the cholera epidemic that struck Charleston four years later than it had struck other major cities. Secular
sources do not speak of the work of the sisters in this field. Apparently
the sisters nursed the poor Irish in Charleston. The Irish themselves
did not write about the work of the sisters and other citizens were more
concerned about their house slaves than the poor Irish. In 1838, Bishop
England founded a Benevolent Society, the Brotherhood of San Marino, and
then rented and converted a house on Queen Street in Charleston as a

---

[64]Cf. Ibid., p. 34.

[65]ASCLM. Copy of "Act of Incorporation."

[66]Cf. Campbell, p. 64.

hospital which the sisters operated until 1841. In 1839, they were called to Augusta, Georgia to nurse the victims of a yellow fever epidemic.

After Bishop England's death, 11 April 1842, the development of the community came to a standstill. The bishop had never given them a constitution and had allowed their superiors very little authority. While the See of Charleston remained vacant, the sisters had no retreat and were unable to renew their vows. When Bishop Ignatius Reynolds took possession of his see in April 1844, he set about placing the sisters on a more solid foundation. He required them to make a retreat, wrote a constitution based on that of St. Vincent de Paul, and then had the sisters elect their own officers. They were, for the first time, given some measure of independence in the conduct of their lives. The Minutes of Council Meetings begin with the meeting of 16 May 1844.[67]

In 1845, Bishop Reynolds informed the sisters that they were well enough organized to send six sisters to Savannah, Georgia to open an establishment there. A year later the sisters in Savannah requested that they be separated from Charleston and be considered an autonomous community. The separation, as provided for in the constitutions, was completed in 1847.[68] After the Ursulines left the Charleston diocese in 1847, the bishop and clergy voted to give the Sisters of Our Lady of Mercy further support, that is, they wanted the curriculum of the Academy broadened to fill the gap caused by the closing of the Ursuline Academy.

---

[67]ASCLM.

[68]ASCLM. Council Minutes, 5 December 1846 - 5 July 1847.

CHAPTER II

THESE NEW SISTERHOODS -- CATHOLIC AND AMERICAN

Constitutions

The most obvious exception to Wach's three-stage model (disciples, sisterhood and institution) is that there was a basic written rule
of life or constitution for each group from the earliest stages. Religious life, in itself, had attained a degree of institutionalization
within the Roman Catholic Church by the close of the eighteenth century.
In the United States it was a new facet of the institutional Church, but
the importance of conforming with a general structure recognizable as
"religious life" as it was already known in Europe was not only an accepted fact, but usually a real goal from the beginning of each institute.
As a result there was an equivocal attitude toward "Constitutions." To
be recognized by the Church it was necessary to have a written rule of
life or constitutions that were approved, at least by the local bishop.
In some cases the approval of Church authorities in Rome was also sought
at an early stage. It was only in the later stages of development, however, that these written rules actually took on the character of a pri-
ary force in the lives of the individual sisters.

Because the first Carmelites came as professed religious with some
years of experience, there is not much parallel between their development
and the model. Within the other seven religious communities the adoption
of written rules and constitutions came about in the first stage. Nevertheless, it is clear that the founders' and foundresses' ideals were the

53

binding force at this stage. Where older rules were adopted the interpretation and adaptations of the founders and foundresses were of great
importance. Only after the death of the founders and original members,
and when the community was expanding, did it become necessary to refer to
the written documents, and even look for written records of the original
interpretations.

The constitutions of the eight religious communities can be
roughly divided under three classifications. The first class is that of
well-developed constitutions for the old religious communities with
solemn vows and strict enclosure. The Carmelites and Visitandines followed such rules and constitutions. The Rule and Constitution brought to
the United States by the Carmelites in 1790 was a French edition of about
1600 which came from Antwerp. As a community of Carmelite nuns they were
firmly established in the third stage and proudly traced their origins
directly back to St. Theresa of Avila.[1] As an American foundation there
was a renewal of the three stages; now, however, it was more a question
adaptation to the American scene. Even these adaptations were minor in
the overall picture; the means of support was the only obvious adaptatio
During the first four decades the nuns supported themselves by the work
their own hands as well as from the plantation. During the last years a
Port Tobacco the plantation was a financial burden rather than an asset
and was one of the factors in the decision to move to Baltimore. Once i
Baltimore, they were forced to find means to provide their full support,
not simply supplement a guaranteed income. The rules that had been observed for about two centuries had not provided for this necessity in a

[1]ACM-B and conversation with the archivist, Sister Constance
Fitz Gerald, 1977.

potentially hostile environment. Teaching school seemed the only viable means. Unlike the other religious communities, the Carmelites had only a day school. This minimized the time spent away from the common life. In this instance, the foundresses' goal for a Carmel in America took precedence over a rule set down more than two centuries earlier. But the rule not to engage in distracting works was merely put in abeyance, it was not discarded.[2]

The Visitation Convent at Georgetown had a unique development when one considers their status as nuns with solemn vows from 1816 onward. At first, as in the six religious communities founded between 1809 and 1829, the women came together to live a life of dedication and conduct a school for girls. Leonard Neale and the first sisters looked forward to the time when the community would be recognized on all ecclesiastical levels as Visitation Sisters. While they had a copy of the rule from an early date, they were unable to make any contact with Visitation Sisters in Europe. There is no doubt that the charism of the founder and foundresses was a major force in the development of the community. The Visitation Constitution gave them a framework in which to work, but certainly the greater force in the life of these women between 1799 and 1816 was the ideal of Bishop Neale and the original members. Neither the prodding of Archbishop Carroll, nor the example of Mother Seton, nor the lack of formal approval could deter them from their commitment, as cloistered Sisters of the Visitation, to the education of girls. Their growth as a community began when they initiated the practices of a Visitation convent as given in the rule and Constitutions in their possession. The formal approval of Rome

---

[2]Ibid., cf. First Rule and Constitution used by the nuns – a French edition of about 1600 which had been brought from Antwerp. See also, above, p. 18.

in 1816 brought with it the recognition of the clergy as well as the pri
vilege of solemn vows. A short time later, Archbishop Neale finally made
contact with a European convent and they were introduced to the official
habit, but the presence of three Visitation nuns from Europe in 1831 had
little lasting effect. A personal contact between the European and Amer
ican convents and the impetus for the first foundation outside of George
town as important as they were, could not be considered essential change
The gnawing question as to whether they were interpreting the constitutions correctly seems to have been resolved. The spirit, or essential
characteristics of the Georgetown community had already been established

The Constitutions of the Visitation Sisters, as written by St.
Francis de Sales, provided for a life free of "exterior rigors and aus-
terities" in order that women with natural infirmities or older women
could live the religious life.[3] Women with contagious diseases were not
to be accepted, nor was anyone whose infirmity was so great that she cou
not follow the ordinary routine of community life.[4] The young sisters
who died of tuberculosis within a year or two of their entrance seem to
be an indication of the general lack of recognition of the contagious
character of tuberculosis rather than a relative indifference to this
point in the constitution.

There is no mention in the constitution that the education of

---

[3]AGVC. St. Francis de Sales, Rules of St. Augustine, with the
Constitutions and Directory Composed for the Religious Sisters of the
Visitation, Translated into English from the French edition printed at
Paris, by Herissant, 1783 (Georgetown, D.C.: Joshua N. Rind, Congress
Street, 1832), p. 47.

[4]Ibid., p. 49.

young girls was to be a particular work of the sisters, but some schools had developed even during the life of St. Francis de Sales and by the time of the French Revolution many Visitation monasteries had schools connected with them.[5] Undoubtedly the Rule and Constitution of the Sisters of the Visitation were adaptable to the American scene in the early nineteenth century. Not only the Georgetown Visitation Convent and schools filled a need within the young American Church but the foundations made before 1850 show that the life and work of the Visitandines were suitable in many areas of the United States.

Three religious communities used the Rule St. Vincent de Paul had written for the Daughters of Charity in France. While the need for schools was the primary need to be met and other work such as nursing and directing orphan asylums seemed a remote possibility in 1809 when Elizabeth Seton began her work, Bishop Carroll and others were interested in having women religious with sufficient flexibility to meet the demands of a growing Church. The clergy who were familiar with the Church in continental Europe were familiar with the work of the Daughters of Charity, a community without solemn vows and, therefore, not bound by strict enclosure. After Benedict Flaget was named as the first bishop of the newly erected diocese of Bardstown, Kentucky, he travelled to Europe. He was asked to procure a copy of the Rule of St. Vincent de Paul.[6] He also tried to procure Sisters to provide the initial formation for the American community. The

---

[5]Cf. Sullivan, p. 51. Also a personal interview with Mother Mary Leonard Whipple, 1976.

[6]ASJCH. Annals, Vol. I, 91st sheet.

French rules arrived in August 1810, but the sisters never came. Every-one concerned was satisfied with this situation. The Rule, as given by St. Vincent de Paul, was a valuable guide. What is more, it had stood the test of time and was recognized by Church authorities. A few changes were considered necessary in order to meet the needs of the American Church. These changes were made in Baltimore specifically for the sisters in Emmitsburg, but they were almost immediately requested by Father David for use in Bishop Flaget's diocese of Bardstown.[7] Bishop England had the model of the Sisters of Charity in view when he formed the community of the Sisters of Our Lady of Mercy in Charleston (cf. p. 50, above), but apparently intended to make more significant or different changes in St. Vincent de Paul's Rule than was done in Emmitsburg or in Kentucky. Only one clear reference was located. In a letter to Bishop Bruté, Bishop England wrote: "I am endeavouring to put in order . . . my convent, my Sisters of Mercy, for whom I am endeavouring to compile a rule, princi-pally taken from that of the Sisters at Emmitsburg ."[8] Around the turn of the century Sister Mary Charles Curtin (Belmont, North Carolina) wrote

> I found about fifteen Sisters [ca 1841] who had made
> temporary vows, not much form but a great deal of good sense
> and piety. . . . They had a few pages of St. Vincent's Rule in

---

[7]UNDA. Fr. David (St. Thomas near Bardstown) to Fr. Bruté, Baltimore, 3 November 1811. (Flaget) B.J., Bishop of Bardstown (St. Thomas) to Rev. Mr. Bruté, St. Mary's Valley, near Emmits Bourgh, 13 July 1813 [the bishop was still waiting for the rules of St. Joseph's house near Emmitsburg. He would also like Sr. Fanny Jordan or Mrs. George to take charge.] Fr. David, St. Thomas Seminary (near Bardstown) to Fr. Bruté, Mt. St. Mary's Seminary, Emmitsburg, 7 September 1813. [Fr. David was still asking for Rose, or Fanny or Kit and the Rule.] See p. 38 above.

[8]ADC. Bishop England to Bishop Bruté in Vincennes, Charleston, South Carolina, 16 February 1835. Photostat, Box 3, N5.

manuscript, but no constitutions or governing Rules. . . .
Several of the Sisters copied these Rules and tried to enter
into the spirit of them. On a visit to Charleston after
settling in North Carolina, I looked for one of these little
books but could not find one.[9]

The most important changes centered around the need for schools
and the necessity of being self-supporting. Chapter I, Article I of the
Constitutions of the Sisters of Charity of Nazareth reads as follows:

> . . . Their institute is the same as that of the Sisters of
> Charity in France, with this difference, that the education which the
> Sisters of Charity there were bound to give only to the poor orphan
> children, will be extended here to all female children, in whatever
> station of life they may be, for which the Sisters shall receive a
> sufficient compensation, out of which they will endeavor to save as
> much as they can, to educate also gratis poor orphan children. There
> will also be adopted such modifications in the rule as the differ-
> ence of country, habits, customs and manners may require.[10]

Article 3 elaborates on the work of the sisters and adds:

> Accordingly, the care of the poor of all descriptions and ages, sick,
> prisonners [sic], invalids, foundlings, orphans, and even the insane,
> in hospitals and private houses shall be the oject of the sollicitude
> of the Sisters of Nazareth and exercise their zeal gradually, as
> openings and means of doing either shall be afforded to them by
> circumstances.[11]

In spite of Archbishop Carroll's pessimism, the opportunity and the means

to provide homes for orphans and hospitals for the sick and the insane

were given to the Sisters of Charity from Emmitsburg and Nazareth before

1850. The Sisters of Our Lady of Mercy cared for orphans almost from the

---

[9]Sacred Heart Convent Archives, Sisters of Mercy of North Carolina (Belmont). "Annals of the Sisters of Mercy, 1840-1910."
Unpublished manuscript.

[10]ASCN. Handwritten copy of the Constitution, 1827. Cf. ASJCH.
Letters, V, 90b, "An Abridgement of the Constitutions of the Sisters of
Charity established in the United States." Also Charles I. White, D.D.,
Life of Mrs. Eliza A. Seton, Foundress and First Superior of the Sisters
or Daughters of Charity in the United States of America; with Copious
Extracts from Her Writings, and an Historical Sketch of the Sisterhood
from Its Foundation to the time of Her Death, 10th ed., (New York: P. J.
Kennedy, 1901. [First edition, 1852]), pp. 284-285.

[11]ASCN. Ibid., Art. 3.

beginning. They nursed the sick during epidemics before 1850, but it was 1882 before they opened a permanent hospital.[12]

Another American adaptation that is clearly stated is that of shortening the five-year probationary period called for in St. Vincent de Paul's Rules to one or, at most, two years. The Constitutions state:

> But this privilege of being allowed to make vows one year, or at most 2 years after their admission into the Sisterhood, being a deviation from the rules of the Sisters of Charity in France, which require 5 years probation; which deviation is made only to obviate to [sic] the apprehension, which Novices might have, that after spending in the Sisterhood the best years of their lives, they could be excluded from it, without committing a Capital fault.-- Should experience hereafter show the necessity (perhaps felt in Europe) of requiring 5 years probation, the Superior General, the Mother and Council if unanimous in this opinion are hereby authorized to require that 5 years probation, and their doing so shall not be considered as an infringement of the Constitutions; . . .[13]

The registers in the motherhouse at Nazareth and Charleston indicate the general practice was to have the sisters pronounce their first vows at the end of a one- or two-year novitiate. There were exceptions t this practice in Charleston, but the lack of a written constitution before Bishop Reynolds' accession led to periods of uncertainty. No profession dates are recorded in the Emmitsburg register. When Sister Ann McAleer wrote about her first assignment, 1839, she said: "[we] were much depressed in leaving home as we were permitted at that time to remain at home two years, and 3 months & at the end of this time we made our holy vows, & went after on Mission, . . . "[14] No other clear reference was

---

[12]Campbell, p. 238.

[13]ASCN., Constitution, 1827, Ch. I, Art. 10.

[14]ASJCH. Notes of Sister M. Ann McAleer, p. 8.

made to the practice before 1850, but the impression was that the probationary period was about two years. It would seem it was not always spent
entirely at the Central House.[15]

The most striking difference in the Constitutions of the Sisters
of Charity from Emmitsburg or Nazareth and the Constitutions as given to
the Sisters of Our Lady of Mercy by Bishop Reynolds was in Chapter 4,
Article 3--"Of the formation of independent establishments." In this
article Bishop Reynolds outlines the steps to be taken if an independent
establishment is deemed advisable. These steps are: 1) The sisters of
the "colony" are to send a petition to the Motherhouse, signed by at least
a majority of them. 2) The Council of the Motherhouse will consider the
petition at three meetings (with at least four days intervening between
each meeting). 3) If the Council assents, the matter is to be submitted
to the Bishop and his judgement will be final. No sister is bound to remain with the newly separated establishment "unless when she took her
vows, or at the time of such separation, she consented thereto; . . . "
Questions concerning the dowry, or money or property given to the Motherhouse were to be considered by the Council in the light of "the expenses
and services of all the separated sisters while they were members of the
Mother-House, . . . but in no case shall there be any claim upon the
Mother-House, beyond its own conscientious judgement, all circumstances
being considered; --and should any difficulty arise, the Bishop will be

---

[15]Ibid., Typescript copies of two letters of Mother Rose White
were bound with the typescript copy of her "Journal." The identity of
the two addressees-both being granted permission to make vows, apparently
for the first time--is too vague to be definitively verified. It would
seem the two sisters had completed their probationary period in the active
apostolate.

the final judge.-"[16] The difficulty between Bishop Hughes in New York

and the Sisters of Charity in Emmitsburg was two years in the future.

Did Bishop Reynolds find distant establishments impractical or did he re-

cognize that many bishops preferred to have authority over the sisters in

their own hands? No motivation for including these provisions in the

Constitution was found. The first application of these regulations came

in 1846-1847 when the Sisters in Savannah, Georgia petitioned to be a

separate foundation.[17] At the time the state of Georgia was still part

of the Charleston diocese so there was no question of conflict between

the local ordinaries.

Three communities--the Sisters of Loretto, the Dominican Sisters,

and the Oblate Sisters of Providence--had constitutions written by their

founders specifically for them. All three founders, of course, had some

familiarity with the rules of religious societies. Only Father Nerinckx

was not a member of a religious community himself. Father Wilson, the

founder of the Dominican Sisters, was one of the founders of the first

Dominican priory, St. Rose, in the United States. At the time he founded

the women's congregation he was prior of St. Rose and the American Pro-

vincial. Father Joubert, the founder of the Oblate Sisters of Providence,

was a Sulpician. The constitutions of all three communities show the

influence of the common aspects of religious life as it had developed

over past centuries in Europe and yet each constitution is unique. Even

---

[16]ASCLM. Manuscript copy of the original Rule, written by Bishop
Reynolds and copied by Rev. T. J. Sullivan, Ecclesiastical Superior,
1844, pp. 47-50.

[17]Ibid., Council Minutes, particularly 5 December 1846, 29 March
1847, 5 July 1847. The text of pertinent letters are inserted in the
minutes.

63

a cursory analysis reveals much about the character of the founder and how he proposed to meet particular needs of the American Catholic Church.

Father Nerinckx was concerned about the lack of basic education in Kentucky before Mary Rhodes arrived there. She not only tried to meet an immediate need for her nieces, but showed a willingness to continue the work and inspired other young women to join her. Father Nerinckx then sought to regularize their life in order to assure the official approval of the Church for their life and also provide continuity and permanence for their work. The rules reflected a stern asceticism and the rough frontier conditions of Kentucky in 1812. Father Nerinckx wrote of the first sisters, "Already they live a life secluded from the world which would serve to fill the first devout Christians with awe and admiration."[18] Many of the ascetical practices such as going barefoot, were not exceptional on the Kentucky frontier. What was exceptional was that these practices became part of the rule. Much of the correspondence between diocesan officials and the Roman authorities (1820-1851) found in the files of the Propaganda Fide are concerned with the particulars of poverty and penitential practices as written into the constitutions.[19]

---

[18]ASL. RGsp III - Sr. Sarita Verstynen, Trans. (1962), Nagelaten Brief van den Weleerw. Heer Carolus Nerinckx in leven Missionaris in Kentucky aan zyne Bloedverwanten en Vriended in Nederland (Te's Gravenhage Ter Drukkery van geb.s Langen huzzen Achter de Groote Kerk, No 23, 1825). The translation was made from the New York Public Library copy. Typescript, 31.

[19]Cf. Finbar Kenneally, O.F.M., United States Documents in the Propaganda Fide Archives: A Calendar, (Washington, D.C.: Academy of American Franciscan History, 1966-1977), Vol. I: pp. 32, 54, 60, 117, 168, 333, 334, 335, 337, 339. Vol. II: pp. 141, 143, 241, 242, 245, 246, 247, 251, 258. Vol. IV: p. 119. Propaganda Fide Archives was not consulted beyond 1851 because of the chronological limitations of this study.

The Rule, as written by Father Nerinckx, was seen as too idealistic:
". . . it is supposed to embrace the customs and Constitutions both of
contemplative and of the active life, as though these women were en-
dowed with seraphic natures: . . . "[20] These critiques of Father
Nerinckx's rules for the Sisters of Loretto bring into bold relief his
lack of familiarity with practices and forms of constitutions that were
generally acceptable to those who had the responsibility to recommend
that the Holy See grant formal approval. Between 1825 and 1849 there were
four revisions of the Rule as written by Father Nerinckx. These were
followed by a new constitution in 1896--"Bishop Byrne's compilation, made
by Apostolic appointment." The basis for every revision was the Holy
Rule of 1816 as printed in London, 1820, and these revisions were concerned with deleting excessive rigorous details, adapting to the changes
from a frontier society, and the government of the congregation.[21]

Ten years after the foundation at Loretto, Father Wilson founded
the Dominican Sisters at St. Rose. The rules he gave the sisters are also
greatly concerned with an asceticism that was quite incompatible with the
work he envisioned for them. Father Nerinckx had requested solemn vows
for his community (cf. p. 102) because he was requested to do so.
Father Wilson provided for solemn vows when conditions made it possible
(cf. above, p. 41). He, himself, according to Webb was a learned man and

---

[20]Augustin C. Wand, S.J., and Sister M. Lilliana Owens, S.L.,
Documents: Nerinckx - Kentucky - Loretto, 1804-1851, in Propaganda
Fide, Rome, (Nerinx, Kentucky: Loretto Literary and Benevolent
Institution, 1972), p. 208. "Scritture Riferite nelle Congregazioni
Particulari (1816-1818)," J. Cardinal Fesch to Msgr. Charles Mary
Pedicini, Secretary of the Congregation of the Propagation of the
Faith, Rome, 8 November 1819 (translation).

[21]ASL. RGsp. Notes on Constitutions compiled by Sister
Antonella Hardy.

'an accomplished theologian."[22] He was also highly regarded within the
Dominican Order itself, having been president of the college conducted by
the English Dominicans in Belgium before it was seized by French revolutionary forces.[23] He explicitly stated that the sisters were to follow
the Rule of St. Augustine[24] which the Sisters of Loretto did only after it
was required by Rome.[25] The Constitution, while referring to the Third
Order, is directed more to a contemplative life than an active one. As
Dominicans their rule and constitution were given the approval of the
Master General of the Dominican Order. In the introduction Father Wilson
wrote:

> The general end, or intention of your holy institute is, as ought to
> be in all good works the honour and glory of God. . . . Now the par-
> ticular aim of our order of St. Dominick is the salvation of souls,
> . . . We of the first branch by administering the Sacraments, by the
> mission &c. The other two by offering up their office and for the
> conversion of souls, by instructing young persons of their sex in
> piety and religion, and by helping their Brethren while occupied in
> their studies in all several services that are peculiar to your
> sex. Thus our Blessed Saviour during his mission was accompanied by
> some pious Women who waited on him, and who are frequently mentioned
> in the Gospel; the Apostles, we read, followed the example of their
> Divine Master and in after times we find frequent mention of the
> Deaconesses or pious Women who devoted themselves to God in the ser-
> vice of the Clergy in visiting the sick, the Confessors of the faith
> in prison, in instructing young Women for Baptism &c. Such was also
> the origin of the Tertiarians of diffenrent [sic] third Orders in
> later times.[26]

---

[22]Webb, p. 208.   [23]Ibid., p. 200.

[24]AOPStC. "Rule and Constitution as found in the Profession
Book, 1822-1919."

[25]Rev. John Rothensteiner, "Father Charles Nerinckx and His
Relations to the Diocese of St. Louis," St. Louis Catholic Historical
Review, (April 1919), p. 164. Letter of Father Nerinckx to Bishop
DuBourg, 29 April 1823.

[26]AOPStC., Rule and Constitutions, p. 7.

The remainder of the constitutions say nothing about an apostolate; they are largely concerned with monastic practices. Appended to the constitutions were Father Wilson's directives: "Distribution of Time." These, too, were monastic in character, including the recitation of Matins and Lauds at midnight. The introductory paragraph says this daily order was kept until the sisters' strength gave out--"the practice of it was for a short time."[27]

Under the heading, "Some Further Regulations," is found the directive: "Your number may not at present exceed 13, without particular leave from the Provincial [of the Dominican priests]."[28] There is no evidence that this particular directive ever resulted in the limitation of candidates. Moreover, this constitution makes no provision for determining the government of the community. Certain offices such as Prioress and Novice Mistress are assumed. The greatest detail is found in Chapter XII, "Of such as are to be Received." Here the prioress and her council, as well as the mistress of novices are mentioned.[29] From all available records and accounts it is certain that from the very first years it was the practice of the community to elect a Prioress General every three years. Of all the rules examined these rules and constitution said the least about the end for which the particular religious community was formed. The charism of Father Wilson and the founding members was so strong, however, that the manuscript rule "was kept by the Sisters of Saint Catharine

---

[27]Ibid., p. 20.

[28]Ibid., pp. 18-19. In 1825 they had seventeen members.

[29]Ibid., Chapter XII.

of Siena Congregation from April 7, 1822 to April 3, 1895."[30] Some

seventy years after the foundation the deficiencies in the primitive

rule caused difficulties in the community which led to a request for

an investigation and finally resulted in a decree issued by the Apos-

tolic Delegate "providing for your Congregation a Rule which may be

observed by all the Sisters belonging to it."[31]

The original Constitution of the Oblate Sisters of Providence is

a succinct, carefully written document. The archives at the Motherhouse

contains the original handwritten copy, written by Father Joubert in

French and English. Archbishop Whitfield placed his signature and

approbation on this copy 5 June 1829.[32] Unlike the Constitution for

the Sisters of Loretto and the Dominican Sisters, there was no mention

of solemn vows. In fact, the original Constitution says: "they make

no Vows, but merely a promise of obedience to the Reverend director -

. . . hence their annual engagement, instead of profession, is called

Oblation."[33] The old French Diary notes that on 22 March 1832 the Sis-

ters received the approbation of the Holy See. This had been dated

at the Propaganda Fide 2 August 1831, and had been obtained through

the efforts of Father Michael Wheeler, the chaplain of the Visitation

---

[30]Ibid., "The Story of the Little Chapel," 76. Several copies of this rule, in manuscript and typed copies are in the archives. There is almost no difference in the various copies beyond spelling and an occasional change from second person to first person plural in the pronouns.

[31]AOPStC. Letter and Decree of Archbishop Francesco Satolli, Apostolic Delegate (#1554), Washington, D.C., 27 March 1895. The "Authentic Translation" 29 March 1895. AAC. Elder Papers, 1894, Sisters of St. Dominic vs. Bishop William George McCloskey (Louisville).

[32]AOSP. Original Constitution.   [33]Ibid., introductory paragraph.

Convent in Georgetown and Father Kohlmann who was then residing in Rome.[34]

In Sister Theresa C. Willigman's history she gave the following account

of this event.

> Oct. [sic] 2. 1831. The approbation of the Community took place.
> Pope Gregory 16th of happy memory gave this great favor through the
> request of Rev Michael Wheeler and Rev F. Anthony Kohlman, S.J.
> Father Joubert lost no time communicating the good news to the
> Archbishop. . . . now said he, they are formally recognized by the
> Holy See. I cannot refuse them any favor. no more can they be op-
> posed. I permitted them establishment but today they are confirmed
> by the Holy See the affair is more serious. May these good women
> whom I esteem very much continue to make themselves more and more
> worthy of the Graces of God. The Sisters were overjoyed.[35]

As a result of the approbation by the Holy See, vows were made for the

first time on 2 July 1832.[36]

The Constitutions clearly stated the purpose of this religious

community and gave directives for carrying it out. The Superior was to

be "nominated" by a vote of all the sisters every three years. The

Director would then confirm their choice if "he thinks proper." At the

conclusion of the portion of the constitution which outlines the structur

of the religious life and work of the sisters is a section entitled "Gene

Observations." This section contains specific directives for the educa-

tional work of the sisters and their relationship with parents and the

general public.[37] The difficulties these sisters experienced over the er

suing years did not result from problems with their constitutions. The

effective charisms of Father Joubert and Mother Mary Lange along with ver

realistic constitutions, on the contrary, helped this community surmount

---

[34]Ibid., French Diary, p. 23.   [35]Ibid., A Short History, p. 5.

[36]Ibid., French Diary, p. 26.

[37]Ibid., Original Constitution.

the difficulties connected with being "a religious Society of Coloured Women"[38] in a nation where even after the Civil War they were second-class citizens. The Catholic Church in the United States showed little concern for their welfare. Speaking of the necessity of closing schools in the 1860's and early 1870's, a recent biographer of Mother Mary Lange wrote:

> The story of one "failure" after the other goes on and on. The work undertaken by the Oblates was never diocesan; it was always financed out of the Baltimore house. And the Baltimore house itself existed with financial stress as daily fare. The Sisters were black; the students were black. This kind of apostolate was a priority of no group in the country at the time. . . .[39]

One of the most striking features of these three "American Rules," when compared with the rules and constitutions of the other five communities is that there are, at most, minimal provisions for governmental structure and details needed for administrative efficiency. Father Nerinckx, in his "Rules for the School," did add a "Catalogue of Lists to be made and preserved." The nineteen lists which are included cover everything one might want recorded in such a form concerning people and property[40] and certainly have aided the Sisters of Loretto in filling the gaps caused by fires at the Motherhouse.

The monastic character of the Dominican Sisters' rule made autonomous houses an acceptable procedure. In fact, the sisters who left Kentucky to make the foundation in Somerset, were an autonomous community from the beginning, but in the early years members were exchanged or loaned as circumstances dictated. Father Nerinckx was uncertain about the

---

[38]Ibid.

[39]Maria M. Lannon, Mother Mary Elizabeth Lange, Life of Love and Service, Black Catholic Sercies, No. 2 (Washington, D.C.: The Josephite Pastoral Center, 1976), pp. 25-26.

[40]ASL. Father Nerinckx, "Rules for the School".

advisability of such a practice and the resulting directives were ambiguous. Some of the consequences of this are considered in Chapter III.

The Carmelites and Visitandines required a dowry. No specific
amount is stated but clearly a substantial sum was expected since the
dowries were prime sources of income. From the beginning, however, excep
tions were made in both communities. The three congregations which based
their constitutions on the Rule of St. Vincent de Paul did not require a
dowry as such, but expected the young woman to pay her board the first
year and to defray her expenses for clothing and bedding unless she broug
sufficient articles with her.[41] Father Nerinckx wrote: " . . . they are
to be received gratis, having with them the religious dresses and bedding
a free gift as an alms may be accepted, but no Stipulation made."[42] Only
the Oblates had a stipulated dowry: "This Sum fixed, in the beginning at
four hundred dollars, may at the desire of the whole Community and with
the consent of the director, be increased or diminished, according to the
capacity and means of the Candidate, or the Services She may be able to
render to the institution."[43] This one statement is certainly the exception to the realistic character of the constitutions. The requirement of
such a high dowry in 1829 would assure the sisters of at least a minimum
financial security. Very few candidates, however, were able to bring a
dowry. Most of them, after all, came from families in which slavery was
closer to their experience than a life of affluence. The readiness to
dispense candidates from the requirement of a dowry or even initial ex-

---

[41]Cf. ASCN. Constitution of 1827, Article 5.

[42] ASL. Original Rule. Chapter 3, #2.

[43]AOSP. Original Constitution, "Of Postulants."

penses is apparent in all eight communities. The unwillingness to do so was apparently at least a partial factor in the failure of the Ursulines to make a permanent foundation in New York in the second decade of the nineteenth century.[44] Persons well acquainted with conditions in America knew that few Catholic women would be able to bring cash that could be invested, but they came willing to do any work necessary. They did not expect to live comfortably themselves and were at ease with the idea of conducting academies which would draw most of their students from among the Protestants since few Catholics were among the affluent. Instead of supporting themselves from the income of dowries, they would support themselves and very likely some orphans as well with income from the academies.

Act of Incorporation

Seven of the eight religious communities were incorporated in the early years of their existence. The Oblates were incorporated only after the Civil War. The Sisters at Emmitsburg received their Act of Incorporation, dated 18 January 1817, from the state of Maryland under the title of "The Sisters of Charity of Saint Joseph's."[45] This enabled them to hold property in their own name. In 1826 Daniel Carroll offered land and a house on Capitol Hill in return for the education of his seven daughters at Emmitsburg. This led to the question of whether the Act of Incorporation in the state of Maryland would empower them to have the deed in their name in the District of Columbia or whether they needed an act of incor-

---

[44]Cf. "Non-Permanent Foundations," p. 43.

[45]Cf. Annabelle M. Melville, Elizabeth Bayley Seton, 1774-1821, (St. Paul, Minnesota: Carrillon Books, 1976; originally published by Charles Scribner's Sons, 1951), p. 321 and note 133; p. 459.

poration from Congress.[46] The legal advice sought on this matter began

action not only in behalf of the Sisters of Charity, but also for the

Visitation Sisters. It was a slow moving process. The "Petition of the

Sisters of the Visitation of Georgetown, D.C. Praying that an Act of

Incorporation May Be Passed in their Favor" is dated April 7th, 1828. On

8 April 1828 it was referred to the Committee on the District of Columbia

and ordered to be printed.[47] On 24 May 1828 John Quincy Adams signed "An

Act to incorporate the Sisters of Charity of Saint Joseph, and the Sisters

of the Visitation of Georgetown, in the District of Columbia."[48]

The petition for an act of incorporation for the Sisters at

Nazareth and Loretto made to the Kentucky General Assembly, 6 February

1830, occasioned a debate concerning the propriety of such a bill on con-

stitutional grounds. Two points were highlighted in the debate as it was

reported--fear that such an act would be an opening wedge for the Pope in

Rome to gain more power, and the fact that the academies at Nazareth and

Loretto were the only good institutions for female education in the state.

The prior passage of similar acts by the Maryland Assembly for the Sisters

of Charity in Emmitsburg and by the United States Congress for both the

Sisters of Charity and the Visitation Sisters was used as an assurance

that such a bill was constitutional as well as the fact that no ill ef-

---

[46]ASJCH. Letters, II, 24c, d, e, "Foundations." DuBois to
Daniel Carroll, 22 February 1826; Daniel Carroll to DuBois, 3 March 1826;
DuBois to Mr. Ironsides, 12 March 1826; the last letter is marked "Confi-
dential," and is one which poses the question concerning incorporation.

[47]Georgetown Public Library, Peabody Room. "Petition of the Sisters of the Visitation of Georgetown, D.C. Praying that an Act of Incorporation May Be Passed in Their Favor" (Washington: Printed by Duff
Green, 1828).

[48]"Notes and Comments," Catholic Historical Review VI (October
1920), pp. 384-386. The Text of the Act is printed in its entirety here.

fects would result from the passage of the bill.[49]

The Carmelites did not petition for incorporation until after the move to Baltimore and the opening of their school. They were incorporated under the title, "The Carmelite Sisters of Baltimore." This act is interesting for its stress on their position as "unmarried women, and above the age of twenty-one." In the statement of their purpose this same point is reiterated: ". . . which association, from its nature and objects, as well as its positive regulations must always be composed of unmarried women."[50] In South Carolina the Sisters of Our Lady of Mercy received their first act of incorporation in 1835. It came under the heading of Act Number 2669 of 1835 entitled "An Act to Incorporate Certain Towns and Villages; to amend Charters of Certain other Villages; and to Incorporate Certain Societies." The incorporation was limited to fourteen years; it was renewed by Act Number 3-72 of 1849. Again it was an umbrella act that included a number of societies and companies.[51] The Dominican Sisters received their initial act of incorporation under the title of "the

---

[49]Sister Columba Fox, The Life of the Right Reverend John Baptist Mary David (1761-1841), Bishop of Bardstown and Founder of the Sisters of Charity of Nazareth, (New York: The United States Catholic Historical Society, 1925), United States Catholic Historical Society Monograph Series IX, "Appendix," pp. 215-220.

[50]ACM-B. "Annals," 5 May 1832. The entire Act of Incorporation is copied into the Annals, along with a preliminary explanation. The Act is dated 17 February 1832.
Compare this emphasis on unmarried women with the statement of Mary Jane Hamilton in "A History of Married Women's Rights." She wrote: "The law generally assumes that the single woman is an anomaly which does not require special legislation. Thus, for purposes of this paper I will dispose of her as the Common Law did: a single woman is a man, legally speaking!" Dana V. Hiller and Robin Ann Sheets, eds., Women & Men: The Consequences of Power. A Collection of Essays (Cincinnati: Office of Women's Studies, University of Cincinnati, 1977), p. 168.

[51]ASCLM. Photostat of the Act of Incorporation.

Literary Institution of Saint Magdalen, in Washington County [Kentucky],"
19 December 1839. Unlike the Dominican Rule and Constitutions followed b
the Sisters, the act of incorporation left no doubt about the purpose of
their religious community.[52]

Thus by 1839 each of the communities except the Oblate Sisters
could own property and carry on business in their own name. This insured
permanence and prevented misunderstandings resulting from property being
held, or loans being made, in someone else's name. The Visitation Sister
for example, had difficulties with at least two priests who as spiritual
directors also became involved in the management of their temporal affair
Mother Teresa Lalor wrote to Archbishop Maréchal: "it will not do to have
Revd Francis Neale to manage our temporal affairs." She and her councillors had dreaded his involvement earlier and now they were convinced
that he was mismanaging their temporal affairs. The details would be lef
for a personal interview. Five years later the sisters were being
threatened with dissolution because of their debts. Mother Harriet Agnes
Brent wrote to beg the same Archbishop's help because the "Spiritual
Father" [Father Clorivière] insisted on building and improving the lot "a
what cost soever" and was "chagrined" if she or her councillors said "a
word against his views."[53] Some of these women had managed households,
or even estates, before they came to the Visitation Convent. The needs o
the convent, academy, and school for poor girls tended more to sharpen th

---

[52]St. Catharine Convent, Office of the President. "Act of Incor-
poration." An amendment of 11 March 1851 changed the title from the
Literary Society of Saint Magdalen to the Literary Society of Saint
Catharine of Sienna.

[53]AAB. A[lice] Lalor to Archbishop Maréchal, 10 June 1818
(18 B 78); Sister Harriet Agnes Brent to Archbishop Maréchal, 30 October
1823 (13 N 7).

to dull their sensitiveness to prudent practices in the management of
their monies and property.

Slavery

No aspect of the life of the women religious in the eight communities under consideration in this study so emphasizes the fact that they
were women of their times, influenced by the culture they lived in, as the
issue of slavery. Only the last two to be founded—the Oblate Sisters of
Providence and the Sisters of Our Lady of Mercy—never possessed slaves.
The time of their founding, however, has no relationship to the question;
it was, rather, their own unique situations. It is unlikely that for most
of the Oblate Sisters their status as free blacks had its origins much
earlier than their parents' generation. The Sisters of Our Lady of Mercy,
on the other hand, were chiefly Irish immigrants who served the poor Irish
in Charleston, South Carolina. Checking catalogues and finding aids in
Charleston libraries and manuscript depositories leaves one with the impression that the welfare of the house slaves was more important to leading
Charlestonians than the welfare of the poor Irish. All eight communities,
however, were founded within the slave states and if there were any
question about the morality of this "peculiar institution" no trace of it
was found in any of the archives. While the annals and traditions of the
first six communities refer to negro or colored servants brought by some
women as part of their dowry, neither the Carmelites nor the Dominicans
(the only two institutions that recorded individual dowries for posterity
to see) ever mention a slave as part of a dowry. In the letters from the
Mother Superior at Georgetown to the Archbishop of Baltimore which mention
the dowry cash and property are mentioned, but slaves are never specified.

Most of the annals or early histories were written at a later date which might account for oblique references to slaves, but if individual dowries were recorded at all, they were recorded at the time they were presented, not years later.

The Carmelites had slaves when they lived in southern Maryland. They were supporting themselves just as most of the people in the area did--by the working of a plantation. Their plantation, however, had to be worked by others under a manager. Currier, who wrote the history of the Carmelites less than sixty years after the move to Baltimore, says th many novices brought their slaves with them. The slaves were "comfortabl lodged in quarters outside of the convent-enclosure and did the work of the farm."[54] As long as Father Charles Neale was able to act as the mana ger as well as the spiritual director of the nuns this seemed a suitable arrangement. Mother Clare Joseph wrote to England in 1807:

> Without rent or revenues we depend on Providence, and the works of ou hands, productive of plentiful crops of wheat, corn and tobacco, . . We raise a large stock of sheep, yielding a considerable quantity of wool, black and white, which we spin and weave, to clothe ourselves and negroes.[55]

In the Carmelite Archives are two letters from Bishop Carroll to the Superior concerning the donation of slave women. The nuns had apparently agreed to the conditions of one offer when Carroll was told that the dona tion would "take place only at the death of her present Mistress, who, fo ought I see, is as likely to live as long as most of your holy community." Nonetheless, whether the slaves came along with the original property,

---

[54]Currier, p. 83.

[55]As quoted in Currier, p. 115.

[56]ACM-B. Bishop Carroll to Mrs. Bernardina Matthews, 28 January 1797; 7 June 1798. Also found in Currier, pp. 96, 97-98.

ere donated, or came with the novices their presence was part of the
urden facing the nuns about 1830.

Before leaving Charles County, a great source of anxiety to the
nuns was the disposal of their slaves. They could not grant them
their freedom, being too poor to provide means of subsistence for
them; but desirous of giving them every possible satisfaction and
ensuring their comfort and happiness, they allowed them to choose
their own masters, and contented themselves with receiving whatever price those persons were willing to give. Several of the
servants who were superannuated were left to the care of competent persons. Their board was paid and all their necessities
provided for, until the death of the last one in 1838.[57]

It is also evident that the Visitation Convent had slaves from an
arly period. It is not possible to say when the first ones came. As
arly as 1818 Mother Teresa Lalor wrote to Archbishop Maréchal that a
eighbor, Parson Addison, had decided to sell his servant woman. She was
he wife of George who had always been so faithful to Archbishop Neale and
he sisters. George was distressed since he feared his wife would "be
old away." The sisters wished to save him from this distress but did not
eed a servant woman. They sought the Archbishop's permission to buy her
nd hire her out. The plea was urgent since Mr. Addison had only given the
oman until Saturday to find a master. The postscript on a letter dated
ust three weeks later notified the Archbishop: "We have purchased George's
ife and children and got the Necessary papers according to law."[58] When
other Agnes Brent outlined the financial difficulties of the community to
rchbishop Maréchal in 1823 she spoke of income from "rents, bonds, notes
nd hire of negroes." The income from all the sources should have been

---

[57]Currier, p. 192.

[58]AAB. Visitation Sisters. A. Lalor to Maréchal, 27 October
818 (18 B 22); Lalor to Maréchal, 10 November 1818 (18 B 23).

about $1433.06 but they did not get one-third that amount.[59] In Sulliv

research concerning convent affairs during the Civil War she found the

petition sent by the sisters in order to receive the reimbursement for

slaves emancipated by residents of the District of Columbia. Four of t

slaves had been given to Martha Young (Sister Mary Ellen) as her share

her father's estate in 1841. Since that time seven children had been b

to one couple. Another slave had been a gift to Sister Regina (Margare

Neal) by her father, John Neal, in 1842.[60]

The Sisters of Charity in Emmitsburg have very little documentat

concerning slaves. There is no mention of them in the annals nor in th

Diary of 1836-1841 which was written by the Treasurer at that time.

In this diary there is an entry for Monday, July 27, 1840 which include

the sentence: "The Treasurer had a good lot of Darkey's [sic] come up

to get their pay for harvesting, which en passant, I must say had cost

more this year than for many preceding."[61] Two letters between Father

Deluol and Sister Margaret George, the treasurer, were found that refer

to the sale of slaves. On 15 November 1839 Father Deluol wrote to

Sister Margaret:

> My dearest child,
> . . . .
> To come to business, all at once, this I will say: If you choose to
> keep your yellow Boys, you may do it; But if you find it more con-
> venient, or advantageous, or both, you may sell the fellows and get
> 10 or 12 per cent premium, without doing an injustice to any body.

---

[59]AAB. Visitation Sisters. Sister Harriet Agnes Brent to
Archbishop Maréchal, 30 October 1823 (13 N 7).

[60]National Archives. Records of the Board of Commissioners for
Emancipation of Slaves in the District of Columbia, 1862-1863, as quote
in Sullivan, p. 106. (Sr. Mary Ellen died in 1849 and Sr. Regina went
to the Wheeling foundation in 1852.)

[61]ASJCH. "Diary of St. Joseph's, 1836-1841."

There is a nobbin of theology for you.

bout two weeks later (28 November 1839) he wrote to report the results.

Your yellow fellows which had leapt out of pandora's box, arrived
safe - pity that you did not send them down ten or twelve days sooner -
They would have brought from $75 to $100 more- As it is, it is pretty
well. They were sold on monday at 10% premium.[62]

he culture of the slave states had so colored the thinking of French-born

nd educated Sulpician, Father Deluol, that he could deal with black people

s a commodity. Could one expect more of women who were born and raised in

lave states and whose level of education was lower? In defense of Father

eluol, it must be mentioned here that the evidence in the archives of the

blate Sisters shows a different attitude. In the brief account of the years

n which these sisters were virtually abandoned, for example, Sister

heresa Catherine Willigman wrote: "The good Father Deluol did all in his

ower but no one dared come forward to take up the work."[63]

It is not surprising that slavery was not an important factor at

mmitsburg. We know that at least 29.7% of their members came from out-

ide the United States and at least another 8.5% came from Pennsylvania

.lone (cf. Table 1a, p. 93). Much of their work was done in the north, as

ell, thus slaves would not even have been a consideration. The community

lid have a few women, however, who came from southern families who may have

;iven their daughters slaves as a part of a dowry or, since no specified

lowry was required, sent a young slave with the woman at the time of her

ntrance in lieu of a cash payment for her initial expenses.

The three sisterhoods in Kentucky are all on record as slave-

---

[62]ASJCH. Letters, III. Father Deluol to Sister Margaret George
5 November 1839, p. 5; 28 November 1839, p. 6.

[63]AOSP. "A few facts . . .," p. 7.

holders in various degrees. The earliest records of both Loretto and Nazareth tell of early members either selling slaves for the money that would otherwise have been almost totally lacking or freeing them. Ann Rhodes, the first superior of the Lorettine Sisters (d. 11 December 1812 less than six months after their foundation) bought fifty acres for the Society for $75., gave her negro (who was sold for $450.) and her household goods in 1812.[64] At Nazareth, the only record that was found of a woman bringing slaves with her is in the biographical data concerning Sister Scholastica O'Connor (Ann Hall) who entered in 1821. Sister Scholastica was a widow and a convert, and a woman of considerable means; her fortune paid for the present Motherhouse grounds. Besides the fortune she also brought a piano and a sideboard as well as a woman and two children as slaves. These slaves were given their freedom a year later.[65] Sister Scholastica, as the first music teacher and art teacher, was certainly one who made it possible for the academy, the principal source of income for the sisters, to attract girls from the upper classes. At Saint Catharine the tradition, and the history which was written much later, indicate the presence of slaves who had come with the young women within a few years of their foundation.

In practice the presence of slaves in these three communities, as it comes to us through surviving documents, is truly a triptych. At Lore there is at least one Bill of Sale in the Motherhouse Archives; in it Mary Jane Buckman (Sister Laurentia), about the time of her entrance, "in consideration of one dollar," gave to the trustees of the Society

---

[64] ASL. (Sister) Ann Rhodes, Bill of Sale.

[65] ASCN. Cf. OLB-XVI: 9-10. Sister Scholastica O'Connor.

of the Sisters of Loretto "her undivided interest in the slaves willed

by John Vowles (?) to Charles Buckman & herself" as well as any that

may come to her in the future from her father's estate.[66] The biographi-

cal data concerning Sister Angelica (Christina Clements - entered 1816)

relates that:

> Old Aunt Nancy Clements was Sister Angelica's negro woman.
> When Sister Angelica made her vows of course she had to dispose
> of her Nancy, whom she sold with all her children "Jesse, Jerry,
> GEORGE, John, Francis and all her increase" to Father Nerinckx
> for Four Hundred Dollars. George became a very dignified
> representative of Loretto in after life, living thus till his
> death; he acted in the capacity of overseer, and the name of
> "Black George" or "George of Loretto" was respected everywhere.[67]

A future Superior General of the Sisters of Loretto, Sister Berlindes

(Lucy Downs) came to Loretto as an orphan. The biographical data pre-

served about her relates that she was well liked by Father Nerinckx and

also that, as a child, she was a companion, "in work and mischief," of

little black George, son of Sister Angelica's negro woman.[68]

Besides these accounts found among biographical data there is a

paragraph in Father Nerinckx's Journal under the heading "Remarks on

the School & Rules":

> No blacks on the place are allowed to go from the place without leave
> & this leave, the Superiours and Overseers is [sic] answerable to me.
> They are to be catechised every sunday twice, and every other day
> once; the women by the Sisters, and men by the Overseers; morning
> and night prayers, duties performed. with a pious short chapter,
> the whole may last one quarter. Instruction for Confession and
> communion, and sacrements frequented every Month.[69]

---

[66]ASL. Sister Laurentia Buckman "Bill of Sale", 16 June
1838.

[67]Ibid., Sister Angelica Clements.

[68]Ibid., Sister Berlindes Downs.

[69]Ibid., Father Nerinckx' "Journal".

Beyond this the records are silent about slavery.

At Nazareth there was no record of anyone except Sister Scholasti

O'Connor having slaves when she entered the community. There is an entr

in Mother Catherine Spalding's journal (which according to Sister Elizab

Suttle had "only about five fragmentary entries") for 1840 - August.

Mother Catherine noted that the sisters had made improvements on the far

and purchased land.

> We also, in the course of the year, bought five negro men; two women
> two girls, and two boys. This year the price of property was very h
> throughout the country; of course we paid high prices for all they
> bought; the prices of hire were also very high; and the Council deci
> it was better to buy servants for the farm, etc., than pay so much f
> hire and then often get bad ones.[70]

The sisters apparently had slaves prior to this purchase in 1840. A

letter from Sister Ann Spalding at Lexington to Sister Claudia Elliot at

Nazareth has no date but seems to have been written shortly after Sister

Claudia left Lexington in 1839. Sister Ann wrote to Sister Claudia:

"All the little Nigs had the whooping cough, and Ed had like to die.

They have all got well." There are other references in the same letter

to serving people who were probably slaves.[71] Most of the other ref-

erences to slaves, whether referred to as nigs, darkies, or negroes,

etc.[72] are found in the many letters to Sister Claudia Elliot. (If

the other archives contained such a file of informal, friendly letters

---

[70] ASCN. DLB-IV:1. See p. 3 for Sr. Elizabeth Suttle's
editorial note.

[71] Ibid. OLB-I:126 (DLB-I:190), Sr. Ann Spalding to Sister
Claudia Elliot, n.d. [1839?].

[72] Uncomplimentary "names" or references were not reserved for
black people. A letter of Sr. Mary Leake to Sr. Claudia tells about all
the new sisters at the Motherhouse since Sr. Claudia left. "all - most
all - New Yorks, You might suppose coming from such a distance, they
were real beauties, but I declare, some of them make the big rats run."
(OLB-V:100 or DLB-I:154, February 1846)

the picture might change.) As business manager at Nazareth, Sister Claudia dealt with the slaves and when she left the sisters were aware of her continued interest in them. The letters she saved tell not only of whooping cough but of weddings, births, baptism, and of such things as the sister who patched their clothing.[73] Mother Frances Gardiner wrote in August 1845 saying: "When I came home from Nashville every negro in the place wanted to go and live with you."[74] But everything did not always go smoothly. Sister Ann Spalding, the sister of Mother Catherine, died 15 May 1848, of poison given her by a colored servant girl. A notation on the record of Sister Ambrosia Abbot says she, too, received a dose of poison from a slave girl at the same time. While Sister Ambrosia did not die until 1872, she never fully regained her strength.[75]

The Dominicans at Saint Catharine received slaves that came with the young women who entered. According to the Chronicles "the original farm house was occupied by the colored people" sometime before 1830 (no exact date is given).[76] Sister Margaret Hamilton wrote that about 1825 "[T]he community had grown until it now numbered seventeen members; and

---

[73]Ibid. Letters to Sr. Claudia Elliot, OLB-I (DLB-I-150), 24 October 1845; OLB-I:126, Mother Frances Gardiner, ca. January or February 1848; OLB-I:146 (DLB-I:148), Sr. Scholastica Fenwick, 18 September 1845; OLB-I:145 (DLB-I:178), Sr. Euphrasia Mudd, 22 March 1849.

[74]Ibid. OLB-I:68 (DLB-I:146), Mother Frances Gardiner to Sr. Claudia Elliot, 14 August 1845.

[75]Ibid. Annals-B, p. 157 and individual's records.

[76]AOPStC. "Chronicles, 1822-1847," p. 54. These chronicles were first written from the dictation of Sister Angela Lynch, the last of the early sisters to die. The copy now in the archives says those papers were consumed by the fire of 1904 (p. 72). The context of the quotation given here would indicate the fire had not yet taken place. It may be that the present reconstructed chronicle incorporated one or more pages saved from the fire.

as a few colored servants had been brought by the young ladies who had entered the novitiate, the Sisters were relieved of hard labor connected with the farm and domestic affairs of the house."[77] By early 1847, the sisters had decided they needed a proper church even though they had no cash. They began to dig the foundation themselves and then begged for money, supplies, or labor from friends and relatives. Sister Margaret Hamilton wrote: "It is recorded that a score or more slaves given to the sisters by their parents voluntarily offered to do without new clothes for a year, that the money might be donated to the chapel fund."[78] The chronicles state: "The colored people were so anxious to have a church that they gave their year's earnings and help to assist in the work which God blessed."[79] In 1937 Sister Margaret Hamilton wrote that her information about "the colored people who belonged to the institution" came from Sister Mary Pius who was a young sister before the Civil War. "These servants were singularly devoted to the sisters, who in turn, regarded them not as mere property, but as human beings requiring care of soul as well as body with no hard task-master over them, . . ."[80] In the lack of any contemporary evidence it may be surmised that the strong tradition of the willingness of the slaves to donate what they could to the erection of a church in 1847, plus the fact that some remained with the sisters until their deaths, even after emancipation,[81] indicate

---

[77]Ibid. "The Story of the Little Chapel," pp. 15-16.

[78]Ibid., p. 51.

[79]Ibid. "Chronicles, 1822-1847," p. 76.

[80]Ibid. Sr. Margaret Hamilton, "In my Time, A Diary," Book I, June 1, 1937, (unpaginated).

[81]Ibid.

that the slaves at Saint Catharine's probably were better situated than most slaves.

The Oblate Sisters did not, of course, have slaves. They were not untouched by the slave-state culture, however. As free black women themselves, their purpose was to educate girls (cf. above, p. 46), who would either be mothers of families or servants. During the very first year, as related in the first history,

> June [1829]. Rumors of disapproval of the project at this time became very alarming. some well intentioned persons objected to the wearing of the religious habit, etc. so Rev Mr Joubert called on the Archbishop [Whitfield] and disclosed his fears. he listened to all. in answer these are his words. Mr Joubert this work has not been entered upon hastily and without reflection; I have approved it. I see the finger of God there. do no oppose his holy will. I am no stranger to all these reports. Besides am I not free to establish an order in my Diocese, no matter for what purpose? Your's is unique and cannot harm any one. I conjure, I even command you to continue the work you have undertaken, [I] promise you to protect this new work. The day will come when you will be justified. It was for the glory of God you acted. He will manifest it one day.82

Early in 1830 a notice was published in the <u>United States Catholic Miscellany</u> in which the editorial comment seems to reflect a similar racial bias.

> The Oblates
> This is a religious society of coloured females who bind themselves by annual vows.* . . .
> *Note.--We doubt if the oblates are permitted to make vows.--Edit. Miscel.83

Father Deluol, superior at Saint Mary's Seminary, Baltimore, requested sisters in 1835 for the management of the housekeeping and the

---

82AOSP. Sr. Theresa Catherine Willigman, "A few facts relating to the Oblate Sisters of Providence of Baltimore Md.," p. 17.

83USCM (12 February 1830), p. 259. In fact the original constitution provided only for annual promises. The sisters began taking vows in 1832, after their constitutions received the approbation of the Holy See.

infirmary at the seminary. In the only extant business letter of Mother

Mary (Elizabeth) Lange she reflected the effect the common attitude

toward women of color had on these same women.

> . . . As persons of color and Religious at the same time,
> and we wish to conciliate these two qualities as not to ap-
> pear too arrogant on the one hand and on the other, not to
> miss the respect which is due to the state we have embraced
> and the holy habit which we have the honor to wear. . . .[84]

The author of this letter was the leader of the original band of women

about whom the United States Commissioner of Education was to write in

his report (published 1871) that "some of them, certainly, [had] been

educated in France."[85] This statement seems to have been a conclusion

drawn from the quality of education at Saint Frances Academy in Balti-

more. When Currier, on the other hand, was writing the history of the

Carmelites for their centennial (1890) he disregarded the very existence

of the Oblate Sisters. He wrote that the Sisters of Charity were the

"only religious in the city" when the Carmelites arrived in 1831.[86]

The Oblates had been established in 1829. And, in writing about Arch-

bishop Whitfield's relationship to the Carmelites, he said: "During the

whole of his administration, Archbishop Whitfield took a lively interest

in the three female religious communities in his diocese, namely, the

Carmelites, Visitandines and Sisters of Charity, . . . "[87] It is very

clear from what has been said above that Archbishop Whitfield not only

took a "lively interest" in the Oblate Sisters as well, but considered

them a fourth religious community in his diocese. In an age when Cath-

---

[84]AOSP. Mother E. Lange to Very Rev Louis Regis Deluol, S.S.,
20 September 1835. Translation from the French as filed in the archives

[85]Special Report, 1871, p. 205.

[86]Currier, p. 192.   [87]Ibid., pp. 168-169.

lics, in general, were often the victims of prejudice, it is an ironic
wist to find a full and very positive assessment of the work of black
omen religious in an official report to the Federal Government while
n Catholic sources there is, at best, a very hesitant acknowledgement
f the same work.

The experience of the Sisters of Our Lady of Mercy in Charleston
as different. It is true they were living and working in a southern
ity in which slavery was a seemingly integral part. They were, however,
utsiders to the local culture on two counts—they were Catholics and
ost of them were Irish. Since Bishop England founded them for the spe-
ific purpose of "educat[ing] females of the middling classes of society
lso to have a school for free colored girls, and to give instruction to
emale slaves, . . ."[88] they were not in a situation in which having
laves would be appropriate. The only record of the offer of a slave
or the sisters themselves is found in the Council Minutes of 6 July 1850.
arie Kennedy who had been professed in 1832 and left sometime later to
ecome a Visitation nun (she had not stayed there either) was seeking
e-admission. She wrote that she was reasonably well but unable to do
eavy work. She "intended to purchase a competent Negro Woman to fill
y place in these employments if the Bishop and you will consent to have
slave in the community. . . . " She was not looking for security
ince she had a fine place with a family and was well provided for. The
ecision was deferred to another time, but there is no record that she
as accepted.[89]

The first eight permanent communities of women religious in the

---

[88]ASCLM. "Bishop England's History," p. 261.

[89]Ibid. Council Minutes, 6 July 1850.

United States followed the basic form of religious life as it had developed in Europe, but all of them also had distinctive American characteristics. The rules and constitutions of the individual communities varied in the degree in which they reflected the American character. The failure to question the propriety of a community of women religious owning slaves is an outstanding example of adaptation to American customs, but one that was comparatively short-lived. The more important adaptations, and those that have had an effect on the way women religious have lived and worked in the United States since the early nineteenth century are found in part in the Acts of Incorporation received by the communities from the states or the federal government from 1817 onward. Many adaptations that were required by pioneering conditions or the pluralistic society often went unrecorded.

CHAPTER III

WHO WERE THESE INTERESTING INDIVIDUALS?

When news of the work of the Sisters of Charity among the cholera
victims in 1832 reached Boston, Levi Bartlett wrote to the superior in
Emmitsburg: "Many of my friends, as well as myself, are desirous to know
more about these interesting individuals: --the name of each, her native
place; . . ."[1] Almost a century and a half later we are asking similar
questions, not only about the few sisters who attracted widespread public
attention, but about all the women who entered these eight religious communities before 1850.

In my search for this information I began with the official register of each community. Even when extensive record keeping was not considered important every community took great care to preserve the official
registers. It is important to understand that the data collected are not
definitive. The absence of absolute accuracy, however, hardly seems reason enough to ignore what is available. Before proceeding to the conditions the data indicate, it is important to know some of the variables in
the registers themselves.

1. The various communities placed names on the official registers
at different times. For example, the Carmelites have no record of any young woman before she took vows while the records

---

[1]ASJCH. Letters III:54. Levi Bartlett to Madam Superior,
7 November 1832. (See also Chapter V, p. 232).

of the Sisters of Charity of Nazareth usually indicate the
date of entrance, beginning of the novitiate, and first vows.
The more common practice was to enter the young woman's name
on the register at the time she became a novice. This was the
date I tried to use. Where the register gives only the date of
first vows I back-dated one year to determine the date of
"entrance." In some cases, particularly when a woman left the
community, the information was incomplete and/or ambiguous.

2. The Sisters of Loretto had a fire at the Motherhouse in 1858,
and the register had to be reconstructed after this. Basic
information concerning those sisters who had left or died
prior to this time was not always available.

3. The Sisters of Charity at Emmitsburg had the register with the
most complete information. This register was set up, however,
only about 1850 when they were united with the Daughters of
Charity in France. The form, as developed in France, reflects
the needs of a large community for a certain administrative
efficiency. Deficiencies in this record can easily be accounted for by the widespread missions staffed by these sisters and
the many members who either had left or died by 1850. In reading early Catholic almanacs, for example, I found the names of
several sisters from Emmitsburg among the obituaries that I had
not found in the register. The Sister Archivist, however,
located the names on the Cemetery Register.

4. Information such as place of birth, family status, amount of
education, and cause of death, which interests us today was
not of great concern in those first years, at least as far as

record keeping was concerned. What information was found in

these areas was often obtained from other sources—obituaries,

personal letters, annals, etc.—or deduced from the work assigned

them. The latter was often used in this study as a measure of

the educational level of some of the sisters. When a woman

could begin teaching advanced classes almost immediately it

was evident she herself had an advanced education.

Unless otherwise noted most of the material for the information used in the

statistical study came from cummunity archives, i.e. registers, annals,

and extant letters. In addition some information was found in diocesan

archives, newspapers, almanacs and directories, and the published his-

tories of the communities. These latter sources were most helpful in

the area of family background and the cause of death.

The total number of women whose names were found on official re-

gisters between the dates of the founding of each of the eight religious

communities and 1850, was 1,441. Of this number over 1,100 spent the re-

mainder of their lives as religious. When one considers that numerous

other communities of women religious were either founded in the United

States or came from Europe during the last two decades of this period, it

seems remarkable that so many would choose what some have referred to as

an "incomprehensible" life during a time when Nativism and its accompany-

ing anti-Catholicism were so prominent.

The documented transfers of women from one religious community to

another are not included in Table 1 (see p. 92). Several women trans-

ferred within the three communities in Kentucky. They were counted only

once. Because the Carmelite and Visitation Nuns as well as the Dominican

Sisters and the Sisters of Our Lady of Mercy, provided for the autonomy

TABLE 1

Number of Entrants - Number of Departures

	Entered	Left
The Carmelite Nuns - Port Tobacco/Baltimore	53	3 (5.7%)
The Visitation Nuns - Georgetown	178	9 (5.1%)
The Sisters of Charity of St. Joseph - Emmitsburg	680	206 (30.3%)
The Sisters of Loretto - Loretto, Ky.*	215 [246]	9 (4%) [41 - 16.7%]
The Sisters of Charity of Nazareth - Nazareth, Ky.	198	74 (37.4%)
Dominican Sisters - St. Catharine, Ky.	49	9 (18.4%)
Oblate Sisters of Providence - Baltimore	27	5 (18.5%)
Sisters of Charity of Our Lady of Mercy - Charleston, South Carolina	41	10 (24.4%)

Table 1 indicates the number of young women who entered each of the communities and remained long enough to have their names placed on the official registers. It also indicates the number, and relative percenta of those who left after officially becoming members of the community. *See the note following Table 1a for an explanation of the figures for the Sisters of Loretto.
N.B. In subsequent Tables and Graphs the religious communities will be designated by the underlined portion of the title given here.

of daughter houses, either immediately or when circumstances made it feasible, the sisters who left for these houses are simply included with the group who lived and died in one community. Table 1a gives the break-down of the sisters within each community who left religious life accordi to the number of years they spent in religious life where that is known. It is clear that there was no pattern, but that a variety of factors must have been the causes of the departures. Some possible factors will be discussed later in this chapter.

The variation in actual numbers as well as percentages of those who left the various religious communities is cause for some reflection.

TABLE 1a

Those Who Left Religious Life - By Community

By Years as Religious

CARMELITES

Departures	3
unknown	1
4 years	1
15 years	1

VISITATION

Departures	9
unknown	6
7 years	1
17 years	1
29 years	1

EMMITSBURG

Departures	206
unknown	162
1-5 years	23
6-10 years	5
11-15 years	5
17 years	1
21-25 years	3
26-33 years	6
38 years	1

LORETTO*

Departures	9
unknown	2
1-5 years	3
8 years	1
12 years	1
16-20 years	2

NAZARETH

Departures	74
unknown	5
1-5 years	49
6-10 years	11
11-15 years	6
16-20 years	3

DOMINICANS

Departures	9
unknown	6
1 year	2
3 years	1

OBLATES

Departures	5
unknown	3
1 year	1
10 years	1

OLM

Departures	10
unknown	4
1-5 years	3
7 years	1
29 years	1
34 years	1

*Besides the data for the 215 members listed in the reconstructed register where there were at least dates of entrance and the date of death or departure from the community, two additional lists of names were found. The first list names twenty-one women who left religious life and two who transferred to the Religious of the Sacred Heart. This list also named some who were among those in the reconstructed register and died as religious. These names came from various lists found with information about the house at Bethlehem, Missouri, 1823-1844. During these years the Sisters of Loretto in Missouri were, for all practical purposes, autonomous. Another thirty-four names were found, but only two names were unquestionably on other lists. It is known that all of these women left before 1858, but that is all that is known. Many of these thirty-four women probably had left as novices. Estimating that the twenty-one names from Bethlehem, Missouri, plus nine from the other group had entered before 1850, it would raise the percentage of departures for the Sisters of Loretto to 12.2%, a number that is more comparable to that of the other non-cloistered communities. The numbers are not used for other computations since no other information is available, but the numbers in brackets in Table 1 take this estimate into account.

At the outset it might be noted that one reason for the Sisters of Charity of Nazareth having a noticeably higher rate than others can well be traced to the fact that names were placed on the register at entrance and some-times it was difficult to determine whether the women actually became novices or not. Aside from that it might be noted that the sisters in Emmitsburg, Nazareth, and Charleston all followed the Rule and Constitu-tions of Saint Vincent de Paul which provided for an annual renewal of vows so both the individual and the religious community could reassess con-tinued membership. Nothing in other written sources of the early nine-teenth century would indicate that there was any serious thought given to anything comparable to the concept of a "temporary vocation." On the con-trary, references to vows were very similar to those given in instructions to young religious of the late 1940's and early 1950's. The implication was strong that if a young woman was serious about dedicating her life to the service of God by serving his people, her commitment to God was made for life from the very beginning regardless of the legal time limit ex-pressed in the vow formula. In a letter to Mother Rose White, Bishop Rosati (who had come to the United States as a Vincentian priest) wrote:

> . . . I have never had much faith in second vocations.
> . . . what I cannot understand is this: that a Sister who has
> had a vocation, desired to make her vows, considered it a great
> favor and grace to be permitted to make them; who has passed several
> years in the community, and renewed her vows once or many times,
> finally discovers that she has no vocation! This is what I cannot
> conceive. . . . [2]

---

[2]As quoted in [Daughters of Charity]. Mother Rose White.
(Emmitsburg, Md.: Saint Joseph's, 1936), p. 241. (n.d.) While Bishop Rosati could not understand a person discovering she had no vocation to religious life, he apparently had no difficulty with someone who wished to transfer from one community to another. The evidence indicates that it was he who encouraged several Lorettines to become Religious of the Sacred Heart. Cf. Flaget-Rosati correspondence.

It was, however, certainly easier to leave such a community at the end of the year than apply to the bishop for a dispensation if a woman concluded this was really not the way she wished to live for the remainder of her life. No doubt the necessity of applying for a dispensation kept some women from leaving other religious communities, but other factors seem to present themselves when one tries to look at the total picture. Some sisters were dismissed by the superiors as well. The register at St. Joseph in Emmitsburg does not indicate a dismissal; the word "Left" was written in the record whether the initiative came from the individual or the community.[3]

Information about dismissals was found in some episcopal correspondence preserved in the Archives at the University of Notre Dame. Information about several dismissals was found among letters to Bishop Anthony Blanc of New Orleans. Bishop Portier's letter to Bishop Blanc blames the problems which led to the dismissal of Sister Abraham Hoey on three other sisters whom he names. He thinks she should go to the Visitation Convent. Father Deluol's explanation of the same Sister Abraham's dismissal, after thirty-four years in the community, was that she had become very lax in receiving the sacraments and had spent her inheritance. No other information was found about this particular case among these same papers and it did not seem pertinent to initiate any further search. While the records are insufficient to indicate a clearly formulated policy, they do show that the superiors were willing to dismiss members they considered unfit. The letters also indicate that the sisters

---

[3]St. Joseph's Provincial House, Emmitsburg, Md. Records of the Provincial Administration. Original Register.

sought support for their actions wherever they could find it.[4]

The Emmitsburg papers show that those in authority attributed some of their losses, that is, those who left the Sisters of Charity of St. Joseph to join another religious community, to members of the clergy who encouraged the sisters to become "nuns." The register provided verification for only two such departures. The only information in the register concerning Sister Eulalia (Mary Ann McGerry) is: "Left in order to be a Visitation Nun." The position of her name in the register indicates that she probably entered the Sisters of Charity in the early 1830's and she most certainly had left before 1850. Sister Beatrix (Martha Tyler) entered 20 July 1827 and "left to be a nun." We are able to follow her life a little more in detail since her sister was Sister Mary de Sales, and both were cousins of the Visitation Nun, Sister Mary Augustine Barber. There is a series of letters from 1848 to 1849 concerning her. In the first letter, 24 January 1848, Sr. M. Augustine Barber wrote from St. Louis to Sister Mary de Sales that her sister's health was failing, while at the same time Sr. Beatrix was convinced she had made the right decision when she transferred to the Visitation convent. By the end of February she was well enough to write a letter herself.[5]

A good example of the Emmitsburg authorities' attitude toward such transfers is found in a letter of Bishop John DuBois of New York. This former ecclesiastical superior at Emmitsburg wrote to Mother Rose White

---

[4]UNDA. Archdiocese of New Orleans Collection. Bishop Michael (Portier), Mobile, Ala. to Bp. A(nthony) Blanc, N. Orleans, February 4, 184(. Deluol to Bishop Blanc, N. Orleans. December 6, 1846 and January 6, 1847. Fr. John Power, V.G., New York to Bp. Blanc, N. Orleans, October 11, 1847. Etienne Hall to Bp. Blanc, August 2, 1847.

[5]ASJCH. Original Register. Letters, Vol. III: 126-7; 129; 131.

on January 5, 1838:

> I have seen with much pain, Bishops and confessors utterly unac-
> quainted with religious establishments, encouraging, or at least
> conniving at Sisters' removing to convents under the pretext of
> leading a more perfect life; I say under pretext, because every
> case that came to my knowledge and examination, was the result of
> indolence, aversion to charitable exertions, and sometimes to
> secret vanity. In this country, convents are not what they imagine
> --a refuge for the contemplative life. Obliged as the nuns are to
> gain their livelihood by teaching, their situation in this respect
> differs very little from that of our Sisters; and in some cases,
> as with the Carmelites, it is in opposition to the spirit of their
> rules; the only difference is the perpetuity of their vows.[6]

Bishop DuBois apparently did not consider frequent transfers, whether to
far distant places or in the type of work the sister did, as a factor that
might leave some sisters unsettled. Even if they themselves were not being changed, the rate at which new works were inaugurated from the middle
of the 1820's onward must have threatened the stability of life some undoubtedly had sought in joining the community.

In the same letter Bishop DuBois states that he considers perpetual vows a dangerous thing in this country. "A troublesome temper
that cannot be expelled is a thorn in any Community, and a constant
scandal; a discontented person is miserable and she cannot free herself
from her misery but by the worst of evils--a breach of her vows--which
leads to reprobation."[7] Bishop Rosati's letter, quoted above (p. 94)
is the more typical attitude toward vows found in the various sources
both at Emmitsburg and other communities.

One other point made by Bishop DuBois is that he considers it dangerous to offer hospitality to "traveling nuns" or for the Sisters to
visit convents. His argument is that the nuns wore "pretty dresses" when

---

[6]Mother Rose White, p. 214. Also found in ASJCH, Seton Papers,
Book V - DuBois, p. 69.

[7]Ibid., pp. 214-215.

traveling and spoke of their comfortable situation, and this "turned the heads of our Sisters."[8] This criticism by Bishop DuBois is difficult to reconcile with what was found in the archival records of any of the eight religious communities in this study. Nothing that was in the annals, typed, printed, or handwritten histories, or the many letters that were read made one suspect that this was a problem. The Carmelite Nuns had worn secular clothes when traveling to America, but the account of the reaction of strangers to them makes it clear that the clothing was out-moded.[9] Ewens relates the experiences of religious of other communities who wore secular clothing, but again, what is known would not indicate that many Sisters of Charity would be tempted by their "pretty dresses." The Carmelite and Visitandine nuns, as well as the Sisters of Loretto and the Dominican Sisters, wore habits and veils. The other four communities wore a common dress that was recognized by many Catholics, at least, as religious habit and some sort of bonnet. With the exception of the Carmelites, the sisters wore what was available in the very beginning of all of the communities' existence in the United States. It was 1817 before the Visitandines had an accurate copy of their official habit. The copy came in the form of a doll dressed in the Visitandine habit by the sisters at the convent in Paris.[11] According to the first history written about the Oblate Sisters, it was in June 1829, that "some well-intentioned persons objected to the wearing of the religious habit, etc.

---

[8]Ibid., p. 215.

[9]Mary Ewens, O.P., "The Role of the Nun in Nineteenth-Century America: Variations on the International Theme" (Ph.D. dissertation, University of Minnesota, 1971). Currier, p. 65.

[10]Ewens, pp. 120-121.   [11]Cf. Sullivan, pp. 62-63.

Rev. Mr. Joubert called on the Archbishop and disclosed his fears."

he Archbishop replied that he was "no stranger to all these reports."

evertheless, Fr. Joubert was to: "Go quietly, humbly and pay no attention

o anything that may be said."[12] Since the Sisters of Charity of

mmitsburg, and also the Sisters of Our Lady of Mercy according to their

radition, consciously adopted the widow's dress as worn by Mother Seton,

hose unfamiliar with Catholic women religious could have mistaken them

or widows.[13] At least one such occasion was recorded by Sister Francis

avier in the account of the journey from Emmitsburg to St. Louis by the

irst sisters who were sent there to open the hospital in 1828. She wrote

hat while traveling through Illinois an aged man remarked that it was a

very uncommon thing to see four old women traveling together."[14]

The modern historian also has a problem with Bishop DuBois

riticism that the "traveling nuns" spoke of their "comfortable situa-

ion." It is difficult to understand how the nuns could speak of their

ife as comfortable unless they were referring to the greater stability

f place and colleagues than was enjoyed by the Sisters of Charity. Both

he archival sources and the traditions of the eight religious communities

ndicate that none of the women were living in what might be considered

---

[12]AOSP. "A few facts relating to the Oblate Sisters of
rovidence of Balt. Md." by Sr. Theresa Catherine Willigman.
17 June 1829) Typescript, p. 4.

[13]Cf. Melville, p. 202. Campbell, p. 13.

[14][Daughters of Charity], Mother Augustine Decount and Mother
avier Clark (Emmitsburg: St. Joseph's), p. 55. In this same account she
elated the day spent with the Sisters of Charity in Nazareth in
incennes, Ind. as they waited for the stagecoach to continue the journey.
When they finally arrived in St. Louis the hospital was not
eady and the bishop was absent so their only alternative was to accept
he hospitality of the Ladies of the Sacred Heart, (pp. 54-55).

comfort, even by early nineteenth century standards. In a letter from the Counsellors of the Visitation to Archbishop Maréchal, 5 November 1823, the nuns presented several alternatives that were possible in order for them to overcome the poverty they were experiencing at the time. The one suggested by the Spiritual Father (which was most unacceptable to them) was to leave the enclosure and teach in other schools. Their response was:

> We left the world not to get bread for most of us could have lived comfortably in the world, but to perfect our souls in the harbour of Religion: from which security it seems we are to be torn.
> It is indeed hard never did we think it would come to this pass,
> . . . We will never willingly consent to go into the world to keep schools here and there. . . .[15]

The continued demand for more space and physical improvements for the students and orphans left little more than what was essential for the sisters themselves. Sometimes, as indicated in the correspondence quoted above, even the essentials were scarce. It is not difficult to understand, however, why the relative stability of place and membership in a specific house that would be found in cloistered communities such as the Carmelites and Visitandines would attract Sisters of Charity. Frequent changes were necessitated by the need for the sisters to staff houses as the superiors tried to keep apace with the ever-expanding Church on the frontier as well as in already settled areas.

The question of perpetuity of vows versus annual vows, or solemn vows versus simple vows, seems to have been largely a clerical problem. The Sisters of Loretto and the Dominican Sisters took simple, perpetual vows from the beginning, but in both cases there were requests

---

[15]AAB. Visitation Nuns, 18 B 26. Counsellors of the Visitation to Maréchal, 5 November 1823.

to be permitted to take solemn vows. There is surprisingly little concern about these questions in the archival holdings of the eight religious communities.

Even a cursory look at the Calendar for the Propaganda Fide Archives, on the other hand, indicates that the question of vows and the power of the bishop in granting dispensations was often on the mind of the nation's bishops.[16] The earliest questions were raised because the nuns who fled the French Revolution had no possibility of living as religious within an enclosure in the United States. Bishop Rosati raised the question of whether the Visitation nuns in his diocese had the privilege of solemn vows in 1843.[17] The question was not settled until 1864.[18]

Two incidents which involved the sisters themselves are important as exceptions to the relative indifference of the sisters. In 1841 Sister Mary John O'Sullivan, a Visitation nun at Georgetown, desired a more penitential life. The account of her departure in the Visitation archives relates that she went to Cuba since the Baltimore Carmelites did not make solemn vows at this time.[19] In 1848 the Dominican Sisters petitioned

---

[16]Kenneally, Volumes 1-7.

[17]Ibid., Vol. I, p. 315 (#2140: Fol. 702 rv.)

[18]UNDA. The Calendar of holdings indicates episcopal correspondence on this question. For a more detailed treatment of this topic see Ewens, pp. 108-113; 202-203. On page 118 Ewens says: " . . . the fact that only those who profess solemn ones [vows] had a strict enclosure and were true religious in the eyes of the Church, . . . " In commenting on a similar statement of the present author's, Kevin Seasoltz, O.S.B. wrote (October 1979) that a declaration of Pope Gregory XIII in 1584 had affirmed that religious with simple vows were true religious. Canonists, however, continued to see in this only a special privilege. This would account for the variety of opinions given by the hierarchy in the United States, as quoted by Ewens in her work, when they were asked for their opinions on the subject during the 1850's and 1860's.

[19]AGVC. Cf. Also with Currier, p. 129. He quotes a letter of Arch-

Pius IX for permission to take solemn vows without the obligation of the choir and the enclosure as related above (p. 44). For the most part, however, the women do not seem to have been much concerned during this period about the legal questions concerning vows. They had committed themselves to a specific way of life and then lived and worked within these bounds. At times priests became involved either because of their own concepts of religious life or because the bishops insisted on answer In 1823 Father Nerinckx sought approval from Rome for the Constitution which he had written for the Sisters of Loretto. He wrote to Bishop DuBourg: "Their vows are simplicia, sed perpetua. I wrote to have them solemnia because requested to do so. Rome, I think, will not agree, unless they be sub stricta clausura."[20]

bishop Maréchal to the Mother Prioress at Port Tobacco (19 December 1817 in which the Archbishop says: " . . . lest for want of temporal means persons bound by solemn vows . . . "

Chapter XXVIII, "The Vows of the Carmelites," discusses in detail the question of solemn versus simple vows. On page 274 Currier states: "In the United States, as we have already seen from the petition addressed t Rome by Archbishop Kenrick in 1853 (cf. p. 249), the vows taken by the Carmelites of Baltimore were always considered solemn." In 1866, the Second Plenary Council of Baltimore, acting upon a decree of the Sacred Congregation of Bishops and Regulars (3 September 1864) decreed that the vows of nuns were simple unless they had a rescript from Rome. The Visitation Nuns in Georgetown had a rescript, the Carmelites did not. Sister Constance Fitz Gerald, Prioress, stated in a letter of 5 December 1979: "The question of Solemn Vows for our nuns was settled only in 1883 by the Holy See at the request of Cardinal Gibbons. Until then, both Archbishop Maréchal (1828) spoke of solemn vows and also Archbishop Kenrick in 1853. These were used as proofs that the nuns had solemn vow when Gibbons wrote to the Congregation. However in 1883 it was settled that the nuns did not have solemn vows . . . because they did not have t original "Apostolic rescript" that had supposedly been issued at the tim of the foundation in Port Tobacco." The nuns took solemn vows again in mid-twentieth century. It would appear that Sister Mary John O'Sullivan in 1841, was following the advice of someone who was misinformed at the time.

[20]This quotation proves Father Nerinckx definitely asked for solemn vows, he was not confusing it with perpetual vows as Wand and Owe say is most probable (notes #17, p. 33; #19, p. 34). St. Louis Catholic

It is most probable that a few who were simply listed as having
left a particular community did transfer to another community. Definite
information about transfers was found for only forty-eight women. Several
other women joined one of these eight religious communities when the one
they originally entered was disbanded. For example, the Sisters of
Charity in Emmitsburg received four members from the Trappistine community
in New York, although only two persevered. The Sisters of Loretto received three former Poor Clares.[21] Several transferred within the eight
communities. When one considers that the forty-eight women who transferred to other communities include those Sisters of Charity who were noted
as having left Emmitsburg for either New York or Cincinnati, and the sisters of Charity of Nazareth who began the community later known as the
Sisters of Charity of Leavenworth, the number is almost insignificant.[22]
The surviving correspondence indicates that at the very least, transfers to
another community appeared as a real threat. Perhaps a reason that transfers from one community to another seemed to take on such importance in
archival sources is that most of the annals were compiled in the second
half of the nineteenth century and by that time the stories had taken on

---

Historical Review (April 1919), p. 164. Nerinckx to DuBourg, Loretto,
29 April 1823.

[21]ASJCH. Chronological Record of the Sisters of Charity of St.
Joseph, November 17, 1814, as quoted in Melville, p. 210. ALM. Sisters'
Records.

[22]For this study the registers or other archival material of the
original communities were used. In addition, the Emmitsburg records were
compared with the results of the "New York Secession" as given in: Rev.
Dr. Joseph B. Code, Bishop John Hughes and the Sisters of Charity, Reprint
of the Miscellanea Historica in honorem Leonis Van Der Essen, Universitatis
Catholicae in Oppido Louvaniensi, Iam Annos XXXV Professoris. n.d. (ca.
1946, the centennial of the event). Code lists thirty-three sisters whereas the Annals at Emmitsburg, 1846-1851 (p. 45) give only thirty names. In
a few cases the fact that a sister transferred to another community was
discovered from personal correspondence that has survived.

the air of the unusual and were thus unintentionally magnified. Another
reason for the air of importance in transfers from one community to
another seems to be that in many of the cases the transfers could be
traced, at least in part, to the influence of a bishop. Thus not only d
the new communities that were formed result from such action, but also t
few sisters who left the Sisters of Loretto to become Religious of the
Sacred Heart did so because Bishop Rosati seemed to encourage this trans
fer.[23]

One other statistic that paled almost into nothingness when it
emerged from the computer was that of known converts who entered these r
ligious communities. There were only sixty-eight sisters out of the entire 1,441, a mere 4.7%, who were converts. The study of the records ha
left the impression that there were considerably more. Two conditions
may account for this small number. First, the membership of the
Georgetown Visitation Convent was the first to be studied. The number o
converts in this community was fifteen, or 8.9% of their total. Second,
in this same community some of these converts, for example Mrs. Jerusha
Barber (Sr. Mary Augustine) and Wilhelmina Jones (Sr. Stanislaus), the
daughter of Commodore Jacob Jones, became outstanding teachers and were,
therefore, highly regarded both in and outside the convent. Most of the
converts who entered the Visitation Order came from families of a high
social standing. A few, on the other hand, were from rather poor backgrounds. In either case it is easy to understand why convent life would
be attractive. Recent historical studies of early nineteenth century
American women stress the emphasis that was placed on religiousness for

---

[23]Cf. "Historical Studies and Notes" (November 1969), pp. 243-24
Calvary, August 16, 1825; (December 1969), pp. 279-280, November 22, 182

the woman who was to find her place and her moral influence in the home.[24] As men tended to be separated more and more from the home by their work women had to seek companionship in the "sisterhood" of other women. If a woman became a Catholic she also set herself apart from the society she had known up to that time. The Visitation Convent with its Young Ladies' Academy would certainly appeal to the well-to-do convert. In some cases, the young woman had been educated there, but the Georgetown Visitation Convent was also more visible than other communities to women from old, prominent families as well as to those whose family's position brought them to the capital in the pursuit of their profession, and unlike the Carmelites the Visitandines were dedicated to education.

There is some interesting correspondence in the archives at Emmitsburg regarding one young woman who entered that community after she had been a student in one of their schools and had become a Catholic. The young lady, Araminta Taylor, Sister Sebastian, according to the register was born in 1823, baptized a Catholic in 1837, entered the community in 1841 and died in 1844, just three months after her twenty-first birthday. Two letters are preserved from her cousin and guardian, William Taylor. In the letter of August 10, 1841, he wrote:

> . . . in case you are determined to stay where you are to serve the priests during life this course is condemned, you know, by all your relations and as far as I have heard them express themselves do think there was a good deal of meanness in Reilly the Priest at Wilmington and the teachers in St. Peters School to influence a girl of your age to such a course and sending you of[f] without letting your Relations know anything about it until

---

[24]Cf. Nancy F. Cott, The Bonds of Womanhood: "Woman's Sphere" in New England, 1780-1835, (New Haven: Yale University Press, 1977). Kathryn Kish Sklar, Catharine Beecher: A Study in Domesticity, (New Haven: Yale University Press, 1973). E. Amanda Porterfield, "Maidens, Missionaries, and Mothers: American Women as Subjects of Religiousness" (Ph.D. dissertation, Stanford University, 1975).

you were on your way. And you must know if your Father was a
living he would have you out of that at the risk of his life . .

The remainder of the letter is of a religious nature and of the type

found in much of the anti-Catholic literature of the period. The

second letter has no year on it, but was apparently written in 1843

because of its reference to Araminta's twentieth birthday. It is

mostly business and then simply states ". . . let both Land and Slaves

remain as they are in case you left the institution you could get it.

Your Relations are all well at present . . . "[25] The feelings ex-

pressed by William Taylor in the 1840's are very similar to feelings

expressed by persons in our own day about young people who become mem-

bers of a cult. The only knowledge of the Catholic Church for many

Americans in the early nineteenth century was what had been distilled

through several centuries of English and American Puritan, anti-Catholic

literature, including the so-called "convent literature."[26]

Certainly such experiences, whether they came by post or the irate

parent or relative came in person, were practical lessons for the com-

munity in working within the pluralistic society. On the other hand, the

young woman herself probably realized more than ever the problems she

would face if she tried to live among her relatives and profess the

Catholic Faith. The difficulty was clearly expressed by Rev. Bernard

P. Cavanaugh, the Catholic pastor in Hartford Connecticut, when he wrote

to the superiors in Emmitsburg, in behalf of a widow who was a recent

convert and considered entering a convent (there is no record that she

did). Father Cavanaugh wrote that Mrs. Whitney "is _persecuted_ here in consequence of her late renunciation of heresy." And he added the post-

script: "Sister Genevieve can tell you of Yankee heretical persecution."[27]

Family Status

Data regarding family background was found for only 37.6% of

the 1,441 women involved in this study.

Table 2

Unknown	899
Planter Class	50 - 9.2%
Established Family	167 - 30.8%
Professional (law, medicine, teacher)	28 - 5.2%
Military	9 - 1.7%
Merchant, Small Business	59 - 10.2%
Artisan	81 - 14.9%
Farmer	136 - 25.1%
Common Laborer	12 - 2.2%

Table 2 indicates the actual number within the total group who were
known to have come from each class listed above. The percentage is
the relative percentage, i.e. the percentage of the known family
backgrounds.

The class headings are broad and some would certainly overlap if

more information were available. A farmer might be a subsistence farmer,

or as is clearly stated in the obituary for Sister Mary George Smith of

the Sisters of Charity of St. Joseph, her father was a "wealthy farmer of

Adams County, Pennsylvania."[28] Some of the fathers of Irish-born sisters

[27]ASJCH. Letters, III:56. Sr. Genevieve was a member of the
Tyler family, a New England family who all became Catholics. They
were cousins of the Barber family.

[28]Niles Weekly Register (Baltimore), October 27, 1832 as quoted
by Sister Bernadette Armiger, "The History of the Hospital Work of the
Daughters of Charity of St. Vincent de Paul in the Eastern Province of
the United States, 1823-1860" (Master's Thesis, Catholic University of
America, Washington, D.C., 1947), p. 38.

TABLE 2a

Family Status as Represented in the Individual Communities

	Carmelites	Visitation	Emmitsburg	Loretto
Unknown	19 - 35.8%	97 - 54.4%	376 - 55.3%	159 - 73.9%
Planter Class	20 - 37.7%	18 - 10.1%	9 - 1.3%	2 - 0.9%
Established Family	10 - 18.9%	52 - 29.2%	21 - 3.1%	41 - 19.1%
Professional (law, medicine, teacher)	1 - 1.9%	3 - 1.7%	19 - 2.8%	2 - 0.9%
Military	0 - 0	3 - 1.7%	4 - 0.6%	1 - 0.5%
Merchant, Small Business	2 - 3.8%	2 - 1.1%	48 - 7.1%	0 - 0
Artisan	0 - 0	0 - 0	78 - 11.5%	3 - 1.3%
Farmer	1 - 1.9%	0 - 0	116 - 17.1%	7 - 3.2%
Common Laborer	0 - 0	3 - 1.7%	9 - 1.3%	0 - 0

	Nazareth	St. Catharine	Oblates	OLM
Unknown	162 – 81.8%	29 – 59.2%	18 – 66.7%	39 – 95.1%
Planter Class	0 – 0	0 – 0	0 – 0	1 – 2.4%
Professional (law, medicine, teacher)	3 – 1.5%	0 – 0	0 – 0	0 – 0
Military	1 – 0.5%	0 – 0	0 – 0	0 – 0
Merchant, Small Business	3 – 1.5%	0 – 0	4 – 14.8%	0 – 0
Artisan	0 – 0	0 – 0	0 – 0	0 – 0
Farmer	10 – 5.1%	2 – 4.1%	0 – 0	0 – 0
Common Laborer	0 – 0	0 – 0	0 – 0	0 – 0

whose occupation was listed as farmer may have been tenant farmers. Th

occupation of only nine fathers of women at Emmitsburg was listed as

"Planter." One of these was the father of Mother Etienne Hall whose

family background was given in the Maryland Heraldry columns of the

Baltimore Sun in October 1906.[29] Sister Lucy Gwynn was a convert from

Jefferson County, Virginia; Sisters Mary Austin Mudd and Regina Smith

were from Grand Coteau, Louisiana, and Sister Joanna Smith from Marylan

The one strange entry is for Sister Mary Thomas McSwiggin from County

Tyrone, Ireland. There is no indication that she was a convert (as the

was for at least one who was born in Ireland), but as only nine fathers

the entire 680 members were listed as Planters there is no indication t

anyone was inflating family status.[30]

The designation of Planter Class was applied to members of other

communities only on the basis of data indicating unusual wealth and/or

social standing in the southern states or the West Indies. The Carmeli

listed the monetary portion of the dowry in the Profession Book. Thus

Sister Joseph of the Sacred Heart (Jane Hamersley) who was professed in

1794, it is written after signature that "she brought to the monastery

£2000."[31] The Visitation Nuns did not record dowries in such a way tha

the amount brought by individuals could be determined today. The corres

pondence of the superiors with the Archbishop of Baltimore, found in the

Archdiocesan Archives, provided some information. When Mrs. Elizabeth

Neale, a widow, desired to follow her two daughters to the Georgetown

---

[29]Mother Etienne Hall, p. 4.

[30]ASJCH. Original Register.

[31]ACM-B. Professional Book.

onvent (having already provided each of them with a dowry) Mother Teresa
alor wrote to Archbishop Maréchal that according to Father Francis
Neale] she "had three thousand dollars in Cash besides Land."[32]   In some
nstances this status was inferred from information such as that about
he family home and foreign education for other members of the family.

The category, "Established Family," includes anyone for whom there
s evidence of moderate wealth, an environment that favored education, cul-
ure, and an acquaintance with persons who were influential, at least in
he local area. Because evidence points to strong family ties, at
east among those families descended from early Catholic settlers in
aryland, a few were placed in this category whose immediate family was
ctually poor. These sisters clearly had a background of education, cul-
ure, and an acquaintance with other families among the leading classes.

The small number of those who could be listed as "Common Laborer"
as unexpected. It cannot be attributed to a hesitancy to list poor Irish
r German immigrants' backgrounds. The Sisters of Charity at Emmitsburg
re the only community whose register regularly gives the father's occu-
ation as well as the only community, other than the Sisters of Our Lady
f Mercy, with a large proportion of immigrants, therefore, it is their
ecords which must be checked. The records indicate that most of the
nknowns are among the sisters who either left the community or died be-
ore 1850 when the register was set up in its permanent form. The fathers
f most of the immigrants who were in the community after 1850 are listed

---

[32]AAB. Lalor to Maréchal; 1-22-1818 (18 A 13). Another source
or information that was not found elsewhere was the Lathrops' history of
he Visitation Convent, A Story of Courage. In preparation for their work
he Lathrops interviewed the sisters, some of whom knew the early members
ersonally. Information about some of the more colorful members of the
ommunity is found here, but is not in the community records.

as farmers or artisans of one kind or another. The large percentage of sisters whose family status is unknown in the three Kentucky communitie can be assumed to have come largely from farms. This will be discussed further detail later. The Sisters of Our Lady of Mercy in Charleston were almost all Irish immigrants recruited by Bishop England. In keepi with the purpose of the religious community he founded he apparently re- cruited mostly women from middle class families, that is, women who cou come with some education and some ability in management. His was not a community for the upper classes, but impoverished and illiterate women would be limited in their activities without time-consuming training. Bishop England wanted workers.[33] It might be noted in conclusion that majority of the unknowns in reference to family status may well be what was most common in the individual religious community. The practice of not making family status important is certainly an indication of the "leveling" that was an implied ideal within each of the religious com- munities.

Even though seven of the eight religious communities did not have a practice of noting the occupation of the father or otherwise giving a indication of the family status the information that is available gives

---

[33]ASCLM. Manuscript notes entitled "Historical Extracts." The source of the following quotation is given as "Bishop England's History the Diocese of Charleston," p. 261.

A congregation of Sisters of Our Lady of Mercy has been formed within three years and has at present ten sisters, who have made annual vows; they reside near the Cathedral in a house for which they pay a high rent, the object of their institution is to edu- cate females of the middling classes of society also to have a school for free colored girls, and to give religious instruction female slaves, they will also devote themselves to the service of the sick, and they have been very useful in the management of the seminary.

picture that seems to be in harmony with what is implied about the charac-
er of the community from other sources. Both the Carmelites and Visitation Orders dated back to a period in Church history when women religious
were required to live a strictly enclosed life. Their monasteries were
funded by regular gifts from the aristocracy and they often had land from
which they could expect a regular income to supplement their dowries.
Membership in either the planter class, or what has been designated in
this study as an established family, did not necessarily mean the young
woman could bring a substantial sum of money with her when she entered.
The planter class had large estates and slaves. While this class consciously imitated the life of the English gentry, they also worked hard.
By the time of the American Revolution many were heavily indebted. This
did not change their style but did mean there was very little cash available. While most of the women in this society were raised in relative
ease and comfort, they were not burdened by a concept of labor as
degrading.[34] While there is no official record of slaves received as a
part of the dowry, the references to the fact that the sisters were relieved of some of the heaviest labor because there were slaves to do it
support the tradition that some women brought slaves with them. This was a
welcome development since it freed the sisters for work more proper to
their calling.

Other factors also favored an upper and upper-middle class orien-
tation in the Carmelite and Visitation monasteries. The Carmelites were
first established in Port Tobacco, Maryland—a location near many of the
old Catholic families of the planter class. The original four Carmelites

---

[34]Cf. Carl Bridenbaugh, Myths and Realities: Societies of the
Colonial South (Baton Rouge: Louisiana State University Press, 1952), p. 14.

in the United States included three members of the Matthews family.

Currier says of this family: "The Matthews family were among the oldest

Maryland, and probably belonged to the first settlers. Ann Teresa Matt

was born in Charles Co., Maryland, in the year 1732, of parents who en-

joyed a high social position, and were at the same time most pious and

virtuous." The monastery records tell us that the mother of the two

younger Matthews women was Mary Neale,[35] that is,. a member of another v

old and highly respected family. The older Matthews family may have ha

more available cash; Mother Bernardina, the Ann Teresa referred to abov

had a brother Ignatius who had been a Jesuit priest. The younger famil

like many other families in the Chesapeake society, apparently had its

share of indebtedness. Their grandfather, William Neale, at his death

his sone-in-law "all he owes me."[36] Nevertheless, a brother William wa

priest in Washington, D.C. and, at the very least, the two young women

needed sufficient money for passage to Europe and their initial provisi

In the entry in the "Death Book" on the occasion of Mother Bernardina's

death it is also related that at the time the American foundation was

planned "her two nieces were only 3 or 4 years in Religion, but the bis

[in Belgium] thought it best for her to bring them for the good of the

house as their friends in Charles Co. were very influential and they we

excellent religious."[37] Because of this background it is not surprisin

that many who entered the community came from the planter class. The

foundresses of the Georgetown Visitation Convent were Irish immigrants

---

[35]Currier, p. 51, and ACM-B.

[36]Raphael Thomas Semmes, The Semmes and Allied Families
(Baltimore: The Sun Book and Job Printing Office, Inc., 1918), p. 269

[37]ACM-B. "Death Book."

pparently had more advantages than the majority of Irish Catholic women of
heir day. Since they were the first to open a Catholic boarding school,
atholics of the planter class in Maryland soon became acquainted with
hem. Their first additional members, even before they were officially
ecognized as Visitation Nuns, were from this class of people. In time,
lue largely to their school, so near the national capital, they attracted
. number of members from the upper or upper-middle class. Both monasteries
ollowed a natural pattern of attracting new members from among the rela-
:ives and acquaintances of those already there. The Visitation Monastery
also attracted a number of their students.

The available information suggests that Mother Seton's community in
Emmitsburg and the three religious communities founded in Kentucky were
more predominantly middle-class. To a great extent this would seem to reflect the major thrust of their work. While all four communities were required by necessity to conduct at least one academy that attracted the
more affluent, many of whom were Protestants, they all had branch establishments which met the needs of the middle and lower classes in towns and
rural areas, as well as the struggling pioneers on the frontier. They
educated girls from families who were rising on the social scale as well as
orphans. The Sisters of Charity of St. Joseph from Emmitsburg were the
first to nurse the sick in hospitals on a regular basis, but the Sisters of
Charity of Nazareth were also involved in this work before 1850. At the
time of the cholera epidemics all four communities (as well as the Oblate
Sisters of Providence and the Sisters of Our Lady of Mercy) helped nurse
the victims in emergency hospitals and private homes.[38] In short, these

----

[38] Archives of the four communities. The work of the sisters
will be considered in more detail in later chapters.

sisters were visible to all classes.

The three Kentucky foundations, as indicated in Table 2a, have
very little information about individual family backgrounds. Bishop Ma~
J. Spalding in his Life of Bishop Flaget wrote: "One feature, common to
both the sisterhoods above mentioned [Loretto and Nazareth],--and also ~
that of the order of St. Dominic,--is the fact that their members have ~
mainly recruited from the country itself."[39] The annals and various pie
of information that have been preserved confirm this. When looking at ~
family names of the early members of these three communities one sees th
repetition of many names that were on the registers of the Carmelites a~
Visitandines and even a few from the Sisters of Charity at Emmitsburg.
The settlers in Kentucky, and in Missouri (as seen in Loretto records)
before 1850, often were younger members of the old planter families in
Maryland. They had come west because good land was scarce in the east.

Undoubtedly the families had little they could give their
daughters in the formative years of these three religious communities.
The foundresses of all three communities had come from Maryland with som
education, but none had much more than a minimum of property of any kind
A pamphlet recounting the foundation of St. Catharine's, which was print
in 1924 but was based on an oral account given by Sister Rose Tenley who
had received the habit in 1824 (d. 1886) contains two facts that seem, a
first glance, to be contradictory. First, " . . . I will say here that
was country girls [italics mine] who were the founders of the three
Kentucky communities--St. Catharine's, Nazareth and Loretta [sic]. The

[39]M.J. Spalding, D.D., Sketches of the Life, Times and Character
of Rt. Rev. Benedict Joseph Flaget, First Bishop of Louisville (Louisvil
Ky.: Webb & Levering, 1852), pp. 293-294.

ndy city ladies had no hand in it, of which I am very proud."[40] Later

is related: "With but one or two exceptions all the manual labor of the

rm was done by the Sisters, many of whom had been delicately reared,

talics mine] but they were strong in the strength of God."[41] Sister

rgaret Hamilton who made great efforts to study and preserve the history

the community in the time available to her from 1918 to the 1940's wrote

at the first sisters "had no dowry, for their parents were struggling and

uld do nothing for the child who had chosen to separate herself from

e common life."[42] As early as 1825, some of the young women had brought

gro servants[43] and by 1833 the sisters had improved living conditions

r themselves, but even more importantly, for their students. This was

t only possible, but necessary to maintain the prestige of the school

cause "[T]he natural resources of the land made the accumulation of

alth easy for the descendants of the early settlers."[44] In 1847, when

e sisters wished to build a suitable chapel they began with only one

llar in their treasury. They began to dig the foundation themselves but

re able to beg the necessary money, provisions and labor from relatives,

riends and former students so that a fine chapel was dedicated less than

o years afterwards.[45]

It is clear from these statements that the living conditions of

e Kentucky settlers became noticeably better from the mid-1820's onward.

---

[40]Sister M. Stephana Cassidy [from the verbal account of Sr. Rose
enley], The Foundation of the Pioneer Sisters of Saint Dominic in the
nited States, 1822 (St. Catharine, Ky.: Dominican Sisters, 1924), p.4

[41]Ibid., p. 5.

[42]AOPStC. Sr. Margaret Hamilton, "The Story of the Little
hapel" (typescript), p. 9.

[43]Ibid., pp. 15-16.   [44]Ibid., p. 40.   [45]Cf. Ibid., p. 50.

Farming retained its importance as cities, viz. Louisville and Lexingto

began to grow at this time. The demand for foodstuffs and other farm p

ducts helped raise farming from a subsistence level to a profitable ent

prise.[46] Thus the settlers were able to provide an increasing financia

support for the various religious, educational and social institutions

which they deemed important. The sisters came from pioneer families.

They were farmers but, as far as possible, the women were relieved of

labor and provided for in the tradition of the Chesapeake society from

which many of their families had come. The sisters in all three com-

munities struggled through the days of subsistence living and as better

times came the needs of orphans, students and patients were met first.

The Sisters of Charity from Emmitsburg had the most diverse mem-

bership. As mentioned above, most of the women for whom there is no

indication of the occupation of the father had either died or left the

community before 1850. It seems worth noting that of those whose back-

grounds are known there are equal numbers, even though very small, of w

can be considered the highest and lowest of the social classes. The fa

that these sisters were working in some of the fastest growing urban

centers and staffed institutions from New England to the Gulf of Mexico

and from the Atlantic seaboard to the west bank of the Mississippi Rive

by 1850 also encouraged diversity of membership.

The Oblates of Providence were women "of color" and, therefore,

very limited in attracting new members. Throughout the period under co

---

[46]Richard C. Wade, The Urban Frontier: Pioneer Life in Early
Pittsburgh, Cincinnati, Lexington, Louisville, and St. Louis (Chicago:
The University of Chicago Press, Sixth Impression, 1972. First publish
by Harvard University Press, 1959). This monograph traces the developm
of the cities from 1790 to 1830. In so doing it also shows the depende
of the urban centers on the rural areas.

ideration they did no work outside the city of Baltimore. In spite of
hese handicaps about one-third of their membership came from families of
iddle or upper-middle class. The foundress, Mary Elizabeth Lange,
ndoubtedly was well educated before fleeing to the United States. She
nd other black refugees found they were discriminated against in
altimore. Whatever social status they may have had in San Domingo was
gnored in the southern states of the United States. The experience of
he Noel family--the mother and two daughters became Oblate Sisters--was
omewhat different. Mr. and Mrs. Noel came from San Domingo to
ilmington, Delaware, where they settled and were respected members of
he local French community. The oldest girl, Marie Louise, knew the Sis-
ers of Charity and visited them at their convent, but "owing to the re-
ulations of those days there was no school but the Friends or Quakers"
here both girls "received a first class education" which included all the
ancy needlework being taught at that time.[47] When Madame Noel requested
dmission to the community Father Joubert noted in the diary that she was
ighly recommended by Father George A. Carrell (later bishop of Covington,
entucky), the Keating family and other highly respectable persons.[48]
ost of the young women apparently came from families of free negroes, but
he Motherhouse archives contain the Manumission-Identification papers for
ister M. Louise Gabriel (Georgianna Addison) who was manumitted by
ichard Caton in 1832, just ten years before she entered the community
nd for Sister M. Ellen Joseph (Marie West) who was manumitted in 1830 by

---

[47]AOSP. Cf. Willigman, "Short history," pp. 51-55.

[48]Ibid., "French Diary" August 18, 1834, p. 56. Father Carrell was
a priest of the Philadelphia diocese when he became acquainted with the
Noel family. He later became a Jesuit.

A. P. West. She was the last to be solemnly received by Father Joubert

1838. A third set of papers are the manumission papers of Angelica Gide

who apparently had been purchased by Father Joubert so he could free her

The front cover states: "Manumission/ J.H.N. Joubert/ to/ Negro Angelica

Gideon.: The document is dated March 1st, 1833 when she was "about

fourteen years of age."[49] Sister Angelica was received into the novi-

tiate in 1839.

If class distinctions were to be applied to these communities, i

might be said that the majority in the two cloistered communities, the

Carmelites and Visitandines, came from the upper and upper-middle class;

in the Sisters of Charity from Emmitsburg and the three Kentucky communi

ties the majority were middle class. In the Oblate Sisters and the

Sisters of Our Lady of Mercy, in spite of the unique situation of these

two communities, the majority were middle or lower-middle class. It is

important, however, to stress that apparently all eight communities had

members of all classes. The middle-class origins of the American plante

class were never completely overshadowed by the accumulation of wealth a

prestige,[50] and this would lead to the blurring of distinctions once you

women from various backgrounds lived together. The Carmelites and

Visitandines had distinctions set down in their Rules between choir sis-

ters and lay sisters, but all the communities needed sisters to devote a

their working day to hard, physical labor. Even the presence of slaves

did not totally overcome this necessity in any community. No records,

however, even implied any disdain for hard work. Whether the labor was

[49] Ibid., Manumission Papers.

[50] Cf. Bridenbaugh, pp. 12-13.

one by slaves or fellow sisters an attitude of gratitude pervades the re-
ords. All the women came to pursue a life of prayer and service; those
ho were prepared served by teaching or being administrators of the
arious institutions.

Place of Birth

able 3 - Place of Birth

Unknown	664 -	46%
Maryland	200	(25.7%)
Pennsylvania	70	(9.0%)
Kentucky	110	(14.2%)
Other - U.S.A.	97	(12.5%)
Ireland	229	(29.5%)
Germany	27	(3.5%)
France	13	(1.7%)
West Indies	10	(1.3%)
Other - Non-U.S.A.	21	(2.7%)

he percentages in parentheses are the relative percentage of those whose
lace of birth is known.

The place of birth of the sisters is closely related to family
tatus in delineating some observable characteristics of the eight re-
igious communities. As indicated in Table 3 the place of birth is
.nown for 54% of all the women covered in this study. Again it is
.ssumed that the unknowns within any given community probably would
.ot differ much from those that are known. This assumption is based on
.he same references given above in the consideration of the family background of the women. Table 3 shows that close to two-thirds of the
.embership came from native-born women. It is not surprising to find
.he Irish the most numerous among the foreign-born members since before
.he late 1840's they were the only Europeans to emigrate to the United
'tates in vast numbers. Considering the large proportion of French
.ishops in the United States in the early nineteenth century and the

influence of French priests in the formation and development of several
of the communities, one might expect to see more French women represented. While the West Indies have the lowest proportion of members,
émigrés from there were largely responsible for the foundation and earl
development of the Oblates of Providence and Sister Benedicta Datty
who had fled from the West Indies to Charleston was the one member of
the Sisters of Our Lady of Mercy who could make a considerable financial contribution when she entered. Even more importantly, she not
only came with an advanced education herself, but she had already established her reputation as an excellent teacher.[51]

Table 3a compares the place of birth of the members of the
individual communities with one another. When the Carmelites came to
the United States in 1790, they came as Americans returning to a fun-
damentally Catholic community in Charles County, Maryland. Throughout
the sixty years covered by this study they retained not only their
predominantly American character, but forty-one of the fifty-three
women who entered during this period came from Maryland. The four
Irish immigrants entered the monastery only after their move to Baltimore in 1831. Three of these women came as lay sisters.

The Visitation nuns in Georgetown were also predominantly
American-born. The founding members of the monastery were Irish
and they continued to receive Irish immigrants throughout the period
under consideration. There is no birthplace known for over half the
membership during this period. The District of Columbia had no port of

---

[51]ASCLM. "Miss Datty: Her Identity and a Short Sketch of
her Activities in Charleston," Joan B. Williman (Unpublished Manuscript)
See also: Mrs. I. M. E. Blandin, History of Higher Education of Women
in the South Prior to 1860 (New York & Washington: The Neale Publishing Company, 1909), pp. 251-252.

TABLE 3a

Place of Birth as Represented in the Individual Communities

	Carmelites	Visitation	Emmitsburg	Loretto
Unknown	2 – 3.8%	101 – 56.7%	279 – 41.0%	131 – 60.9%
Maryland	41 – 77.4%	35 – 19.7%	84 – 12.4%	12 – 5.6%
Pennsylvania	0	3 – 1.7%	58 – 8.5%	1 – 0.5%
Kentucky	0	2 – 1.1%	0	59 – 27.4%
Other – U.S.A.	5 – 9.4% (90.2%)	19 – 10.7% (76.6%)	56 – 8.2% (49.4%)	4 – 1.8% (90.5%)
Ireland	4 – 7.5%	14 – 7.9%	156 – 22.9%	4 – 1.8%
Germany	0	1 – 0.6%	22 – 3.2%	1 – 0.5%
France	0	0	9 – 1.3%	1 – 0.5%
West Indies	0	1 – 0.6%	3 – 0.4%	1 – 0.5%
Other	1 – 1.9% (9.8%)	2 – 1.1% (23.4%)	13 – 1.9% (50.6%)	1 – 0.5% (8.5%)

Table 3a. The actual numbers and percentages are given for the various places of birth of the entrants into each religious community. The percentages in parentheses are the adjusted frequencies for the American born and immigrant entrants to each community.

TABLE 3a, continued

	Nazareth	Dominican	Oblates	OLM
Unknown	124 - 62.6%	11 - 22.4%	16 - 59.3%	0
Maryland	11 - 5.6%	11 - 22.4%	5 - 18.5%	1 - 2.4%
Pennsylvania	5 - 2.5%	2 - 4.1%	0	1 - 2.4%
Kentucky	28 - 14.1%	21 - 42.9%	0	0
Other - U.S.A.	6 - 3.0% (67.6%)	1 - 2.0% (92.1%)	2 - 7.4% (63.6%)	4 - 9.8% (14.6%)
Ireland	16 - 8.1%	3 - 6.1%	0	32 - 78.0%
Germany	2 - 1.0%	0	0	1 - 2.4%
France	3 - 1.5%	0	0	0
West Indies	0	0	4 - 14.8%	1 - 2.4%
Other	3 - 1.5% (32.4%)	0 (7.9%)	0 (36.4%)	1 - 2.4% (85.4%)

entry, nor vast tracts of land, nor factories to attract large numbers of destitute immigrants. The foreigners who came usually came because it was the nation's capital. It is particularly noticeable that despite the French background of the Order itself (not the Georgetown monastery), no member is known to have come from France, except the nuns brought to Georgetown by Father Wheeler in 1829. (These three nuns, because of the temporary nature of their presence, are not included on the membership rolls.) So while the form their life took was regulated by Rules, Constitutions and some customs that evolved in a French culture, in their actual life they were essentially Americans working with and for other Americans. No extant records were located that implied any desire to encourage other French women to come. There seems to have always been as many candidates as they could accommodate and so priests or bishops did not seek to recruit members when abroad as they did for the seminaries. Still, the French language was regularly taught in the Academy,[52] so there must have been at least one sister who was well acquainted with the language after the early years.

The three religious communities in Kentucky were founded in strongly Catholic settlements, but they were not isolated from the pluralistic elements in American life. The table indicates that more than the foundresses came from Maryland. Father Nerinckx brought a group of young women from Maryland to become Sisters of Loretto in 1821,[53] and Bishop

[52] The Catholic Almanacs or Directories printed the prospectus each year. These are available on Microfilm and give pertinent information about the convents and academies throughout the United States for any given year.

[53] ASL. Memoirs - Sister Theodosia Kelly.

Chabrat brought two candidates from Maryland also in 1821, along with two French women, for the Sisters of Charity of Nazareth.[54] Overall, however, it is clear both from the known data and from the other contemporary sources referred to above that these three communities received most of their members from families in the area in which they worked. I was only in the 1840's that there was any significant foreign immigration to the Kentucky area. By that time the Sisters of Charity from Nazareth had opened the orphanage, the infirmary and an academy, besides providing teachers for two schools in Louisville. The oldest of these schools had been opened in 1828.[55] The Sisters of Loretto had opened an academy in Louisville in 1842.[56] The more varied work of the Sisters of Charity in Louisville and their presence in the city for almost a decade and a half before the Sisters of Loretto were there could account for the greater proportion of immigrants who entered the Sisters of Charity of Nazareth.

The Oblate Sisters of Providence were limited to the city of Baltimore during this period. Since their members were drawn from a minority that was discriminated against, even in the Catholic community, they could look for support in only a few areas. Aside from the Noel family in Wilmington, the extant correspondence and the report of the United States Commissioner of Education indicate that most of their support came from the free negroes and the priests who worked with them in

---

[54]ASCN. Biographical Sketch of Sister Louisa Dorsey in "Biographical Sketches of Early Members," pp. 17-21.

[55]Sister Agnes Geraldine McGann, Sisters of Charity of Nazareth in the Apostolate: Education, Health Care, Social Services, 1812-1976 (Privately Printed, 1977), pp. 14-15.

[56]ASL. "Foundations of the Loretto Society, Chronologically Arranged."

the city of Baltimore and the District of Columbia.[57] The Sisters of

Our Lady of Mercy, on the other hand, were a community that was substan-

tially composed of Irish immigrants. It was the only one of the eight

religious communities to be founded outside a predominantly Catholic area.

Charleston, while it had had a small Catholic community since the end of

the eighteenth century,[58] was a southern city that served the plantation

society. There were a few French Catholics who had come to Charleston by

way of the West Indies, but the greater number of Catholics were Irish

immigrants. Bishop England, unlike the bishops and priests in Kentucky,

found no young women in Charleston who were seeking to serve God by living

the life of religious and working for those in need. Of the six American-

born women who entered before 1850, three left religious life and Ellen

Lynch left to become an Ursuline nun.[59] The necessity of depending so

heavily on Irish immigrants to meet the needs of the sisters in serving

the local church continued until almost the end of the century. Sister

Anne Francis Campbell, the community historian, wrote:

> . . . Between 1881 and 1891 sixteen Sisters were professed.
> The remarkable feature of this group was that eight of the
> sixteen were native Charlestonians. Of the remaining eight,
> three came from other parts of the South; one from Belgium;
> while only four were Irish-born. Prior to this time the Irish-
> born members of the Community outnumbered the American-born
> Sisters three to one. Only two native Charlestonians had been
> professed in the Community before 1881. Bishop England had
> once predicted that native vocations would not materialize
> for fifty years, but he could not have realized how accurate
> his statement proved to be . . .[60]

---

[57]AOSP and U.S. Dept. of Education, Special Report, 1871;
pp. 203-206, 211, 216-217, 285.

[58]Pamphlet of St. Mary's Church, Charleston, South Carolina.

[59]ASCLM. Register.

[60]Campbell, pp. 233-234.

It is not difficult to see that the established society of Charleston could easily ignore the presence of this group in their midst unless some unusual occurence called their attention to it.

The only other religious community during this period whose immigrant membership equalled or exceeded the American-born members (which it does among those whose place of birth is known) was the Sisters of Charit from Emmitsburg. Sisters from Emmitsburg began work in Philadelphia in 1814, New York City in 1817, in Baltimore in 1821, and in Boston in 1832.[61] They did, of course, begin establishments in many other places during this period, but the aforementioned cities would have been major port cities where the first large wave of immigrants, mostly Irish, would have entered. New York City and Boston had, by far, the greatest number—many of whom were penniless by the time they arrived. The presence of these sisters in the ports of entry as well as many of the other cities across the land to which large numbers of foreign-born gradually moved would account for the large portion of foreign-born members in the community. Young immigrant women, recognizing the need of their impoverishe fellow-countrymen, could hope to give both spiritual and temporal aid by joining the Sisters of Charity of St. Joseph.

Age at Entrance

One of the most striking characteristics of the total group of women who entered the first eight permanent communities of women religiou in the United States between 1790 and 1850 was the great age span of the

---

[61][Daughters of Charity], 1809-1959 (Emmitsburg, Md.: St. Joseph's Central House, 1959), pp. 11-14.

women at the time of their entrance--between twelve and seventy-six years

of age. While it was not unusual for a young woman to enter religious

life at age sixteen, only the Sisters of Loretto had a significant number

of younger women although the Visitandines also had a few. The Constitu-

tions of the Sisters of Charity of St. Vincent de Paul which had been only

slightly modified for Mother Seton and then adopted by the Sisters at

Nazareth, Kentucky, and used as a basis for the Constitution of the

Sisters of Our Lady of Mercy stated that candidates must be "of an age

commonly neither short of 16 nor exceeding 28."[62] The early Constitutions

of the Dominican Sisters, as found at the beginning of the Profession Book

says: "A person must be 16 years old to make the Solemn Vows [the Sisters

never made solemn vows, but only simple, perpetual vows]."[63] The original

rule of the Sisters of Loretto provided for young girls to become

"Desirants" at age ten and postulants after First Communion but went on to

state that "[the] Habit not to be taken before fourteen, which when taking

they make the following promises, and confirm them after one year's trial,

if of age, which must be sixteen, accomplished." For almost two decades

the Sisters of Loretto took perpetual vows immediately. The register in-

dicates that the first temporary vows were taken in 1829.[64] The

---

[62]ASCN. "Constitutions of 1827;" Ch. I, Article 4. ASCLM, printed
copy of the Constitutions, Ch. III, Art. 4. The original copy of the
Constitutions at Emmitsburg was not examined because of the fragile condition of the copy. The Xerox copy used at Nazareth was made from the
Constitutions as they came from Emmitsburg. ASJCH. Annals, Vol. I, 117th
sheet, gives details of changes made in the French Rule; it quotes the
requirements for entrance which are identical to the above.

[63]AOPStC. Professional Book, 1822-1919, p. 16.

[64]ASL. Original Rule, Chapter 3, #6.

Visitation Nuns also had a custom of allowing a young girl to take the

"little habit." The records indicate that the only very young persons

permitted to take vows were those who were dying.[65] The Carmelite recor

show that the earliest age at which vows were made was eighteen years.[66]

TABLE 4

Median Age of Entrants by Decade

	1790	1800	1810	1820	1830	1840	
Carmelites	19	24	21	17.5	24	21	21.1
Visitandines		28	18	22	21	24	22.6
Emmitsburg			23.5	19	21	22	21.4
Loretto			20	17	19	20	19
Nazareth				18.5	(Insufficient data for all other decad
Dominicans				23.5	19	19	20.5
Oblates		Insufficient data			—		
OLM					28	23	25.5
	19	26	20.6	19.6	22	21.5	21.3

Note: The Sisters of Charity of Nazareth did not have the age of entran
(or birth date) as a standard entry on their records before 1850. 73.2%
of the ages at entrance are unknown. The decade of the 1820's, with
seventy entrants was the exception. Only 22.8% of the ages at entrance
are unknown. The Oblates of Providence had ages for only eight of the
twenty-seven women who entered the community during this period.

In spite of the early age at which a number of the women entered

(cf. Graph 1, p. 131), the median age at entrance as given in Table 4

is lower than eighteen years of age in only two instances. During the

decade of the 1820's only two young women entered the Carmelites; one

was assigned[67] the entrance age of seventeen and the other eighteen year

The median age of entrance for the total group over the sixty year perio

---

[65]AGVC. Official Registers and Conversations with Mother Mary
Leonard Whipple (1976 and 1977) concerning community customs.

[66]ACM-B. "Vow Book."

[67]Cf. above.

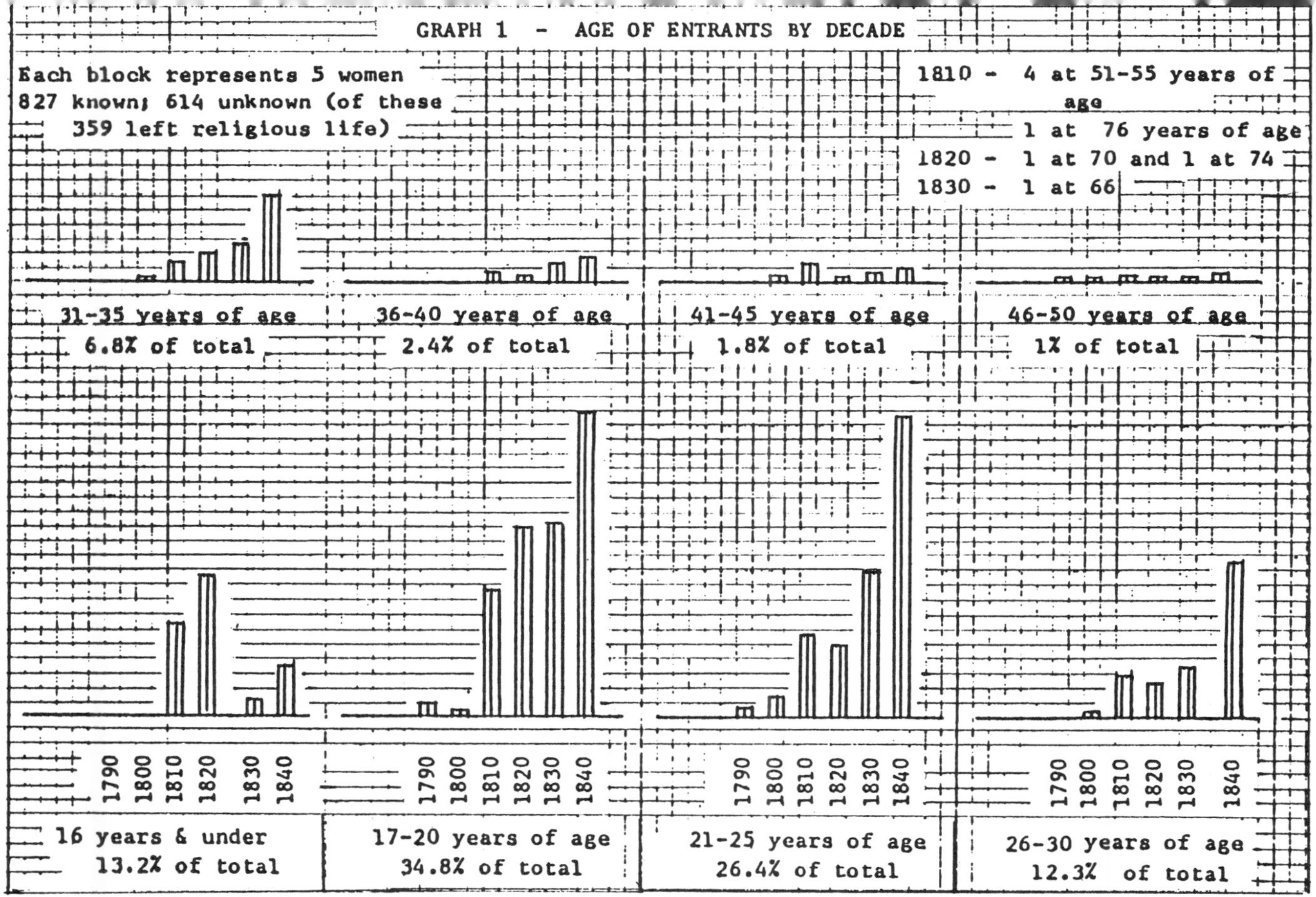

GRAPH 1 - AGE OF ENTRANTS BY DECADE

Each block represents 5 women
827 known; 614 unknown (of these
359 left religious life)

1810 - 4 at 51-55 years of age
1820 - 1 at 76 years of age
1830 - 1 at 70 and 1 at 74
1830 - 1 at 66

46-50 years of age
1% of total

41-45 years of age
1.8% of total

36-40 years of age
2.4% of total

31-35 years of age
6.8% of total

26-30 years of age
12.3% of total

21-25 years of age
26.4% of total

17-20 years of age
34.8% of total

16 years & under
13.2% of total

1790 1800 1810 1820 1830 1840

is 21.3 years.

Graph 1 (p. 131) shows a tendency for the seventeen to twenty-fiv
years age-groups to grow in importance during the 1830's and 1840's. Eve
the actual number of women between twenty-six and thirty-five years of a
increased during this same period. The first decade of a community's
existence usually had less younger women; this follows naturally from th
need for greater maturity in the foundation of a new community. The one
community where this was not evident was the Carmelites who were founded
in the United States by four women who were already professed religious
1790. The actual number of women who entered after age thirty-five is
minimal in proportion to the whole. The Dominicans, however, were the
only community who had no record of anyone entering after age thirty-fi
The oldest record of an age at entrance among the Dominican Sisters was
thirty-four. Most of the oldest entrants are also to be found in the
first decade of a particular community's existence. Several of them wer
foundresses; for example, Sister Teresa Lalor and Sister Mary Frances
McDermott at the Georgetown Visitation Monastery and Sister Mary Lange c
the Oblates of Providence in Baltimore, were past thirty-five when they
began their work. Others among these older women made significant contributions of cash and/or property which helped a struggling community t
continue. The most significant contributions made by these older women,
however, were the experiences they had and were able to pass on the othe
Sister Benedicta Datty who entered the Sisters of Our Lady of Mercy in
Charleston at age sixty-six, is the most outstanding in this regard. It
is, moreover, very probable that at least some of the widows or experienced teachers or nurses for whom no date of birth is known were ove
thirty-five years of age at the time of their entrance. It was while re

cording data such as the age of entrance, sometimes followed very shortly
by death, that it became apparent that the authorities, whether clerical or
not, did not strictly adhere to a legalistic interpretation regarding requirements for entrance into any one of these eight communities of women
religious. The principal criteria, although never expressed, seems ordi-
narily to have been the ability of both the individual and the community to
benefit from the particular woman's membership.

Number of Religious in the Family

In collecting the data on the individual sisters it also became
evident that there were family groupings, that is mother-daughter, sisters,
or cousins in every community. Besides this there were known family re-
lationships among members of two or more communities and some sisters had
relatives among the clergy. The total number known to have other family
members in religious life, which for the purpose of this study includes
the clergy whether religious or diocesan, was only 250. This number
breaks down as follows:

Number of Additional Religious in the family	Sisters in the Eight Communities
1	124
2	47
3	17
4	13
5	3
6	4
indeterminate	42

There were many with the same family name who do not appear in this tabulation. There was no way to determine if the relationship was close enough
that they considered themselves part of the same family. There were also
probably many who were related to other religious on their maternal side,
but without specific genealogical information one is unable to document

the fact. The tabulation, however, confirms the impression that there was a core of families, mostly old Maryland families, whose members actively served the Church throughout the United States in the early nineteenth century.

Education at Entrance

When one seeks to determine the level of education at the time the woman entered a community hard data are lacking. Even among the 17.4% of the total number for whom some information was available the determination of just how much education any woman had was bound to be subjective. There were a few exceptions such as the lay sisters at the Visitation Convent where it is noted that their vow formulas were signed by an X, that is, they were illiterate. At the other end of the scale there are a few accounts such as that of Sister Benedicta Datty of the Sisters of Our Lady of Mercy (see above, p. 122). The most renowned of the early teachers at the Nazareth Academy in Kentucky was Sister Ellen O'Connell (from Baltimore) of whom Webb not only says that she was an experienced teacher before she entered, but wrote:

> Her father was an eminent professor of languages and rhetoric.
> Ellen, his only child, left motherless at a tender age, was the
> object of his greatest solicitude. He cultivated her gifted
> mind with care and delight in her progress.[68]

While the Oblates of Providence have no record of the education of their first members the quality of education they were able to give to those who attended their academy was so high that in the report of the United States Commissioner of Education (1871) it was stated: "The colored women who formed the original society which founded the convent and seminary, were from San Domingo, though they had some of them, certainly, been edu-

---

[68]Webb, p. 247.

cated in France."[69] Once the academies were in existence for a few years
the number with some formal education certainly increased, for vocations
often came from the student body. Nevertheless, other sources must be
consulted to get some idea of what level of education was to be found in
these communities.

Specific information indicating that a particular woman was illiterate was available for only seventeen. An essay, "Illiteracy in the
United States," written by Edwin Leigh was published in the Special Report
of the United States Commissioner of Education, 1871. He wrote: "The
first statistics upon this subject for the United States were gathered
and published in the national census of 1840. It returns 549,850 white
persons over twenty years of age unable to read and write. In 1850 this
number had increased to 962,898; . . . "[70] Writing shortly after the
Civil War the author answered justifications such as: "They are mostly
foreigners, from countries where, in the interests of despotism, the
people are kept in ignorance." His response was:

> This is true of only a small portion of the emigrants from Europe,
> nearly all the European States from which most of them come, having
> efficient systems of public schools. Besides, our illiterate are,
> most of them native born. . . . The foreign-born illiterate are found
> chiefly in the States containing our great commerical cities . . .[71]

Between 1840 and 1850 the number of illiterates grew faster than the population.[72] Moreover, these are the facts as given in the census, "But it
is well known to those who have investigated the subject that these are
far below the truth." Few illiterates would report, or have someone else
report them, as being in this category. Horace Mann thought the 1840 cen-

---

[69] Special Report, 1871, p. 205.   [70] Ibid., p. 801.

[71] Ibid., p. 802.   [72] Ibid., p. 805.

sus figures should be rounded out, not to 500,000 but to 700,000.[73] If

these figures can be accepted for 1840 and 1850, then certainly it is to

be assumed that many young women, especially in the first years of any

religious community's existence came with very little, if any, formal ed

cation. The history of education in the United States shows a very unev

development in educational facilities of every kind before the Civil War

The real demand for public education as it has come to be known, i.e.

state-supported schools that are tuition-free and open to the children

of all social classes, began only about 1830 with the rise of the "comm

man," but it was the mid-nineteenth century before real progress in or-

ganizing state systems of education and actually putting the related

legislation into effect in rural as well as urban areas could be noted i

some states. In other states effective school systems were organized

only after the Civil War.[74]

The educational scene in the United States during the first half

of the nineteenth century will be treated in more detail in a later

chapter. The purpose here is simply to give some background for the low

level of education that is referred to in correspondence. Most of the r

ferences come in correspondence about the Kentucky communities due, no

doubt, in part to the frontier character of Kentucky at the time. In

communities that sent their members to distant missions, particularly th

Sisters of Charity from Emmitsburg and Nazareth, the ability to read and

write was essential if the major superior was to have personal contact

with individual sisters. An early reference to the problems of the chur

---

[73]Ibid.

[74]Cf. H.S. Good, A History of American Education,
Second Edition (New York: The Macmillan Company, 1962), pp. 134-168.

because of the lack of educational facilities in Kentucky is found in a report of Bishop Flaget to Pope Pius VII, dated 10 April 1815. In writing about the Seminary he had opened four years earlier, he said: "The beginnings were very small and the progress slow, for at first very many of the pupils had to be instructed not only in Latin and grammar, but also in the very elements of reading and writing, such is the great and almost barbaric ignorance of this district."[75] About ten years later Bishop Flaget appended a note to a report to the Propaganda Fide in which he wrote of "about twenty young men [at the seminary] who have persevered over a period of two years in the elementary grades. . .in their desire of receiving orders."[76] In 1823 Father Nerinckx wrote to Bishop DuBourg, who had asked for sisters for his diocese, that "you will observe, my Dear Sir, how unaccomplished they must be, being all brought together in such a hurry."[77] Bishop David merely restated the same difficulty when he wrote to Mother Rose: " . . . it is difficult to form good teachers especially in these parts; postulants come to us with little knowledge, hardly able to read."[78]

The more personal aspect of the difficulty of overcoming illiteracy is found in two letters written to Sister Claudia Elliot who entered the Sisters of Charity of Nazareth in 1826. Her father had been

---

[75]"Documents," The Catholic Historical Review (October 1915), I:315. The translation is as it appears in CHR.

[76]Wand & Owens, 59 (trans). Cf. also Kenneally, Vol. I, First Series, p. 168, #1023 (Wand & Owens give 1033) Fols. 80 rv and 81r, 1825 (?) February 4.

[77]St. Louis Catholic Historical Review (April 1919), I:161.

[78]Mother Rose White, Bishop David to Mother Rose, Bardstown 3 June 1824, p. 109.

one of the original settlers at Pottinger's Creek in 1785.[79] Many in-

formal letters to Sister Claudia are extant; they are valuable sources of

information about everyday life in the Nazareth community. A letter of

Sister Clementia Payne (Nazareth, 4 June 1846) begins as follows:

> . . . Anyhow, I hope you will excuse me for not writing to you before
> now. But you know what a job it is for me to write. But this is a
> beginning. I am going to write you often, I think, if nothing
> happens. That is, if you will write to me. If it is but a dozen
> lines, it will please me.
>
> Tell me have you got through with that big book yet. How do you
> come on learning to write. I have been through three or four books
> since you left here, and I have been improving myself, but I cannot
> compose well, that is the hardest thing for me to do. I must now
> tell you all the news.[80]

In an undated letter (internal evidence indicates January or February

1848) Mother Frances Gardiner wrote to Sister Claudia:

> Your kind letter has come as safely as if the telegraph had
> brought it. I must thank you for it, and as I know you do not write
> much, I doubly prize it. In the second place, I was surprised to
> find that you had improved so much in the writing. Indeed you need
> not cover your face with blushes to write to anyone. Thirdly, the
> spelling was pretty good and if you will just put yourself at it like
> a pig "sets to a sty", I am sure you will spell well.[81]

Both Sister Clementia and Sister Claudia entered in 1826, so that these

letters show their concern for their educational handicap twenty years

later. Not only do the letters indicate their ability, but the community

records prove they were recognized as valuable and capable members. Sis-

ter Clementia was twice elected as Procuratrix (business manager), and

Sister Claudia was elected to the same office once. Records, traditions

---

[79]Cf. Webb, pp. 28, 31.

[80]ASCN. OLB-I, 126; DLB-1, 161. Sr. Clementia Payne to Sr.
Claudia Elliot, Nashville, Nazareth, 4 June 1846. The DLB was used
by the author.

[81]Ibid., DLB-1, 197. Mother Frances Gardiner to Sr. Claudia
Elliot, Nashville. [January or February 1848?].

and accomplishments suport an assessment that all eight communities attracted capable women. Deficiencies were the result of the general lack
of educational handicaps. But it was also this great need for educational
institutions that provided the impetus for founding seven of the eight
communities. This need remained constant and the calls for more teaching
sisters did not favor a policy of accepting only those with a good education. Bishop DuBois of New York had been the ecclesiastical superior of
the Sisters of Charity at Emmitsburg from late 1811 until he became
bishop of New York in 1826. In 1832, in great need of sisters to care
for the orphans and nurse the ill he gave a recommendation for a young
woman who wished to enter the Sisters of Charity even though she was de-
ficient in "money and education."[82] Six years later when he seemed much
more concerned with having teaching sisters who would equal or excel any
teacher in the Protestant schools, and somewhat resentful that sisters
were being sent to the west and south instead of New York, he wrote
to Mother Rose White:

> If you have received candidates not fitted for the schools, you
> must blame yourselves; you know that it was understood that no re-
> commendation from clergymen would avail unless the postulant had
> been examined by one of your Sister Servants.
> As for the numberless calls upon St. Joseph's this is the result
> of the unwise and impolitic extension you have given to your mis-
> sionary labors. Had you left Kentucky to provide for the Western and
> Eastern [sic] establishments you could have given yourselves time to
> prepare your subjects.[83]

The tension between trying to meet the immediate needs and giving the
sisters adequate training was met in the most practical terms at any

---

[82]ASJCH. Seton Papers; Book V - DuBois, p. 61. Postscript - DuBois
to Mother Augustine, New York, 21 October 1832.

[83]Ibid., 69. DuBois to Mother Rose White, New York,
5 January 1838, as quoted in Mother Rose White, p. 215. Cf. Ibid.,
p. 68, 18 December 1837.

given time. Over the years training programs were developed in all the

principal houses to prepare young members. The successful completion of

a specific level of education was apparently never made a prerequisite

for entrance into any community before 1850.

TABLE 5

Type of Work Engaged In As Religious

(Information was available for 723, ca. 50%)

1.	Domestic	94	13%
2.	Needlework or Craft*	4	0.5%
3.	Education	156	21.6%
4.	Asylums	67	9%
5.	Nursing	81	11%
6.	Teaching & Asylums	73	10%
7.	Nursing & Teaching	14	2%
8.	Nursing & Asylums	47	6.5%
9.	Nursing, Teaching & Asylums	52	7%
10.	Administration - Local	74	10.2%
11.	Administration - Central House	61	8%

*Needle work or Craft work was almost always included in the prospectus o
a school and, at times, it was an important source of income even though
it does not figure as an important work for individual sisters.

A large proportion of the sisters for whom no principal occupation

could be determined were very probably teachers since that was the prin-

cipal work of all the communities in this study except the Carmelites.

number engaged in administration on the level of the central house is pro

ably the most accurate since such offices were usually recorded or have

been documented by a community's historian from signatures on such docuents as council minutes or financial accounts. The multiple listings

#5-9) are limited. Anyone listed under Administration engaged in some

ther work at least for a time. When a sister was engaged in a second

ield of labor for only one short period this was disregarded in the tabu-

ation. The purpose of the multiple listings is to give some indication of

he flexibility needed within the communities which were engaged in

ultiple ministries--the Sisters of Charity from Emmitsburg and Nazareth,

nd the Sisters of Our Lady of Mercy. Since these three communities had

he highest rate of attrition (cf. Table 1: Emmitsburg 30.3%; Nazareth

7.4%; OLM 24.4%) the question arises: did this kind of professional in-

ecurity contribute to the greater number of departures as much as, or

ven more than, the fact that the sisters took annual vows instead of

erpetual vows? There is no documentary evidence to answer the question.

he closest evidence that might support an affirmative answer is found in

 letter of Mother Etienne of Emmitsburg to Bishop Blanc in New Orleans.

he calendar entry for the letter notes the sisters were dying so fast,

specially in the south. "They cannot force their Sisters under such cir-

umstances. Sister Georgia Ann left the Community because she was mis-

ioned to Baton Rouge to teach music. For the last ten years she had been

onstantly teaching here every branch of English, French, Spanish, and

usic. She is now with the New Yorkers."[84] In the narrative work on the

ife of Mother Xavier Clark it is related that in 1844 while Sister

oyola Ritchie was serving as Procuratrix of the community in Emmitsburg,

ishop Peter Paul Lefevre appeared at St. Joseph's Convent on 20 May 1844,

ith a letter from the Reverend Superior, Father Deluol, in which the

---

[84]UNDA. Archdiocese of New Orleans Collection. Calendar entry:
tienne Hall to Bishop Blanc, 2 August 1847.

petition for sisters for a school in Detroit had been granted. Sister
Loyola was proposed by Father Deluol as the superior of the new work.
The call was so urgent that Sister Loyola and three others left for
Detroit that very afternoon with the bishop.[85] The answer to the
question posed above is purely speculative; however, as one reads the
archival holdings of these early American religious communities, one
senses fluid, changing circumstances that appear more like our contemporary scene which has witnessed so many departures from religious lif
than the apparently stable scene of the 1940's and '50's.

In comparing the type of work done with the place of birth in
those cases where these factors are known it is clear that Americans
most of the administrative offices in the central houses. In this cat
gory we know the place of origin of 86.9%. 62.4% are known to have be
Americans by birth (more than half of them from Maryland). The Irish-
sisters furnished nine higher superiors, or 14.8%. On the local level
know the place of birth of only 64.9% of the superiors; of these 47.3%
Americans and 13.5% were Irish.[86] While only 1.4% of those whose plac
birth was known came from the West Indies, these same sisters filled 8
of the highest offices. Sister Xavier Clark was elected superior of t
Emmitsburg community in 1839, and was several times Assistant Mother.
Sister Benedicta Datty served as superior of the Sisters of Our Lady o
Mercy until her death during the cholera epidemic in 1836. And the Ob
were led not only by their foundress, Sister Mary Lange, but also by S
ter Chantal Noel (Madame Lauretta Noel), and Sister Mary Frances Balas

---

[85]Cf. Mother Xavier Clark, p. 192.

[86]Comparison with Table 4 will show that 29.5% of those whose
place of birth is known were Irish while 61.3% were Americans.

Number of Women Who Entered Each Decade

	Unknown	pre-1790	1790	1800	1810	1820	1830	1840
Carmelites	1	4	9	10	8	2	5	14
Visitation	–	–	3	3	45	20	43	64
Emmitsburg	16	–	–	13	50	78	246	277
Loretto	1	–	–	–	48	80	28	58
Nazareth	–	–	–	–	24	70	38	66
Dominican	–	–	–	–	–	20	13	16
Oblates	–	–	–	–	–	3	20	4
OLM	–	–	–	–	–	4	17	20
Total	18	4	12	26	175	277	410	519

Offices of leadership, whether on the level of the central house
or at the local level required the sister to be at ease with the pluralistic society and able to do business with persons in other positions of
leadership (9.3% of their total) is further confirmation that these sisters were drawn from the middle class. Another 28.3% of the Irish-born
sisters are known to have been involved in teaching all of their active
lives or a reasonable proportion of it. If the Irish-born sisters had
come primarily from the poorest classes one would expect a much higher pe-
centage of them doing domestic work. Of those sisters for whom we have
information concerning place of birth and their principal work, sixteen
(8%) of the 200 born in Maryland did domestic work, while seventeen (7.4%)
of the 229 born in Ireland were primarily engaged in this work. We know
the principal occupation for 66% of the Maryland-born sisters and 71.6% c
the Irish-born sisters.

Years as Religious

The number of candidates for the eight communities continued to
increase even after other communities began making permanent establishmer
in the United States from 1830 onward. Table 6 (p. 143) gives the actual
number of entrants during each decade for each of the eight communities.
Graph 2, sections a, b, and c, shows the percentage of entrants for each
community in relation to that of the one or two communities founded
about the same time.

In viewing the sharp drop in new membership for both the Carmelites and Visitation communities two points must be considered. The
first point is that both communities suffered financial distress during
the 1820's. Because of the nature of the two communities this meant not

GRAPH 2a - Percentage of Entrants by Decade

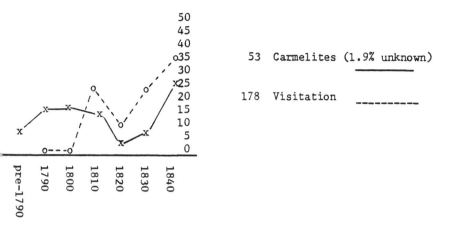

53 Carmelites (1.9% unknown)

178 Visitation

nly a real problem meeting their daily needs at times, but also they were
unable to enlarge their living quarters. The Carmelites' situation did
not really improve until after the court decided in their favor regarding
the ownership of their property at Port Tobacco, followed by their
decision to sell that property, move to Baltimore, and open a school in
831.[87] The Visitation Nuns were aided by the growing reputation of
their academy, the fact that some money belonging to their ecclesiastical
superior, Father Clorivière, was freed and he used it for improvements in
the school, as well as general improvement of the financial scene in the
United States. Adequate physical space for all the members was a real concern at the Georgetown Visitation Convent during the last two decades of
this study. In late November 1832 and January 1833, thirteen sisters
left Georgetown for Mobile, Alabama where the French sister, Mother
Madeleine Augustine d'Arreger, led the first foundation. Four of these

---

[87]Cf. Chapter I, p. 18.

sisters had only been lent and returned to Georgetown at a later date. Mother d'Arreger was recalled to Fribourg, Switzerland in 1833. A new monastery was founded in April of the same year at Kaskaskia, Illinois; the members of this community moved to St. Louis in April 1844 when the flood washed their property into the Mississippi River. Fourteen sister left Georgetown permanently and another four were lent for this Kaskaskia/St. Louis foundation; eight sisters had been in the original group. The Baltimore monastery was opened in 1837 with ten permanent members (three novices) and four sisters who were lent to the foundation Frederick, Maryland was the next foundation, the school being taken over from the departing Sisters of Charity in September 1846. Another eleven sisters formed the core of this community. Apparently four other sister joined them at a later time and three sisters were lent to them. In 1848 a group of about twelve sisters went to Philadelphia. This monastery was closed four years later. The strong Nativist feeling made it impossible to continue there. The last foundation during this period was made in Washington, D.C. in 1850. This time, however, the Baltimore and Frederick monasteries also helped.[88] In the meantime the Georgetown Academy continued to develop, even as the other foundations established academies that also won respect of the parents.

The Sisters of Charity in Emmitsburg did not experience a decline in entrants, but the requests for sisters seemed to be always greater th could be fulfilled. The greatest increase in the number of entrants can during the decade of the 1830's, a decade of great expansion in the Unit States as a whole. By 1830 the Sisters from Emmitsburg were conducting

[88] AGVC. "Georgetown Sisters Sent or Lent to Other Foundations."

GRAPH 2b - Percentage of Entrants by Decade

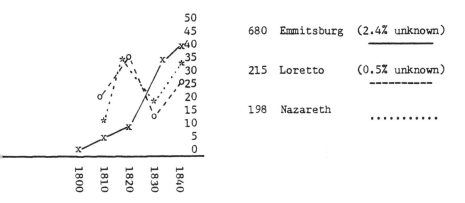

680	Emmitsburg	(2.4% unknown)
215	Loretto	(0.5% unknown)
198	Nazareth	

schools, hospitals, and orphanages in the major cities along the Atlantic seaboard and at such distant points from Emmitsburg as Cincinnati, St. Louis, and New Orleans. The title, "Sister of Charity," had begun to signify a woman dedicated to selfless service. The sisters' increasing visibility was apparently an attractive force for other women who wished to dedicate their lives to serving the needs of the Church. The percentage of increase in the number of entrants slowed down during the 1840's. By that time the number of communities of women religious doing similar work was increasing and some bishops were discouraging any community which was not directly responsible to them from working in their dioceses.

The difficulties experienced about the time of Father Nerinckx's departure from Kentucky and his subsequent death are reflected in the decrease in new members for the Sisters of Loretto during the 1830's. A serious problem among the sisters in Kentucky at this time was the division concerning the direction of the community by Father Guy Ignatius Chabrat, S.S. Should they remain loyal to all that Father Nerinckx had taught or should they accept the new directions of Father Chabrat? No

letters or diaries written by the sisters at that time were found. The
single copy of the Original Rule in the archives at the Motherhouse has
traces of a fire. The tradition is that Bishop Chabrat ordered the sist€
to bring all of Father Nerinckx's writings to him and these writings wer€
then burned. One copy of the Rule fell off the pyre and a sister rescue€
it and hid it. Sister Theodosia Kelly wrote the annals of this period i₦
1901, but they reveal little about the feelings or determination of the ₳
ters in the 1820's and 1830's, although she does refer to the division
among the sisters.[89] It was probably during this time that some women
entered in Missouri, and either left or died before the two centers were
once again definitively united. Somehow these names never seemed to hav€
been entered on the reconstructed register after the fire in 1852. Thei₹
names were found only in some accounts of the western houses.

The Sisters of Charity of Nazareth also experienced a decline in
the percentage of entrants during the decade of the 1830's. No records ₫
tradition of difficulties exists that would compare with those experienc€
by the Sisters of Loretto during this same period. It was, however, a ₫
cade of some uncertainty in the diocese and this did effect the sisters ₳
Nazareth to some degree. The cholera epidemic of 1832 made it necessary
to close the school at Nazareth for a time and many of the sisters nurse€
the victims. Three sisters died in the service of the sick and several
others were greatly weakened for the rest of their lives. When the scho€
was reopened only thirty pupils returned, and the school was always an i₦
portant source of new members. Following this blow came the appointment
Bishop David as Bishop of Bardstown with Father Chabrat as coadjutor.

---

[89]ALM. Original Rule, Annals, and conversation with the
archivist.

is news was especially hard to grasp as it was unexpected. After Bishop

aget was persuaded to retract his resignation it took several months be-

re he was again named Bishop of Bardstown. The conclusion of this situa-

on was that Bishop David resigned as coadjutor and Chabrat was consecra-

d as his successor.[90] About the same time a somewhat mysterious misun-

rstanding arose between Bishop David and some members of the community

ich prevented him from occupying the house that was being prepared for

m.[91] There are also indications in some of the correspondence that there

re difficulties with Father Ignatius A. Reynolds when he was the ec-

esiastical superior.

These are possible explanations, but perhaps both the Sisters of

retto and the Sisters of Charity of Nazareth had reached a point of

nsolidation and a time in which local population could not be expected

provide increasing numbers of members. The Sisters of Loretto in

ssouri, while practically autonomous during some of this time, were ex-

nding their work west of the Mississippi River. This same decade of

e 1830's was one of expanded works for the sisters from Nazareth. It

s during this decade that the orphanage and infirmary were opened in

uisville as well as several schools in various parts of Kentucky.[92]

th of these communities experienced a marked increase in the percentage

entrants during the 1840's.

Both the Oblate Sisters of Providence and the Sisters of Our Lady

Mercy found themselves in a precarious position during the 1840's.

---

[90]Cf. Life of Bishop J.B.M. David, pp. 135-145.

[91]Cf. Ibid., pp. 150-151.

[92]McGann, pp. 14-15.

Bishop England died in Charleston before he had provided the Sisters wi

an adequate Constitution. In Baltimore, the Oblates had lost both Fath

Joubert and Archbishop Whitfield. In an age when neither Church nor

state, nor society in general, looked favorably on women managing all t

own business affairs it was particularly difficult for these two commun

ties, both of whom were in a minority that many considered second-class

GRAPH 2c - Percentage of Entrants by Decade

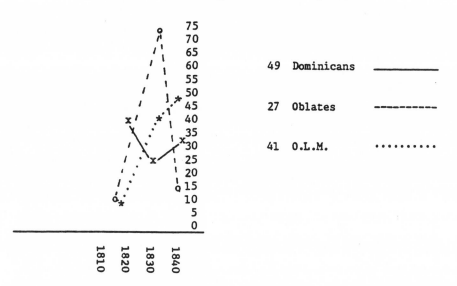

As late as 30 March 1850 Archbishop Eccleston wrote to Bishop Purcell o

Cincinnati:

> So far as I am concerned, I would be much pleased to second your wi
> to have a colony [of Oblates]. In fact, I believe that they could e
> a great deal more good in a Free State than here. I have requested
> Father Anwder [Anwander, CSSR] to exert himself to carry out your
> views. On him mainly will depend the direction given to the minds a
> wishes of those good Oblates—A favorite Spiritual Director is all
> powerful with female communities. . . .[93]

---

[93]UNDA. Archdiocese of Cincinnati Collection. Eccleston, Balti
to Purcell, Cincinnati, 30 March 1850.

Sister Mary Charles Curtin who arrived in Charleston shortly before Bishop England's death wrote about the unsettled condition of that period, and she also indicated the sisters' place in the local social structure. "Ours [the Charleston community of sisters] started in the protestant city of Charleston, where there were but few poor Catholics, surrounded by the wealth of those who looked down upon them."[94] In spite of Eccleston's strong implication that female communities were lacking direction without a priest, both the Oblates and the Charleston Sisters had shown a remarkable strength of purpose and commitment when they were virtually abandoned by the clergy. The Dominican Sisters had shown a similar strength in the previous decade when Father Munos told them to disband because of the debt (cf. p. 42) and the Sisters of Charity of Nazareth left Bishop Flaget no reason to doubt their self-determined direction when they clearly rejected his suggestion about a change in habit and a union with France in 1841 (cf. p. 38).

During the six decades from 1790 to 1850 the number of young women who entered the first eight communities of women religious in the United States continued to increase, but no community was without its setbacks. The first years of any community, because of the initial commitment to shared ideals and the charisma of the foundresses and the founder, would have few, if any, who left the group. None of the original Carmelites, Visitandines, or Sisters of Loretto left their community. Two women who joined Mother Seton at Emmitsburg in 1809 left the commun-

---

[94]Sacred Heart Convent Archives, Sisters of Mercy of North Carolina (Belmont). "Annals of the Sisters of Mercy, 1840-1910." Unpublished manuscript. When this was written Sr. Mary Charles was advocating that the Belmont Sisters, (cf. Campbell, p. 198), who had become an independent community in 1872, adopt the Rule of the Sisters of Mercy.

ity; no information was found concerning Sister Jane Corbet, but Sister

Cecilia O'Conway left after Mother Seton's death. The registers lists

her as having been Sister Servant at the Pay School of the New York

Orphan Asylum in 1822; the date of her departure is not given. At

Nazareth, one of the original members, Sister Betsy Wells (a convert),

left after two years. The Nazareth records tell us that she "was

dismissed having not the religious vocation."[95] The biographical data in

the archives states that she devoted herself to works of charity until

she entered the Dominican Convent. The Dominicans have no record of her

profession but she was buried there as Sister Rose Wells. It is assumed

that she lived with the Dominicans as a tertiary. Webb wrote of her: "She

was a pure and noble soul, somewhat eccentric in her ways, possibly, whic

explains her retirement from the Nazareth community; . . ."[96] and, one

might add, it probably explains why she was not a professed member of the

Dominican Sisters. Among the first members of the Dominican Sisters were

two who transferred to the Sisters of Charity of Nazareth. Sister

Silvilla Tarlton left "of her own accord" within three months, but Sister

Emily Elder remained for twelve years before transferring in 1834, just

the financial difficulties which had threatened the existence of the com

munity were being resolved. Sister Theresa Duchemin left the Oblates of

Providence and founded the Sisters of the Immaculate Heart of Mary in

Michigan in 1845, when the continued existence of the Oblates was very

doubtful due to a lack of approval by Archbishop Eccleston. Sister

---

[95]ASCN, "First Annals."

[96]Webb, 246 (footnote). See also UNDA, Mt. St. Mary's, Emmitsbur
Maryland Collection, Sisters of Charity. Father David, St. Thomas Semin
(Bardstown) to Fr. Bruté; Mt. St. Mary's Seminary, Emmitsburg. 7 September 1813. David describes Betsy Wells in similar terms (the original
is in French).

ugustine Burke, a convert and one of the four women Bishop England brought
o Charleston from Baltimore in 1829, returned to Baltimore in 1833.
ishop England dispensed her from her vows when she decided she could do
ore good among her Protestant relatives than in the convent.[97] The
ommitment to the ideals of the founder or foundress contained within it
ufficient motivating power to overcome the difficulties experienced by
ost of the original members.

As the communities grew in size and lost the founders and foun-
resses through death, they experienced a period of instability. This
nstability was due not only to the absence of the original charismatic
eader but also to the demands of a church that was rapidly growing in
umbers as immigration continued to increase and was expanding geogra-
hically as the Catholics, just as other Americans, followed the westward
ovement. In the decade of the 1820's at least thirty-three women left re-
igious life.[98] The two succeeding decades witnessed 106 women depart--
ver fifty in each decade, but by the decade of the 1850's the known de-
artures were down to twenty-nine. While the number of those who trans-
erred was always minimal, the largest proportion, 47.9% of all who trans-
erred, had entered in 1830. Most of these women were among the Sisters
f Charity from Emmitsburg who remained in New York under Bishop Hughes'
urisdiction in 1846. It is of interest to note that the three communities
hat experienced divisions which led to the founding of new communities of
omen religious had this experience during the stage that Wach calls "the

---

[97]Cf. Campbell, p. 97, referring to information from the "Community
istory 1829-1856" (ASCLM).

[98]Community records give no year of departure for 181 women, of
hese 162 left the Emmitsburg community.

brotherhood."[99] In the case of Sister Theresa Duchemin of the Oblates

of Providence, it was after the death of Father Joubert and Archbishop

Whitfield, but the foundress, Mother Mary Lange was still living and

active. This case, however, was seriously affected by the racial questio

as black women in the slave state of Maryland, the Oblates were even more

dependent on clerical support than other women religious. Sister Theresa

was apparently light enough that when she went to the north her French-

American ancestry and her ability to speak both languages precluded

racial questions. Among the Sisters of Charity, both those from

Emmitsburg and Nazareth, the divisions came during the transition from

"sisterhood" to "institution." The move toward centralization was un-

doubtedly a major factor in the formation of the Sisters of Charity in

New York (1846) and Cincinnati (1852) by sisters who had entered the Sis-

ters of Charity at Emmitsburg. The same is true of the Sisters of

Charity who separated from the Nazareth community in Memphis in 1851, but

eventually moved west and became known as the Sisters of Charity of

Leavenworth. It was a question, not only of a move toward centralization

within the women's communities, but bishops, also were moving to centra-

lize their authority at the same time.[100] This question of whose

authority takes precedence is clearly enunciated in a letter of Father

William McClellan of New York City to Father Francis McFarland in

Watertown, New York.

> . . . The Bishop convened a meeting of the Clergy for New York and
> Brooklyn today at this Church for the purpose of taking into con-

---

[99]Cf. Wach, 137f.

[100]Cf. Jay P. Dolan, The Immigrant Church: New York's Irish and
German Catholics, 1815-1865 (Baltimore: The Johns Hopkins University
Press, 1975), pp. 159-169.

sideration the present position of our charitable Institutions. The
Sisters of Charity after having during the space of nearly 50 years
[sic] managed the male asylums, now consider it proper to leave off.
This sudden resolution on their part of course places the Bishop in
a very embarasing [sic] position, especially as it does not leave him
sufficient time to make adequate arrangements for the care of boys.
However the council of Emmitsburg refuse to wait, and this brings up
a principle for discussion, whether an order after having been re-
received in a Diocese shall whenever they think proper, and without
consulting the Bishop of the Diocese, whether the measure be prac-
ticable or not, or whether it may not entail injurious consequences,
issue peremptory mandates concerning matters which may seriously in-
jure the public order and welfare. . . .[101]

Elizabeth Seton was long dead when the difficulty between the
superiors at Emmitsburg and Bishop Hughes arose. As the two sides
hardened their positions there were sisters who had entered during the
time of Mother Seton on both sides of the issue, and both sides were convinced they were being loyal to her spirit. Code's study, Bishop John
Hughes and the Sisters of Charity, shows very clearly that the correspondence concerning the "secession" of New York was essentially a question of
those authority takes precedence, that of the superiors at the Motherhouse
or the Bishop, in the determination of the kind of work done by the sisters as well as in the assignment of the sisters. This question came to a
head over the issue of caring for male orphans, and this issue was so
emotional that many participants saw it as the main issue. Code also con-
tends, and research verified it, that the issue of union with France was
dormant from the time of Mother Seton until the "secession."[102] It then

---

[101]UNDA. New York Collection. Father William McClellan, New York,
to Father Francis P. McFarland, Watertown, New York, 26 August 1846. The
length of time the Sisters of Charity cared for orphans in New York is considerably exaggerated. According to the Emmitsburg records the first
sisters opened the Orphan Asylum in New York in August 1817, i.e. twenty-
nine years before the separation, not "nearly 50 years" before.

[102]Cf., ASJCH. "Annals, 1846-1851," 368m, Copy of Circular of
Father R. R. Deluol, Baltimore, September 7th, 1849. "During the last
five years [i.e. since 1844], it has been the first and dearest wish of

appeared imperative to effect a union in order to maintain independence
from American bishops in the determination of the work and assignment of
the sisters. Apparently the oral tradition which is strong even to the
present day, that the New York separation took place because of moves t
the Emmitsburg authorities to adopt the unmodified Rule of St. Vincent
Paul,[103] arose because of a failure of the participants to recognize th
real issue at the time coupled with the actual union of Emmitsburg with
France within the short space of the next four years.

There is no doubt that both the separation of New York in 1846 a
that of Cincinnati in 1852 (after the affiliation with France) were emo
tional issues. The emotions were strong enough that tradition is color
by them to the present day. It is beyond the scope of this dissertatio
to make a detailed study of the causes for the two separations from the
Emmitsburg community, but some observations--because of the profound
effect on many individual sisters as well as institutions--are necessar

1. The personal decisions were not made lightly. Most, if not all, th
sisters who remained in New York made the decision in the light of the
needs in New York and despite a real conflict between their loyalty to
Bishop Hughes and their loyalty to the superiors in Emmitsburg, Code

my heart to place the Community under the direction of the Lazarists
[Vincentian priests]." (This circular is also found in Mother Etienne
Hall, pp. 87-91.) The quotation is given here on page 88. While this
might mean Father Deluol wished to have them affiliated with France sin
1844, I found nothing to support that interpretation. The Sulpicians w
being pressured by their superior in Paris to remove themselves from al
works not directly connected with seminaries. It would seem that befor
1846, Father Deluol's primary concern was to see that the Vincentians
would provide the ecclesiastical superior for the Sisters of Charity at
Emmitsburg, as the Sulpicians had done until then.

[103]Cf. Code, "Conclusions," pp. 46-47.

quotes a lengthy letter of Sister William Anna Hickey to Mother Etienne,
19 June 1846. A few excerpts will show a view of a participant who in
the end made the decision to remain in New York.

> . . . I saw the bishop yesterday. He is really in trouble. He says
> he wishes only what you wish. If you cannot see things as he does,
> then let things remain as they are. . . .
> My dear Mother, your heart would break to see the present insti-
> tutions under the care of the sisters broken up--the poor orphans as
> well as others--all this good set aside--and then the state of our
> community after such a scene--all the blame thrown on the superiors.
> . . . I do entreat you, for the love of our Lord, to overcome the
> bishop by a magnanimous act of generosity. . . .
> . . . .
> . . . I cannot remain dumb and see you drawn into difficulties when
> perhaps the little I could impart might be of use to you. . . .
> As for the sisters remaining in New York, I do not think one will
> remain. . . .[104]

Sister Aloysia Lilly (Sister Servant at St. Patrick's Asylum, New York,
1846) who chose to return to Emmitsburg wrote as follows to Father Deluol,
12 December 1846:

> Yesterday your letters arrived with the enclosed dispensations,
> some of the Sisters were much affected and wept bitterly, this is in-
> deed an awful thing to see some of our oldest Sisters, even those of
> Mother Seton's time, remaining here. They are all dearest Father
> pleased with your kindness towards them and all desire to be affec-
> tionately remembered to you. Sisters Lucina & Matilda [who had been
> sent from Emmitsburg to conclude the separation[105]] allowed them to
> keep what clothing they had and three or four of them were in want of
> a few other articles which I gave them as follows. . . . [shawls,
> capes, etc.] they all think very hard of having to part with the
> Community Book and said they knew Father Deluol would not take it from
> them. Please dear Father let it be sent back to them, poor things
> their bitter tears, pale faces and sleepless nights show plainly the
> grief of their hearts, and the work is all their own I suppose only,
> for I do not know, the schools are to be continued, they speak of the
> return of Sisters Betsy and William Anna as a matter of course. I was
> afraid Sister Betsy would be here before I could get off, I shall
> leave in the morning and hope on Wednesday to enter my retreat the
> silence of which will be a balm to my heart. You know well dearest
> Father how delighted I am to leave this house yet I shall feel the
> separation from so many dear old Sisters whom I shall see no

---

[104]Code, pp. 18-19. [105]Cf. Mother Etienne Hall, p. 14.

more, and who no longer belong to our Community, please dearest
Father pray for your devoted

child Lash[106]

2. <u>Administrative concerns appear among the most important reasons for</u>
<u>seeking union with the Daughters of Charity in France at the close of</u>
<u>the 1840's.</u> Two factors concerned Father Deluol as Superior General of
the Sisters of Charity of Saint Joseph at Emmitsburg after 1846. First
of all he, as well as the Mother Superior and her council, was concerned
that other bishops would try to follow Bishop Hughes' example and per-
suade sisters to form independent communities in their dioceses. The
second concern was to assure proper leadership for the sisters after he
left since the Sulpician Superior General had ordered his priests to re-
linquish this responsibility. Those who supported this union seemed
convinced that such concerns would be adequately negated by this move.

Bishop John Joseph Chanche of Natchez was a staunch supporter of
the move toward affiliation, and, in fact, was the one who opened negotiations with the Superior General of the Vincentians, Father Etienne,
in Paris, 1848. Father Burlando, C.M. who became the sisters' confessor
at the time of the affiliation, wrote a history of the event. According
to this history Father Etienne was at first hesitant when Bishop Chanche
approached him. One of his conditions was that the majority of the
American bishops must approve of the affiliation. He was, however, quite
satisfied by the formal petition presented to him by Bishop Chanche.
This petition was signed only by Sister M. Etienne, Mother Superior,
the Very Reverend L. Deluol, Superior General, Archbishop Eccleston, Pro-

---

[106]ASJCH. Letters, V:75. Sr. Aloysia Lilly to Fr. Deluol;
St. Patrick's Asylum (N.Y.), 12 December 1846. The Deluol-Hughes
correspondence (copies) relative to this situation are to be found in
Letters, V:102.

tector of the Constitutions of that Community, and Bishop Chanche.[107]

Another side of the story is mentioned in a letter of Father Mariano Maller, Visitor [Superior] of the Vincentian Province of the United States, who was charged with carrying out the details of the affiliation in the United States. One of his responsibilities was to visit the bishop in each diocese in which the Sisters of Charity worked. On 11 December 1849 he wrote to Bishop Blanc in New Orleans about his meeting with Archbishop Peter Richard Kenrick of St. Louis two days before. As he had done in other dioceses he asked to name, from among his confreres, the confessor for the sisters and novices. Maller reported that Archbishop Kenrick told him several things that made it clear that Kenrick opposed the union and the "imprudent manner" in which it was carried out-- without consultation with the other bishops. He would not oppose this union if the superiors and sisters wanted it "which he doubted very much," but he would never give up his right to appoint their confessors. Although he would not want to give up the sisters he would choose that alternative. Maller was embarrassed by this situation as he was sure Father Etienne would never allow the union to be completed unless the sisters in America were on the same footing as those in France. An understanding should be reached.[108] Apparently such an understanding was reached since the sisters continued their work in St. Louis, and I found no other references to this difficulty.

3. <u>The Sisters had little knowledge of the proceedings.</u> In the letter

---

[107]Cf. ASJCH. Father Burlando's History (manuscript). See also <u>Mother Etienne Hall</u>, pp. 60-64.

[108]Cf. UNDA. Archdiocese of New Orleans Collection. Fr. M(ariano) Maller (C.M.), St. Louis, to Bp. (Anthony Blanc), N. Orleans [French original], 11 December 1849.

of Father Maller to Bishop Blanc referred to above (#2) there is no further explanation of Archbishop Kenrick's statement that he doubted
whether the sisters and their superiors approved of the affiliation.
One can only surmise that he had heard statements of disapproval from
the sisters, either directly or indirectly. Other references (see below) indicate that expressions of disapproval or doubt about the affiliation would not have been unique to the sisters in St. Louis.
Again no other references were found, however, so one must conclude
that the majority of the sisters as well as the archbishop were rather
quickly satisfied by the clarifications that were offered.

Letters of Bishop Chanche of Natchez, now located in the archives
at the University of Notre Dame, show little concern for what have remained emotional issues. In 1850 he wrote to Bishop Purcell:

. . . .
I am sorry any of the Sisters should have made any difficulty about their vow to the Superior General. The Union being
effected, it was the only person they could make it to. They
ought to have more confidence in their superiors than to think
that they would be subjected to the trial which they fear. It
is understood on all sides, that no changes are to be made in
the government of the Sisters in this country, at least for
many years. I am glad that the vast majority of the Sisters
have rejoiced at an event which gives them a real standing
in the church and besides which unites them in good and
prayers to 8 millions of devoted servants of God. It['s]
only carrying out now, what was the anxious wish of the
Founders of St. Joseph: the DuBourgs, the Davids and the
DuBois.[109]

In a letter to Bishop Blanc of New Orleans, 22 December 1849, Chanche
had written that it seemed "this union of the Sisters of Charity of
this country with those of France does not give general satisfaction
among the Bishops. I think those who disapprove it are mistaken." He

---

[109] UNDA. Archdiocese of Cincinnati Collection. John Joseph
Chanche, Natchez, to J.B. Purcell, Cincinnati. 4-26-1850.

considered this union necessary to give the sisters importance. "I
will be blamed, I suppose, for my interference--but I have only been
the weak instrument to carry out the original values of the Founders of
this society, the DuBourgs and the Davids . . ."[110]

Bishop Chanche ignores the American origins of the community,[111]
and the American sensitivity of both the bishops and the sisters involved.
The ideals and spirit of Mother Seton were important to the sisters in
the decisions made by them whether they finally chose to stay in New York
in 1846, or in Cincinnati in 1852, or remain with Emmitsburg at either
time. In 1846, some, at least, of the sisters who worked with the immigrants who were often destitute and seriously ill when they arrived, may
well have seen their needs as concerns which placed considerations of
final authority in specific instances in second place. In Cincinnati by
1850, foreign connections could be a hindrance. "A real standing in the
church" had little meaning among Cincinnati's German and Irish Catholics
who were making strenuous efforts to prove their Americanism. The sisters in Emmitsburg, New York, and Cincinnati, were, and have remained,
convinced of their loyalty to Mother Seton.

Available evidence would hardly support an interpretation of
Mother Seton's attitude toward affiliation with France as decidedly negative for all time, but neither does it support an interpretation that
such an affiliation was her goal. It is certainly clear that Archbishop

---

[110]UNDA. Archdiocese of New Orleans Collection. Bp. Jn. Jos.
Chanche, Natchez, to Bp (Anthony) Blanc, N. Orleans. 22 December 1849.

[111]Cf. ASJCH. Letters, V:50. In the sketch memoir presented
to the Fathers of the sixth provincial council of Baltimore, 1846, it
stated that the "Sisters of Charity in the United States, were founded
by the Most Revd. Archbishop John Carroll, under the direction of the
members of St. Sulpice, . . . "

Carroll was not in favor of such a union.[112] Because conditions had changed so greatly between the time of Mother Seton's death in 1821 and the late 1840's, the question about what she would have done under similar circumstances is a moot one. The different choices made by loyal followers in 1846 and 1852, clearly point to the difficulty.

The move toward affiliation shows a lack of concern for the sisters involved. Again, archival records point to this failure. In the account of the separation by the sisters in Cincinnati, given in the biography of Mother Etienne Hall the cause of the separation is said to have been "the dress."[113] If this seems trivial, a manuscript account of the Union shows how widespread the problem of dress actually was:

> Many of our Sisters, old and young, were very much opposed to the dress--At first hint that we might adopt it.
> In Philadelphia at this time, Sr. Ann Maria said to Fr. Maller, "Father, they are threatening us with this dress! . . . [if the superiors judged it to be good, there was to be no further discussio
> Some few, to whom the thought of the French costume, was a young martyrdom, were spared the trouble of adopting it. They were faithfu and true; and, our good God, in his loving condescension, took them Himself before the black cap was laid aside--. . .[114]

Adopting a French dress, surely meant adopting French customs--and this at a period when nativists had been accusing Catholics of being under foreign domination. The majority of the Sisters of Charity, at least of those who had lived or worked in any urban center, had experienced the scorn of the nativists in some way or other. This reaction to things French may explain the effort made to show how little was changed in the lives of the sisters in written accounts at Emmitsburg.[115] Cincinnati

---

[112]Cf. Melville, pp. 212-219.   [113]Mother Etienne Hall, pp. 94

[114]ASJCH. "Union with France," an unsigned manuscript account.

[115]Cf. ASJCH, "Annals, 1846-1850," p. 358. Much of the compariso of their lives as Daughters of Charity to that before 1850 is based on

ad been a focal point for nativism, especially since Rev. Lyman Beecher

ad settled there about 1830, when he accepted the presidency of Lane

heological Seminary.[116]

. The extent and the meaning of the necessary changes resulting from

ffiliation with France were interpreted differently. The dissatisfac-

ion in Cincinnati stemmed from such differences in interpretation.

ather Maller, during a visit to Cincinnati in the spring of 1850, assured

he sisters "that nothing would be changed, that all things would go on

s before under previous Ecclesiastical Superiors." And then, shortly

efore 25 March 1851 the sisters received an official communication from

other Etienne Hall. "A new formula of vows for each Sister and a doll

ressed as a Cornette Sister accompanied the announcement that the Com-

unity was now affiliated with the Daughters of Charity in France."[117]

ister Margaret George, and those who remained with her in Cincinnati, in-

erpreted the change of habit, the change in the vow formula, and the

hanges in the administration of the community as a sign that Mother

eton's and Archbishop Carroll's concerns for being able to meet the needs

f the American Church were being disregarded. The primary concerns which

hey recognized (like the sisters in New York, six years earlier) included

eaching both boys and girls, and caring for male, as well as female,

rphans.[118] The documents leave no doubt that few, if any sisters, aside

---

he horarium, times of conferences and retreats, etc. There is very
ittle said about the vows, the administration of the community, or the
orks of the community.

[116]Billington, 126f.

[117]Sister Mary Agnes McCann, The History of Mother Seton's
aughters: The Sisters of Charity in Cincinnati, Ohio, 1809-1917 (New York:
ongmans, Green & Co., 1917), Vol. II, pp. 99-100.

[118]Cf. Ibid., pp. 99-120. McCann gives an account of the Cincinnati

from the Mother Superior and her Council in Emmitsburg, had anything to

say about the affiliation. The chief participants were clergymen. When

American women asserted their right to disagree they were not taken

seriously. The letter of Father Maller to Bishop Blanc, referred to abc

seems to indicate that Archbishop P. R. Kenrick had heard complaints abc

a lack of consultation from sisters in St. Louis, too.

5. <u>Reverence for the ideals of Mother Seton was a characteristic of all</u>

<u>three groups</u>. A typescript biography of Mother Margaret Cecelia George

the archives at Mount Saint Joseph (Cincinnati) quotes letters that sho

her conviction that the sisters in Cincinnati, as well as those in New

York, remained faithful to Mother Seton.[119] In a letter to Rev. John F.

Hickey, Sister Margaret wrote: "So we are trying to fulfill the ends of

our vocation calmly and humbly such as Mother Seton wished her children

be--"[120]

The Emmitsburg records, while showing that both separations were

painful, clearly imply a different focus in their view of the causes of

each separation. At the time the sisters in New York separated from

___

separation which agrees with sources found in Emmitsburg and Notre Dame.
She stresses the importance of being an <u>American</u> community, but makes no
connections between this insistence on Americanism and the current nativ
campaigns. Her references to the New York separation are not always
accurate. Code's work on that event is better. It may be time for some
one to do a thorough study of the causes and relationship of the three
events--the New York Separation, Union with France, and the Cincinnati
Separation.

[119]ASCMSJ. Sister Rosanna Barker, S.C., M.A., "Mother Margaret
Cecelia George: First Superior of the Sisters of Charity of Cincinnati,
Ohio," (typescript).

[120]ASCMSJ. Certified copy of the letter, p. 2. Sr. Margaret C. (
to Rev. John F. Hickey, postmarked 30 November 1853. Fr. Hickey had
been the ecclesiastical superior of the Emmitsburg community during
the 1830's.

Emmitsburg, Bishop Hughes was seen as the person primarily responsible for the difficulties. And it is to be remembered that superiors of other communities also looked upon the event as a possible example for other bishops to follow. On the other hand, while there may have been an impulse to make Bishop Purcell primarily responsible for the separation of the Cincinnati sisters, it was Sister Margaret George who was blamed. Bishop Purcell had been president of Mount Saint Mary's College in Emmitsburg and a beloved friend of the community in "the Valley." After he became bishop he always seemed to visit the sisters when business brought him to the East Coast. Sister Margaret George, a close companion of Mother Seton and a former councillor of the community, was viewed as a deserter (an indication of the conviction of the Emmitsburg sisters that they had been loyal to Mother Seton by affiliating with France). In the biography of Mother Rose White a sister companion of Sister Margaret at the time of the secession of St. Peter's Asylum, Cincinnati, gave the following "testimony":

> Sister Margaret was a good soul!--laborious, generous, kind-hearted:--a remarkable financier, yet no manager in domestic affairs and had little control over the children. . . . She rose at three o'clock in the morning to build the fires and have the rooms comfortable for the Sisters; . . .
> And yet, with all this unselfishness, all this earnestness in the works of her vocation, the moment of weakness came--and the vocation went down![121]

----

[121]*Mother Rose White*, p. 122. Cf. ASJCH. Annals, III:255. "Sister Margaret George, who had been a most faithful, devoted member of the Company, had been one of the companions of Mother Seton, took umbrage at our union with France, and particularly at the adoption of the French costume.--We always feared, that she had yielded for the moment, to the influence of persons who preferred to have the Sisters free from the control of the Central House. [At this point there is a pencilled note: "No, see statements of Srs. Eliza Dougherty and W. Gehring."] It was most painful to see this dear old Sister after so many years among us, and filling such important positions, leave her Mother House--and dear vocation--And bitterly she regretted, to the last day of her life--She could never see

TABLE 7

Age at Death by Decade Entered

	Unknown	1790	1800	1810	1820	1830	1840
16 or under	–	–	–	2	5	1	–
17–20	–	–	–	6	11	2	5
21–25	1	–	–	12	11	14	14
26–30	1	1	–	10	7	4	20
31–35	–	–	–	11	6	8	19
36–40	–	1	2	3	5	11	11
41–45	–	–	–	7	7	6	15
46–50	1	–	1	6	14	9	16
51–55	–	1	3	10	11	9	18
56–60	–	1	1	7	15	12	19
61–65	–	2	–	10	12	11	11
66–70	2	1	3	10	6	20	26
71–75	1	1	2	8	16	27	26
76–80	–	1	3	15	13	11	42
81–85	1	–	–	9	13	11	29
86–90	–	–	–	2	8	9	10
91–95	–	–	–	2	4	1	7
over 95	–	–	–	–	2	–	–
	7	9	15	130	166	166	288

Note: Age group within which the median falls _____

In reading accounts written about the early days of St. Joseph Convent, Emmitsburg, it seems that variations of this "testimony" were included wherever Sr. Margaret George was mentioned. That Sister Margaret George regretted the necessity of such a separation is clear, but the continued existence and growth of the community in Cincinnati, as well as their loyalty to the ideals and spirit of Mother Seton strongly support the view that her decision was not a selfish one, but a decision seriously considered from all the various angles as she saw them.

Life Expectancy

Table 7 gives the age at death of the sisters (known for 781 sisters) by the decade in which they entered. The table also indicates the median age at death for each decade. The median age at death for the entire period was sixty-one years; the average age at death was fifty-seven years. The only statistics for life expectancy in the United States for 1850 or earlier are based on statistics for the state of Massachusetts. The average life expectancy for females at birth in 1789 was 36.5 years; this had risen to 40.5 years in 1850. A woman at age twenty in 1789 could expect to live another 34.3 years (i.e. to age 54.3); in 1850 the twenty year old woman could look forward to another 40.2 years (i.e. to attaining age 60.2). Since the median age at entrance was 21.3 years, an average life expectancy of 57.2 years for the women who entered before 1850, compares very favorably with what little is known about all women in the United States at this time.[122]

a Lazarist, without bursting into tears.--To one of them she often said, with heartfelt grief: 'Oh, that I had only gone home, Oh, why did I not go home?' Thus Cincinnati was lost to the Company--"

[122] Warren S. Thompson and P.K. Whelpton, Population Trends in the United States (New York: McGraw-Hill Book Co., Inc., 1933), p. 240.

When one tries to determine the cause of death it is very difficult to get any representative statistics. The tradition in all eight
communities indicates a high incidence of tuberculosis. In Emmitsburg,
one or more members of the Seton family were infected by the disease from
the very beginning. Knowledge of the cause and spread of the disease was
very limited. A professional's view of the disease was found in the
Appendix to the Baltimore City Health Department's report for 1828:

> In the list of mortality, amounting to about seventeen hundred,
> we have to deplore the fact of about 300 persons having died of con-
> sumption. When we look at this widespread "picture of death," and be-
> hold the many interesting groups of female fashion, excellence, and
> beauty, who are laid in the dust by this disease, we are strongly re-
> minded of the admonition of the great and good Dr. Sydenham, who says,
> that more of mankind are slain by exposure to cold, than by war,
> pestilence and famine. And when we see the many, among the male
> groups, who fall by intemperance . . .[123]

If, as the report indicates, the incidence of consumption was higher among
females than among males, the 20.8% of deaths from the disease in the
Carmelite community would not be unusual. This 1828 report speaks of a
percentage for the total population of 17.6%; in 1836 consumption accounted for 13.3% of the total deaths recorded in Baltimore, and in 1845
16.8% of the deaths were attributed to consumption.[124]

Sister Defrosa Onan died of consumption at Nazareth, Kentucky,
8 November 1837. The short account of her life and death--she had en-

---

Cf. also pp. 228-229. J. Potter, "The Growth of Population in America,
1700-1860," in Population in History, Essays in Historical Demography,
D.V. Glass and D. E. C. Eversley (Chicago: Aldine Publishing Company,
1965), pp. 631-688.

[123]MHR. Baltimore City Health Department: The First Thirty-five
Annual Reports, 1815-1849 (Baltimore, 1953), Appendix. "Report from the
Consulting Physician," Baltimore, December 31st, 1828.

[124]Ibid., "Report of Internments in the City of Baltimore, . . ."
(January 1, 1836 - January 1, 1846).

tered the community only six years previously and it was apparently ill-health that delayed her profession until 1 November 1836--relates that she had been the baker until she became too weak. From then until a short time before her death she had charge of the refectory.[125] The evident tone of admiration for her work, in spite of weakness, reinforces the assumption that the manner in which the disease was communicated to others was unknown (and nothing in the Baltimore report of 1828 would contradict this). In a letter of Bishop Flaget to the Propaganda Fide of 4 February 1825 (?) concerning changes he considered necessary in the Constitution of the Sisters of Loretto he wrote:

> However, when I heard that fifteen or sixteen sisters who were not yet thirty years of age had died from tuberculosis within the short space of one year, my heart was filled with sorrow, and I blamed myself for acting the way I did [not commanding Father Nerinckx to make the changes suggested earlier]. I consulted learned medical men and all of them unanimously and without hesitation attributed the deaths of the sisters to the great severity of their rule.[126]

Between September 1823 and September 1824 there were fifteen deaths of sisters under age thirty in the Loretto community. Five of them took place during the month of March 1824. In the records of the Sisters of Loretto, as in the records of other communities, there are indications that good health was not always a major requirement for acceptance. The first superior, Sister Ann Rhodes, died--apparently of tuberculosis--six months after the foundation of the community. Father Nerinckx, himself, wrote that Sister Lucia Calhoun "died with a lingering complaint, which she had before she came to the Society." He also noted that Sister Thecla McSoarley (d. 28 July 1823) died at Gethsemani "5 months after she had

---

[125]ASCN. OLB-XVI:42.

[126]Flaget to the Cardinal Prefect of the Congregation for the Propagation of the Faith, 4 February 1825 (?) as quoted in Wand and Owens, p. 58.

mad [sic] her final vows" [at age 17].[127] The register at Loretto gives
Sister Maxima Sansbury's entrance dates as 3 April 1824 and her death da
as 5 April 1824. And for Sister Everildes Knott the entrance date is
2 July 1824; her death date is given as 21 July 1824. It is possible th
mistakes were made when the register was reconstructed in 1858, but because of the statements in Father Nerinckx's Journal error cannot be assumed. Some of the very early deaths can also be attributed to allowing
the young women to take vows on their deathbed. When a young woman's il
ness appeared grave, but it was still possible for her to return home
she did. One of the more unusual accounts of plans for a return under
these conditions was found in the Council Minutes of the Sisters of Our
Lady of Mercy, 4 June 1846. Miss Riordon who had entered the community
the previous October "has been laboring under mental infirmity for the
last four months." The question before the Council was whether to send
her home to Ireland at the first opportunity or send her to an institution in the United States. The decision was made to send her home since
the physician reported that there would be no risk. Arrangements were t
be made.[128] The young woman died on 30 June, less than four weeks after
the decision was made to send her home. All the extant records show a
serious concern for protecting the health of the sisters and the sick we
given the best care possible. Medical science was not far advanced during this period: "It is unlikely that any weight can be attached to medi
cal improvement as a cause of population increase in the USA in the firs
half of the nineteenth century. . . . [until] the cholera outbreaks in t

---

[127]ASL. Father Nerinckx'."Journal".

[128]Cf. ASCLM. Council Minutes, 4 June 1846.

middle of the nineteenth century, medicine made little or no contribution
to lowering mortality."[129] The sisters lived in close contact with one
another and their students and many of them nursed the sick. Contagious
diseases were certain to take their toll. Even the cloister at Carmel did
not protect the nuns from all contagion. Sister Mary of the Incarnation
(Frasier), the first lay sister to enter the community, died of small pox
(14 December 1831) which she caught from a poor person who came for alms.
The records note that in answer to prayer it did not spread within the community. In March 1850 there were two deaths from typhoid and another
death in 1858 (of a sister who entered prior to 1850) of the same
disease.[130]

Probably the only count that reflects reality for the entire group
is that for the thirty-six who died as a result of epidemics. This
category accounts primarily for victims of such diseases as cholera and
yellow-fever. Deaths in the service of the sick during epidemics were
noteworthy, not only within the religious community, but usually to the
general populace. The obituary at Emmitsburg for Sister Martina
Butcher says that she died of yellow fever (in Mobile, Alabama,
7 August 1849) while nursing the sick. Her grave marker was donated, in
appreciation of her heroism, by the "Can't-Get-Away-Club".[131] The low
number of deaths is quite remarkable since sisters from every community
except the Carmelites and Visitandines went into the homes of the victims,
makeshift hospitals, or over-crowded almshouses to nurse the poorest and

---

[129]Potter, p. 679.

[130]ACM-B, Death Book.

[131]ASJCH, Obituaries.

most seriously ill of the dread disease.

It is interesting to note that of the 341 women known to have been older than seventy years of age at death, there were notations that only twenty-six died of the complications of old age. In general, death was recognized as a fact of life, and not much was made of the age of death or its cause unless there was something of the unusual in the circumstances surrounding it.

Had a person met any one of these women before they entered religious life he or she probably would not have noted anything that would cause the young woman to stand out. After their entrance the women were easily distinguishable by their dress and life-style. The majority of persons who have left a record of their meeting with sisters found nothing to condemn. They may still have wondered why a young woman chose such a life-style, but they did not question her womanhood or the value of the work that was accomplished.

CHAPTER IV

EDUCATION: 1799-1850

Freedom to worship and the freedom to organize the Roman
Catholic Church in the United States brought with it many problems for the
Catholics who were ready to assume leadership. Except for several congregations in eastern Pennsylvania the Catholics were even without parish
churches.[1] The old Catholic families of Maryland had been well served by
the Jesuit priests since the time of the original settlement, but
because Catholics had not been free to practice their faith openly after
the 1690's, no educational institutions had been able to develop.[2]
By the time the United States had won its independence the Society of Jesus
had been dissolved by the Pope. The former Jesuits remained in America to
serve the Catholics and several ex-Jesuits from Maryland families had returned from Europe, but since some Catholics were as ready as other
Americans to look for a better life on the frontier there was a serious
shortage of priests. Immigrants were beginning to come to the eastern
port cities in a steady trickle and native-born Americans were moving westward. How could the Church care for these people? There was no possibility of forming enough parishes within which a resident pastor could
give regular instructions and provide pastoral services for all the
Catholics in the United States.

---

[1]Cf. Ellis, pp. 28-29.

[2]Cf. Ibid., p. 27.

The emphasis on educational institutions appears as a practical
response to the needs of the American Catholic Church and its formative
stage. If Catholics had a solid education one could expect more recruits
for the priesthood and religious life. But lacking sufficient priests
and religious to instruct and serve the Catholic community, the Catholic
laity could receive a great deal of instruction through reading. The
people were living and working among non-Catholics. They needed to be
prepared to find their own answers to questions and fulfill their own
devotional needs when no priest was available.

John Carroll, even before he was named the first bishop of the
United States, led the move to establish Catholic schools. In May 1789 a
prospectus for an academy at Georgetown was published by the clergy and t
school was opened two years later.[3] A year earlier, 26 May 1778, Carroll
had written to his friend, Charles Plowden, in England: "I expect Mr Tha?
very soon. As to his nuns, I hope he will let that alone till he has ma?
some progress in Boston. Mr Chas. Neale of Antwerp is eager to introduc?
Teresians (Carmelites). I wish rather for Ursulines."[4] It would seem c
from other statements to Charles and Robert Plowden in England and Mothe?
Bernardine Matthews in Port Tobacco as quoted above (Ch. I, pp. 3-4) tha?
his preference for Ursulines rather than Carmelites was occasioned by his
sire to have schools established for girls. Before he died (1815) John
roll witnessed the establishment of the academies for girls in Georgeto?
D.C. and Emmitsburg, Maryland; moreover both the Loretto Sisters and the?
Sisters of Charity of Nazareth were teaching young girls on the Kentucky

---

[3]Cf. Documents of American Catholic History, pp. 167-168.

[4]John Carroll Papers, Vol. I:312. John Carroll to Charles Plowde?
Rock Creek, 26 May 1788.

rontier. By 1835 the number and the quality of Catholic schools had made
ufficient impact for Lyman Beecher to use the very existence of these
chools as a warning sign of the Roman threat to America and American
nstitutions.[5]

When Bishop Carroll encouraged the founding of schools his first
oncern was not that Catholic children would be lost to Protestantism as
result of Protestant control of the public school system. Rather, it
as that Catholic children would grow to maturity without any education.
his is not to say that he did not care about their religious training;
t is simply to recognize that there was no school system, either public
r private, in most areas of the United States while he was Bishop of
altimore. The move to establish public schools became significant only
bout 1830. Before the Jacksonian era elementary education was, to a
reat extent, received only in private schools.[6] There are, of course,
umerous references in both published and unpublished documents of the
arly nineteenth century which speak of the danger of Catholic children
ttending "public" schools. The statements of the early nineteenth cen-
ury reflect a belief that the Protestant characteristics of the schools
ould be changed in order that the schools would be acceptable to Catho-
ics. After the two bitter struggles in New York and Philadelphia in
he early 1840's over the question of reading the Bible in public schools
he change in attitude toward public schools is clearly noticeable.[7] But

---

[5]Cf. Lyman Beecher, Plea for the West (Cincinnati: Truman and Smith,
835), especially pp. 71-72; 92-93; 98-100. See also Ch. I, p. 57; Re: the
uality of the schools at Loretto and Nazareth.

[6]Cf. A History of American Education, pp. 134-135.

[7]Ibid., pp. 137-138.

these were two large eastern cities and it was some time before many are
of the United States had sufficiently well-organized public school syste:
to cause grave concern among Catholics.

In the early 1840's the rise of nativism became more pronounced,
and in both New York and Philadelphia the question was raised as to
whether the bible was a sectarian book. The attitude of Catholics
toward public schools began to change in response to these conditions
and is, perhaps, best reflected in the words of the Pastoral Letters issued by the American hierarchy in 1843 and 1852. The letter issued by
the Fifth Provincial Council of Baltimore, 1843, (before the full impact
of the struggle in Philadelphia had made itself felt) admonished parents

> Let them, therefore avail themselves of their natural rights,
> guaranteed by laws, and see that no interference with the faith
> of their children be used in public schools, and no attempt
> made to induce conformity in any thing contrary to the laws of
> the Catholic Church.[8]

The First Plenary Council of Baltimore, 1852, issued a Pastoral Letter i
which the admonition contained a very different attitude toward public
schools. No longer did the bishops see a policy of "no interference wit
the faith" of the children as acceptable.

> Listen not to those who would persuade you that religion can
> be separated from secular instruction. . . . Encourage the
> establishment and support of Catholic schools; make every
> sacrifice which may be necessary for this object; spare our
> hearts the pain of beholding the youth whom, after the example
> of our Master, we so much love, involved in all the evils of an
> uncatholic education. . .[9]

In rural areas and on the frontier, before the middle of the nine

---

[8]Peter Guilday, ed., The National Pastorals of the American
Hierarchy (1792-1919), (Washington, D.C.: National Catholic Welfare
Council), p. 153.

[9]Ibid., pp. 190-191.

.eenth century, even private schools for the affluent were often lacking.
:atholic schools, whether academies, pay schools (schools without boarding
`acilities), or free schools were needed to meet the need for basic educa-
.ion as well as provide a religious education for the young. All the early
.atholic schools seem to have welcomed non-Catholics. The early Catholic
.lmanacs, directories, and newspapers printed the prospectuses for the
`arious academies.[10] Every prospectus made some statement about the accep-
.ance of non-Catholics. In 1828 the Female School of Loretto included the
`ollowing statement in its prospectus:

> 4. The Sisters who have the direction of this Institution
> profess the Catholic religion. . . . They deem it a duty incumbent on
> them to inculcate upon pupils of the other denominations, the general
> principles of Christian religion and morality. They do not, however,
> use any influence with the pupils of other professions, toward in-
> ducing them to join the Catholic religion, without the express will
> and consent of parents.[11]

Iithout non-Catholic students in the academies there would not have been
.nough students to meet expenses and support the sisters and some other
vork. On the other hand, the records imply that the sisters, and the
.ishops and priests who were instrumental in the foundation of various
.chools, were sincerely concerned about the general lack of adequate educa-
.ion and were pleased if they could help overcome this inadequacy. The
.nitial thrust to establish schools staffed by these original communities of
vomen religious was made well before "public school" and "Protestant school"
.ecame synonomous terms in the minds of most Catholics.

The greatest emphasis on the number of conversions that resulted

---

[10]The first Catholic Directory (the title varies--directory or
.lmanac--depending on the publisher) was published in 1817 and the United
States Catholic Miscellany, the first Catholic newspaper, began publication
.n 1822.

[11]"Female School of Loretto," USCM, p. 216.

among the non-Catholic students in the schools seems to have been in rep

to Europe whether they were directly to the Propaganda Fide in Rome or t

the headquarters of the various missionary aid societies. At home the

sisters, as well as the local church authorities, were happy when the su

and good-will of the students and their parents were won. An example of

this may be seen in two reports of Bishop Flaget. The first was sent to

Holy Father and dated 10 April 1815 at Bardstown, Kentucky. The bishop

cluded a paragraph about the two communities (the Sisters of Loretto and

Sisters of Charity of Nazareth) founded in his diocese less than three

years before by saying: "The greatest help, if God favors us is expected

from them for the salvation of our neighbors."[12] The second report, now

found in the Archives of the Propaganda Fide, was written in 1825 and is

a copy of "A Statement of the chief Litterary Institutions and public

Buildings made by the Catholic Clergy of Kentucky, as given in a Letter

of the Right Rev[d]. B. J. Flaget in answer to a Letter directed to him

in the name of the Secretary pro temp. of the General Government of the

United States of America." At the conclusion of the section dealing wit

the institutions of women religious in Kentucky, Flaget wrote:

> All our Institutions are conducted on the most liberal
> principles, and are opened both to Catholics and Protestants.
> These latter are by far the more numerous part of our Pupils,
> and nevertheless live in friendship with their Catholic School-
> mates, and their Teachers who glory in the profession of this
> Religion.[13]

In the Annals written in Emmitsburg, the following entry is found

> In 1832, the city of Boston, the Athens of America, has seen its
> frozen prejudices gradually melt away before the kindly sun of chari

---

[12]"Documents," CHR (October 1915), p. 316 (a translation).

[13]UNDA. Microfilm: Archives of the Propaganda Fide, Vols. 480r
to 483v (27 September 1825). Cf. Kenneally, Vol. I:152, #925.

The dark night of intolerance has passed by, and the enlightened citizens in that capital have not scrupled to entrust the charge of their Orphan Asylum and Benevolent School, in which three hundred children are gratuitously educated to an association, whose religious principles have for centuries formed the theme and terror of the pious bigot and gloomy fanatic--thus much has been written by the public press--[14]

That those who thought the prejudices had melted away were overly optimistic is a matter of record. The Ursuline Academy at Charlestown, Massachusetts, was burned by a mob on 11 August 1834.[15] On the other hand, it is very clear from the above quotation that success was not seen as consisting only in conversions--good-will was a true measure of success.

An entry in the "Diary of St. Joseph's" seems to reflect an attitude somewhere in between satisfaction with good-will and measuring success by the number of converts to Catholicism:

Ap 4th 1941 Palm Sunday

. . . Mary Robert's uncle has come to take the dear girl from school, I suspect the motive is <u>fear that</u> she should imbibe too many Catholic ideas: poor Protestants! I pity you--Mary however has prevailed over her friends & she is to remain until after Distribution & perhaps another year, if she does not during her stay at home during Vacation, manifest too many Catholic notions----[16]

There were very few schools or academies for young women any place in the United States in 1790. An early twentieth century study of the education of women in the early nineteenth century shows a bleak picture indeed. Even in New England where formal education had been provided almost from the foundation of the colonies there were, reportedly, women from respectable families in Boston who were illiterate at the time of the

---

[14]ASJCH. "Annals," III:261.

[15]Cf. "Non-Permanent Foundations," p. 48.

[16]ASJCH. "Diary of St. Joseph's, 1836-1841," 4 April 1841.

Revolution. In the south, elementary education was usually dependent on the family's ability to hire a tutor. Although the Moravians had several fine schools for girls that had been founded in the mid-eighteent century,[17] it is doubtful that Catholics would have sent their daughters to one of these schools because of their clearly sectarian affiliation. Joseph Emerson opened his seminary for young ladies at Byfield, Massachus in 1818, and it was this school that was to become a model for many other in the succeeding decades.[18]

We know that in the leading eastern cities there were private ele-mentary schools and academies, but there was nothing like a school sys-tem. It was by conducting a private elementary school that Elizabeth Seton, after the death of her husband, sought to support herself and her family first in New York City and later in Baltimore.[19] When Ellen O'Connell came to Nazareth, Kentucky from Baltimore in 1814 she was al-ready an experienced teacher;[20] Julia Datty had conducted an academy that was well known in Charleston, South Carolina before she entered the Sis-ters of Our Lady of Mercy in 1832;[21] Mother Augustine Decount "was a teacher of music in a first class French Academy in Philadelphia" before she entered the Sisters of Charity at Emmitsburg in 1817.[22] The first three members of the Oblate Sisters of Providence had been conducting

---

[17]Ethel Margaret Lacey, "Joseph Emerson as Educator: A Study in t Education of Women in the United States during the Early Part of the Nine teenth Century," (Ph.D. dissertation, New York University, 1916), pp. 1-4

[18]Ibid., p. 12.

[19]Cf. Melville, pp. 149-151; 183.

[20]Webb, p. 247.

[21]Blandin, p. 252.

[22]Mother Augustine Decount and Mother Xavier Clark, p. 1.

school under the leadership of Miss Mary Elizabeth Lange in Baltimore
or some time before the decision was made to form a religious community.
The original historian, Mother Theresa Catherine Willigman, wrote:

. . . she opened a school for children of both sexes (in Baltimore),
It was at the time the only Catholic school and as there was a large
number who had emigrated from Hayti, and the Islands, the Parents lost
no time in placing their children at Miss Lange's school."[23]

What we know of the lives of some of the members of these eight
communities of women religious gives a hint of the manner in which the
more affluent citizens educated their daughters. Elizabeth Seton had
been educated at "Mama Pompelion's," a school in which young ladies were
prepared to take their place in society.[24] Sister Stanislaus Jones who
entered the Visitation Convent in 1825 had been educated in the French
boarding-school of Madame Bense in New York.[25] Certainly the knowledge
of French was important to those who sought to take their place in society
in the major cities along the eastern seaboard, but it is also clear that
various types of fancy needlework, painting and music were important
elements. Both Loretto Motherhouse and St. Catherine's in Kentucky
have one or more harps that were brought by early members of the community and several communities have records of the purchase of pianos--
music in the academies was not confined to occasional group singing or
simply what was desired for prayer and liturgical services.

---

[23] AOSP. Original History, pp. 2-3.

[24] Cf. Melville, p. 33.

[25] AGVC. Biographical Sketches.

Academies

In contrast to the picture of attempts at elementary education
in a few free schools in cities such as New York and Philadelphia[26] and
private schools for the elite in some of the major cities, the early
schools of the sisters must have been a welcome sign of progress to many
Even when the sisters were not well educated to begin with there were
priests ready to help them. The formation of religious communities gave
reason to expect not only dedicated teachers but also continuity. The
existence of a school would not be dependent on one person's ability to
continue. The one clear exception to this almost constant quality or
improvement of the schools was the "Young Ladies' Academy" in Georgetown
After the first three women (later to be known as Visitation nuns) arriv
in Georgetown from Philadelphia about 1799, Mrs. Sharpe became the principal teacher. An account written many years later by Sister Stanislaus
Jones says Mrs. Sharpe was "the soul and head of the little academy,"
but that when she was no longer able to direct the school it declined.[27]
The academy never went out of existence but it was an academy in name
only. The very fact that it was not closed during the years that only
a very rudimentary education was offered is a clue to the paucity of
educational facilities available for young women at the time. Georgetow
college was nearby but it, too, was struggling and poorly staffed in the
early years of the nineteenth century. As the second decade of the century drew to a close at least one accomplished teacher, Mrs. Jerusha

---

[26]Cf. Good, pp. 135, 139.

[27]AGVC. Biographical sketches. The quotation in this sketch quo
Sister Stanislaus Jones as saying Mrs. Sharpe directed the school for fi
to six years. Since her death occurred in 1802, this is an impossibility.

rber, entered the community and Father Joseph Picot de Clorivière was

ppointed "Spiritual Father" of the Convent by Archbishop Maréchal.[28]

ce there were well-educated persons to further the education of the

sters the school progressed and through the decade of the 1820's there

re numerous references to it. The Catholic publications have frequent

eferences to it either in the form of a prospectus or articles about

t by contributors. The secular press also began to take note it its

xistence. By 1830 it was beginning to attract the attention of prominent

ersons.[29]

There is a great deal of similarity in the courses offered in

he academies of all eight communities of women. The first academy men-

ioned in the United States Catholic Miscellany (founded 1822) was the

eorgetown Visitation Academy. The academy had been favorably described

y a Mr. Ingersoll in an address before the American Philosophical Society

n Philadelphia (23 October 1823) which was later published. Bishop

ngland stated that Mr. Ingersoll's "facts" were "the best comment on

he text of the pamphleteer (Rev. Mr. McEnroe)" whom he was refuting in

is newspaper.[30] A short advertisement for the school appeared on the first

age of the National Intelligencer (Washington, D.C.) on 18, 19 and 21

arch 1825.[31] Father Michael Wheeler became "Spiritual Father" at the

---

[28]AGVC. "Georgetown Visitation Convent Book of 1816," and the onvent register.

[29]"Young Ladies Academy at the Convent of the Visitation in eorgetown, D.C., 1799-1830" (unpublished paper by the present author).

[30]"Review of the strictures on the letters of the Right Rev. Dr. ngland, and Rev. Mr. McEnroe, " USCM (14 January 1824), pp. 20-22.

[31]National Intelligencer (Washington, D.C.), Library of Congress icrofilm, 18, 19, 21 March 1825.

Visitation Convent after the death of Father Clorivière (1826). Father Wheeler was an American by birth. Although Father Clorivière had done much to encourage the erection of adequate buildings and had helped the sisters become accomplished teachers, Father Wheeler was clearly far superior in the field of public relations. A new prospectus was printe Instead of the previous single sheet this prospectus had six pages of text. It was signed by "Michael F. Wheeler, M.A. President, Of St. Mary's College, Balt. and Director of the Convent and Ladies' Academy of the Visit." It was dated 14 August 1827. The prospectus, in its entirety, was found several times in both the United States Catholic Miscellany and The Truth Teller.[32]

This prospectus not only gives the basic information about the school that compares with the prospectus of almost any other academy-- Catholic, Protestant, or non-denominational--of the same period, but it also states the institution's philosophy of female education. The prospectus of 1827 certainly indicates that the direction of the Academ in Georgetown was in the hands of those who were conversant with current thinking concerning the education of women in the United States as well as the theory of woman's "sphere." This theory seemed generally accept as a means of balancing the equality of women with the concept that wome were different from men.

In Lacey's study of "Joseph Emerson as an Educator" (about 1818- 1830) she quotes his "Address on Female Education" in which he said:

Let our daughters be accomplished as much as you please, the

---

[32]"Prospectus of the Ladies' Academy of the Visitation, in Georgetown, D.C." as printed in the Petition for an Act of Incorporatio (1828). See also USCM (15 September 1827), pp. 82-83; The Truth Teller (15 September 1827), p. 288, and subsequent issues of both papers.

more the better, only let their accomplishments be united with
substantial improvements, with useful acquisitions . . . let
them be accomplished in conversation, in every branch of literature
which they will probably have occasion to use, especially let them
be accomplished in domestic philosophy, in the skilful, judicious,
and dexterious performance of domestic duties, above all, let them
be accomplished Christians.[33]

Lacey also quotes the following maxim of Joseph Emerson: "Improvement
of mankind depends on improvement of mothers."[34]

The Prospectus of 1827 for the academy in Georgetown states:

. . . The taste of the age, however, has obtruded within the circles
of polished life, branches of education, hitherto almost exclusively
confined to Colleges or University [male institutions]. Such is
the nature of the human character, that each individual of the
circle wishes to give marks of information or intelligence on the
subject in question, and none can be found insensible to the re-
proach of utter ignorance or mediocrity, where all would be equal.
. . . Moreover, as to the care of ladies is intrusted the guardian-
ship of society in its earliest age, to them is frequently due the
bias of the growing mind. It is often in their power to refine the
taste, and to whet the appetite, for every virtuous and literary
acquirement. . . .
The expansion of the youthful mind, in the more advanced
stages of life, is generally the effect of impressions communicated
to it, when first awakened to reason. . . . Its form is the form of
the mould, and the man, seen in his important relations in society
was the youth whose mind was quickened in its first operations by
the mother.[35]

This 1827 prospectus for the Ladies' Academy of the Visitation was
the most detailed and complete of any that were examined. The schools,
or seminaries, directed by Joseph Emerson were primarily directed toward
preparing the young ladies to be teachers while the academies conducted
by the various communities of sisters do not seem to have had this as a
specific goal, at least before 1850. The Special Report of the Commissioner
of Education (1871) in the section dealing with the education of black

---

[33]Lacey, p. 26.   [34]Ibid., p. 71.

[35]Prospectus, 1827, p. 5.

children in the District of Columbia up to 1867 leaves no doubt that the Oblate Sister of Providence succeeded well in preparing teachers.[36]

Beyond Emerson's stated purpose of training teachers there are other differences. Nowhere does he seem to have included in his course of study what Archbishop Carroll referred to as "elegant accomplishments." Emerson's work seems to have been directed toward preparing young women from the middle class in New England to support themselves for a few years before marriage by helping others of their sex to acquire an educa tion. The academies conducted by the sisters were meeting the needs and desires of the upper classes. The academies were finishing schools, but they were also dedicated to preparing the young lady for the practical aspects of her future role.

A work published in 1851, that is twenty-four years after the prospectus used here as an examplar, says much the same thing under the sub-title, "The Education of Mothers."

> I have now established two facts which are preliminary to any system of female education. The first is, that human nature is one; and the second, that differences of body do not imply differences of faculties. . . . but if these are facts, then her education should be essentially the same, in all that relates to the culture and strengthening of the SOUL (which includes both the intellect and the affections), as that of man: that is, that the elementary, fundamental, and philosophical part of education which relates to the development of the faculties, and is independent of avocations and professions, should be the same, in reference to all individuals, according to their time and opportunities, in the order of Providence. . . .
>
> . . . It comes to this, then, that women have the same faculties, and are capable of the same culture and acquisitions as men; they are not inferior, or opposite, or totally different from men in the essential elements of character.
>
> We come now to the practical application of this principle. What reason is there why women should be highly educated, or as

---

[36]Cf. Special Report, 1871, pp. 203-285. Not all the schools described in these pages were directed by students of the Oblate Sisters; about six schools were conducted by their former pupils.

highly as the circumstances of their condition will admit? The first thing we observe is, that women are the mothers of mankind. As such, they are the <u>first teachers</u>. . . .[37]

In Emerson's schools in the 1820's the course of study included reading, chirography, arithmetic, geography, grammar, rhetoric, composition, history (English, American, and Ecclesiastical), bible, catechism, dictionary, Watts on improvement of the mind, conversations on natural philosophy, and on chemistry, outline of lectures on astronomy.[38] Emerson's pupil, Zilpah Grant, provided the following additions in the course of study at her school in Ipswich: algebra, modern and ancient geography, botany, government of the United States, human physiology, Euclid's geometry, intellectual philosophy, philosophy of natural history, moral philosophy, geology and analogy. According to Lacey neither French nor Latin was taught but "the study of drawing, painting, and vocal music was urged upon all without extra price."[39] When one compares these courses with what was offered in the academies conducted by the sisters[40] one finds little variation in the core subjects.

Several other differences between the Catholic academies considered here and a few non-Catholic schools might be noted. In most prospectuses from Catholic academies the mention of geography was followed by the phrase, "with the use of maps and globes." The 1827 prospectus for the

---

[37] Edward D. Mansfield, <u>American Education, Its Principles & Elements</u>, Dedicated to the Teachers of the United States (New York: A. S. Barnes & Co., 1851), pp. 301, 303.

[38] Cf. Lacey, pp. 79-80.

[39] Cf. Ibid., pp. 88-90.

[40] The courses of study for the principal academy conducted by each of the eight communities which form the basis of this study can be found in Appendix 2, pp. 272ff.

188

Georgetown Academy notes that popular astronomy is taught "with the
assistance of the newly invented Geocyclic of Delamarche." In an account of the final, public examinations for the girls at the academy in
1830, a "Spectator" wrote: "During the interesting exhibition of the
class of Natural Philosophy, one of the young ladies, explained to the
company, the properties, &c. of a curious and complicated instrument,
called the blow pipe, which by reason of certain improvements (which
the "Spectator" attributes to Father Wheeler) may be used with perfect
security; . . ."[41] This compares very favorably to the announcement
of the Washington Henry Academy in Virginia, 1825, where the course of
study is given as follows:

> The following branches of Education will be taught, viz: The
> Latin, Greek and English Languages, Grammatically; Arithmetic,
> Geography, &c., Translation and composition of the French: The
> Elements of Chemistry and Natural Philosophy, so far as knowledge
> of those sciences can be conveyed without the apparatus necessary
> to their perfect illustration.[42] (italics mine)

The 1830's were the decade in which most of the schools began
offering the more advanced subjects. Neither the School for Coloured
Girls in Baltimore, conducted by the Oblate Sisters, nor the Female
Academy of the Sisters of Our Lady of Mercy offered any science or
philosophy courses before 1850. Only the academy at Georgetown added
specific courses in "Domestic Economy, comprising the various exercises
in Pastry and the Culinary art, Laundry, Pantry, and Dairy inspection,
&c. as conducted at the Academy of St. Denis Banlieue de Paris."[43] All

[41]"Convent of the Visitation," USCM (21 August 1830), p. 61

[42]Richmond Enquirer (13 January 1825) as quoted in Edgar W. Knight
ed., A Documentary History of Education in the South before 1860, Vol. I
"Private and Denominational Efforts," (Chapel Hill: The University of N
Carolina Press, 1953), #17.

[43]Prospectus, 1827, p. 6.

eight communities of women religious offered instruction in the French language and various forms of needlework. By the late 1840's all the academies except the one for "Coloured Girls" listed painting, drawing, and music lessons at least on the piano, if not on other instruments. These latter courses, unlike Zilpah Grant's school in Ipswich, did, however, require the payment of an additional fee.

This brief comparison of the courses offered by these early American Catholic academies with a few non-Catholic schools is derived almost entirely from published sources of the day. It does not seem necessary to go into more depth to show that these academies were prepared to fulfill their purpose of providing a good education to meet the needs and desires of the upper classes. Their success in doing this is attested to by the support given them by non-Catholics as well as Catholics. While some of this support came in the form of public statements which praised the educational institutions, a very important form of support came through the attendance of non-Catholic girls at the academies. If no such written records survived to the present there would still be little doubt that many non-Catholic girls attended the academies. The academies were, after all, the principal means of support not only for the sisters, but also for the day schools for the poor and the support of orphans.

One of the best testimonials of the importance of these academies as a means of support is found in the "Annals of Loretto, 1812-1852" written by Sister Theodosia Kelly about 1900.

> When the Loretto Sisters began to qualify themselves and to teach the arts, music, etc., and pupils came to them from all points, there were many consultations held by those interested in the welfare of Nazareth and the members of that body, the result of whose deliberations was that Bishop Flaget should

come to Loretto and induce Father Chabrat and the superiors
by persuasion if possible, if not by command, to give up their
academies and devote themselves exclusively to teaching the
poor, gratis. . . . But no arrangements were made for the
support of the Sisters, or to build convents thereby to extend
their usefulness, etc. . . .

Since the professors at St. Joseph's College in Bardstown spoke freely
of the scheme, several of the seminarians who taught at the college heard
of it. One of their number, Mr. Charles Carter, went into town, hired
a horse and rode to Loretto to warn Father Chabrat and the sisters of
the scheme. In the meantime his colleagues screened his absence by fulfilling his tasks. When Bishop Flaget arrived at Loretto, Sister
Theodosia related:

He was induced to expose the whole affair, reasons, etc. before
any reply was made. Then to his dismay he found that he himself
had been imposed on by specious reasoning, and was rather glad to
dismiss the subject, etc.[44]

The ability of the sisters to grow and expand their work as rapidly as
they did before the mid-point of the nineteenth century owes much to
their flourishing academies. The Catholic community in the United States
during this period simply did not include a sufficient number of families
in the upper class to keep these academies, and the many others that
were opened during the 1830's and 1840's, in such flourishing conditions.

Although no records could be found at the Visitation Convent in
Georgetown, or the Loretto Motherhouse and St. Catharine's Convent in
Kentucky, both the latter communities consider it very possible that
their foundresses attended school at the Visitation Convent. The Sis-
ters of Loretto have accepted this tradition for many years. At St.
Catharine's the supposition is based on the similarity in the school

[44]ASL. Memoirs - Sister Theodosia Kelly.

programs. A long accepted tradition is probably more reliable than a comparison of school programs. The foregoing comparison of the program at the Visitation Academy in Georgetown with the schools of Emerson and his pupil Zilpah Grant, and the academies conducted by the other religious communities will show the danger of trying to support a connection between two institutes by comparing only their programs. Rather the similarities would seem to stem from exceptional leadership which recognized the most progressive trends in the education of young women in the United States and added to that the refinement of the experience of the Church in some of the finest educational institutions in Europe. Beyond this, the work in all eight motherhouses archives left the definite impression that the communities were willing to help one another in whatever way they could. At times this help took the form of correspondence between members of two or more communities and at other times the communication was between the priest-superior of one community with members of another community. The only record of direct, person-to-person help is Currier's statement concerning the opening of the Carmelites' school in Baltimore. He wrote: "They [Sisters of Charity] aided them in making the necessary arrangements for opening their school, imparting to them much useful information and giving them the benefit of their own experience."[45]

Elementary Schools

All the original communities except the Carmelites taught the elementary subjects in day schools referred to by such terms as pay schools, free schools, poor schools, or benevolent schools. Sometimes

---

[45]Currier, p. 192.

these schools were near an academy. At other times they were connected
to a specific parish in a city or small town. In a few cases the school
for the poor was housed in the same buildings as the orphanage. Since
these schools served the local community there was no need to publish
a prospectus and there is, therefore, little documentation to consider.
While free schools became more and more available, the prejudice against
them often kept children from attending them. This prejudice may have
been a factor in encouraging the development of parish schools although
no documentary evidence came to light to substantiate this idea. The
idea that free, or public schools were pauper schools was overcome earlier
in eastern urban centers than in other areas. Labbé, in her study of
women in early nineteenth century Louisiana, described the condition
there. (The description seems to be quite typical of early nineteenth
century American opinion.)

> Ironically, orphan girls who were sent to the Female Orphan Asylum
> received a better education than poor girls with parents, as they
> were taught to read and write, while   few poor parents wanted to
> call themselves "paupers" in order to enable their daughters to
> attend school.[46]

Article 1, Chapter I of the Constitutions of the Sisters of
Charity, as adapted for the United States reads:

> Their institute is the same as that of the Sisters of Charity
> in France, with this difference that the education which the
> Sisters of Charity there were bound to give only to the poor
> orphan children, will be extended here to all female children,
> in whatever station of life they may be, for which the Sisters
> shall receive a sufficient compensation, out of which they will
> endeavor to save as much as they can, to educate also gratis
> poor orphan children.[47]

---

[46]Dolores Egger Labbé, "Women in Early Nineteenth Century Louisiana"
(Ph.D. dissertation, University of Delaware, 1975), p. 108.

[47]ASCN. Manuscript Constitutions, 1827, Chapter I, Article 1.

This adaptation of St. Vincent's Rule shows a recognition that circumstances in the United States required a different approach to common problems. The possibility of providing an education for the poorer classes
was dependent upon an income derived from conducting academies for the
upper classes. Fathers Nerinckx and Joubert and Bishop England all expressed greater concern for the less affluent and the poor. Father
Nerinckx stated the purpose of the Lorettine Society as:

> . . . the propagation of our holy Religion, by aiming at a more
> perfect life in retirement from the world and his maxims, by
> instructing youth of the female sexe, . . .[48]

and Father Joubert wrote simply:

> the Oblates renounce the World to Consecrate themselves to
> God, and to the christian education of young girls of colour.[49]

Bishop England wrote:

> . . . the object of their institution is to educate females
> of the middling classes of society also to have a school for
> free colored girls, and to give instruction to female slaves,
> . . .[50]

It is clear from the early history of both the Lorettines and
the Sisters of Our Lady of Mercy that academies were established to meet
the needs of supporting the sisters in their primary work even though
no specific provision for such schools was made by the founders. The
case of the Oblate Sisters was different. In light of the increasing
fear of the potential influence of free black persons on the slaves in
the years preceding the Civil War, prudence probably led to a policy

---

[48] ASL. Original Rule, Chapter I.

[49] AOSP. Constitutions of the Oblate Sisters of Providence
(manuscript copy).

[50] ASCLM. Historical Extracts (manscript notes), "Bishop
England's History of the Diocese of Charleston," p. 261.

of very little publicity. Certainly there is no doubt that a solid elementary education and training in the skills that would make it possible for the colored girls to earn a living and be good mothers was paramount. We also know from the Report of the United States Commissioner of Education that the sisters were capable of teaching more and did so in a number of cases. The financial support for the Oblate Sisters may well have depended on the fact that their students could be depended on to be something akin to model house servants for leading families in the Baltimore area. Father Joubert, himself, had proposed this ideal in that portion of the Rule that speaks of the advantages to society as a whole from young girls who had learned not only the common elementary subjects, but also solid virtue. It was this same portion of the Rule that was printed in the early announcements of the school in the Catholic almanacs.[51]

The nuns at the Visitation Convent in Georgetown seem to have had a school for poor girls in the neighborhood almost from the beginning. As early as 1823 Archbishop Maréchal wrote to Rome for permission for "out-sisters" to teach poor girls outside the monastery.[52] (The building used for this school is on the edge of the monastery property. The sisters never left the monastery grounds to teach in this school.) The same year Mr. Ingersoll, in his address to the American Philosophical Society in Philadelphia, said the sisters had "under their care a day school, at which upwards of a hundred poor girls are

[51]Cf. Catholic Almanac, 1834, p. 124.

[52]Cf. Kenneally, Vol. I, 139 (#824, #826). The school was listed among the works of the sisters at the Monastery of the Visitation in the 1822 Laity's Directory, pp. 93-94. At that time they wrote of "upwards of a hundred girls."

educated."[53] In 1829 the <u>United States Catholic Miscellany</u> printed "Nunnery in the United States. Georgetown, D.C. March 13th 1829," with this
introduction: "We copy the following piece from a Georgia paper; we know
not whether it is copied from another, but we know that its outline is
tolerably correct, . . . it is a sufficiently fair exhibition for a person to whom all this is evidently new." The writer had the following
to say:

> The Academy . . . contains a boarding school for upwards of
> one hundred pupils--and a free or charity school of a much larger
> number of day scholars. . . .
> . . . The Charity School embraces about two hundred pupils.
> For their humanity and benevolence in collecting and teaching
> these children the Nuns deserve praise. . . .[54]

This benevolent school is usually mentioned in any report to Church
authorities in Rome and was a visible sign of the concern of women religious, even when living within a cloister, for the welfare of all classes.

The available documents list a number of free schools conducted by
the various communities of women religious in the first half of the nineteenth century. What is very scarce is any account of what these schools
were really like for both teachers and pupils. Early in the nineteenth
century Lancasterian schools were introduced in the United States. The
system appealed to philanthropic societies because it provided a cheap
education for large numbers. The system had been developed by Joseph
Lancaster (1778-1838) in England. The essential feature--not entirely
original with Lancaster-- was that "a part or all of the teaching was done
by the more advanced pupils, those who knew a little more instructing
those who knew a little less." There was rigid discipline and extensive

---

[53]USCM. "Review on the strictures . . ." (14 January 1824),
pp. 20-22.

[54]USCM. "Nunnery in the United States" (13 June 1829), p. 386.

use of punishments, rewards and rivalry. Only one salaried person was envisioned for as many as 500 pupils. Supplies were kept to a minimum and most of the learning was memory work. Literacy was the chief goal.[55] There is no record of any of the sisters actually conducting a Lancasterian school although they certainly were forced by circumstances, at least in the early days, to use similar methods.

Because Sister Anacaria's notes about the beginnings in the Buffalo Diocese about 1848, are the only detailed description of the opening of a day school among the poorer classes, at too great a distance from the central house to get even temporary help, I will quote it at some length. Reading "between the lines" in other motherhouse archives definitely left the impression that this experience was not unique.

> June 3, 1848, six Sisters arrived in Buffalo to begin an Hospital and three for an Asylum and School; - for the latter I was designated. A telegram had been sent from Albany, announcing our arrival for the 2d. but we had boarded a slow immigrant train, and had to remain all night in Rochester. In the morning, we started for Buffalo, and reached there at noon. At the depot, before we left the cars, a tall, young seminarist entered the cars, and said, "Are you the ladies for Bishop Timon?" On being told we were, he ordered a hack, put six Sisters in, and then he got up and rode with the driver. We were the curiosity of the day! We soon reached a small, two story house, the residence of the Bishop and his Seminary. The Bishop had just stepped out after his dinner, so we were received by a priest, whom we took for sexton, or workman, - a red flannel shirt very prominent, etc. . . . Whilst at dinner our kind Lazarist Bishop came in, made us welcome, - expressed great joy in seeing us, said he "was glad we found something to eat, - sometimes, you'll have only a little corn-bread to eat, etc." . . .
> Well, after the "Candy Carnival," where the Bishop introduced us, and told the children "the good Sisters were to teach them" such a school room! Lord deliver us from such now! who would tolerate such! A young priest went over with the Bishop when we went to see our lovely room. He said: "But, Bishop, you will have this cleaned before the Sisters teach!" "O, the good Sisters know what to do," replied the Bishop. The Father begged and pleaded, no use; then he said: "Bishop, allow me to

---

[55] Cf. Good, pp. 136-137.

get it done for the Sisters?" Oh dear! he was soon silenced with what I call "a flea in his ear." We had to clean our school room as best we could. Some of the poor women came and offered their services. The old desks and benches looked as though they came from the Ark. The work of organizing the school came to my lot. A few years experience on other missions helped me along, and with a good will, tho' a heavy heart, I went to tame the Buffaloes, as I called them.

I would go over, heart-sick to the Sister Servant, and tell her I could do nothing with them. The children began to pour in, - over one hundred and twenty-five were counted. To keep them in some kind of order was all that could be done; - they would not kneel for prayers, - just squat back on their heels; - run in and out, without order. At the end of a week or so, the Sister Servant sent the other Sister to assist; classes were formed, and soon all went on well; they became studious and docile. In the course of time, we taught them Sewing and Tapestry-work; - that pleased them wonderfully! The Bishop was for us keeping school all through the Summer; - he was a working man, and why should not his children be the same?

. . . Whilst the Hospital was being repaired, the Bishop thought it would be well for the Sister to gather the children together, and teach them. A room, opening out into the yard was selected, some benches gathered, and put there to make a class room. - it had been a parlor for hens, chickens, etc; they did not like to abandon their home, so they made several encroachments. As soon as the Bishop left the city for a few days, Sister availed herself of the chance to move benches and scholars into a more suitable room. On his return she had to march back to the "Chicken Parlor." 0, the act of humility! No need to say, when he spoke or acted, you would have thought it was St. Vincent himself who was there.[56]

The directions to teachers in all the communities show a great concern that the teachers be well-prepared for their work and be aware of individual needs. Among the directives found at Emmitsburg was one that said: "No Sister shall keep a larger number of children in her class than she thinks she can do justice to. The number assigned by those who have long experience in public school, (Free School) is 40."[57]

---

[56]ASJCH. "Annals, 1846-1850," Sister Anacaria's (Hoey) Notes are appended to the manuscript annals and are entitled, "Notes about Mission in Buffalo," pp. 133-138.

[57]ASJCH. Ibid., "Annals, 1846-1850," General Directions (apparently written before 1850), 8th.

Father Joubert included important directives for the teaching sisters in the Constitutions under the heading, "General Observations." These include such basic directives as: "those Sisters who will be appointed to teach must possess a sufficient knowledge of the different branches of education over which they preside: for how could they possibly instruct the children intrusted to their care, in the things of which they themselves would be ignorant?" He also spelled out very clearly the importance of educating the children in the Christian life and self-discipline. "The surest means of succeeding in this, as well as in all other respects, is to gain the affections of the children." The sisters were to do this not through weakness or by being indulgent, but by winning the children through "mildness and affability."[58] One directive of Father Joubert's is unique: "the Oblates will effectually prevail on such parents [those who do not send their children to school because of their poverty] by courteous and engaging manners, by taking a lively interest in their concerns, and even by paying them some visits [italics mine]."[59] This directive is worthy of special note since the constitutions of all eight religious communities, the Oblate Sisters not excepted, stress the importance of not wasting time by visiting with outsiders. The religious life and the work engaged in by every sister was considered too important to allow useless interruptions. In an age when the common practice seemed to be that parents either came to the school, wrote letters, or communicated through a third person the directive to the sisters to visit the parents shows an exceptional sensitivity

---

[58]AOSP. Constitutions, 1829, General Observations, especially #2 and #6.

[59]Ibid., #7.

to the problems of the people and a great respect for the ability of the sisters and parents to overcome any difficulties themselves. This directive may well have been the result of the special needs of the black community, but it is still remarkable. The Oblate Sisters were not only women religious, but they were black. Their priest-founder seems to have been able to overlook all three categories and consider them as persons capable of exercising full responsibility.

Most of the day schools, like the academies, were schools for girls. During the early nineteenth century this was a common practice even in non-Catholic schools although there seems to have been a sufficient number of elementary schools with mixed classes to arouse the concern of some. Father Nerinckx wrote in his journal: "The request [of Mary Rhodes to teach her niece and a few other girls] was easily granted, with a particular view of keeping some girls from the promiscuous Schooling with the boy so subversive of morality."[60] Roman authorities, as well, did not approve of women religious teaching boys as well as girls. This attitude was clearly expressed in a critique of the Rule of the Sisters of Loretto as found in a letter from the Propaganda Fide Archives, Cardinal Fesch to Bishop Flaget, 8 November 1819. The Cardinal wrote: "It should be made clear that they are not destined to teach in schools to which boys have access. Such mixed assemblies are not to be allowed, lest there might arise future suspicions."[61]

No episcopal correspondence on this subject was located in either motherhouse or diocesan archives. The evidence seems to indicate that

---

[60] ASL. Father Nerinckx' "Journal".

[61] Wand & Owens, p. 208.

the early bishops had no more objection to the sisters teaching boys,
at least in the day schools connected with parishes, than they did to
the sisters caring for orphan boys. The boys, too, needed elementary
education as much as the girls did; it was not easy to find well-prepared
dedicated teachers of boys. Neither of the Pastoral Letters of 1843
or 1852, issued by the Bishops after the Councils of Baltimore, mention
anything about separate classes. Certainly boys and girls were separated
wherever possible, but the more important consideration was providing
for an adequate education that included the teachings of the Catholic
Church.

Most of the archival records indicate that teaching or caring
for boys by the sisters was done only in cases of exceptional need, if
at all. The two most obvious exceptions to this were the records of
the Oblate Sisters and those of the Dominican Sisters in Kentucky. In
the Constitutions written by Father Joubert for the Oblate Sisters he
speaks of "the christian education of young girls of colour" as an aim
of the society, but in his "General Observations" which are primarily
directives for the teaching sisters, he uses the word "children" regularly.[62] Sister Theresa Catherine related that during the eight years
Father Anwander was the spiritual director he built two large additions
to the convent and also a boys' school behind the convent. When he was
transferred in 1850 there were "65. boarders, 100. day scholars, 60.
Boys in the Male School."[63] Nothing says whether the sisters did or
did not teach, but there is also no indication that this was a temporary,

---

[62]Cf. AOSP. Constitution, 1829.

[63]Cf. AOSP. "A few facts," p. 8.

or emergency move. The fact is stated with no apologies.

The only statement in the original Rule and Constitutions of the Dominican Sisters about their apostolate is the general one that says that the second and third orders of St. Dominic work for the salvation of souls "by offering up their office, & for the conversion of souls, by instructing young persons of their sex in piety and religion, and by helping their Brethren while occupied in their studies in all the several services that are peculiar to your sex."[64] In 1833 Dr. John Polin of Springfield, Kentucky, a widower, asked the sisters to teach boys under age twelve. All the references to this school (both boarding and day school), including reminiscences of both former students and the sisters who taught them, are made matter-of-factly. The reason the school was closed (the date is indefinite) was because the girls' school was expanding and the majority of the boys were then about twelve years of age. Nothing indicates that anyone considered it unsuitable for the sisters to be teaching and caring for young boys; it was simply a question of how available resources could be best used.[65]

While both the Dominican Sisters and the Oblate Sisters had had their Constitutions approved by authorities in Rome, neither of them has a record of a stricture against teaching boys such as was made in reference to the Lorettine Constitutions (cf. p. 199 above). This seems to be another instance of a much more exacting scrutiny of the latter Constitutions because it was written in a somewhat unconventional form. Actually the only early expression of concern was found in Father Nerinckx's

---

[64] AOPStC. Profession Book, 1822-1919, p. 7.

[65] AOPStC. "Chronicles, 1822-1847," pp. 57-59.

journal and Cardinal Fesch's critique of the Constitution written by
Father Nerinckx. Once the question was raised (1846) by the superiors
in Emmitsburg concerning the work of the Sisters of Charity in orphanage
for boys, this question became one with which the clergy and women
religious must deal in any apostolic endeavor involving young people.
Many conditions had also changed both in the United States as a whole
and within the structure of the American Catholic Church. Many more
communities of religious—both of men and of women—were conducting scho
and staffing institutions by the middle of the nineteenth century. It
was possible by 1846 for a community, and often quite necessary for a
specific community, to set limits on the extent of their work. The
point of interest here is that after the Sisters of Charity of Emmitsbur
made the decision to limit themselves to the care of girls, other communities apparently felt it was necessary to justify their position in
this regard. The justification was most often in terms of the needs as
the particular group of sisters saw them and not in terms of what they,
as a religious community, were capable of doing with their specific resources. Most of the annals or early histories of these communities wer
written in the latter half of the century and reflect a post-1846 men-
tality.

The council minutes, 15 May 1846, of the Sisters of Our Lady of
Mercy contain the statement: "The Council agreed that it would be very
desirable, if a house could be provided wherein to receive male orphans and to conduct a day school for boys."[66] Apparently it was not
possible to do this at the time for an orphanage and day school for boys

[66]ASCLM. Council Minutes, 15 May 1846.

is not mentioned again before 1850. There was never any serious question of either the Visitandines or the Carmelites teaching boys. The records of the Dominican and Oblate Sisters are remarkable for the fact that both communities were directly involved in the care and/or teaching of boys but make no attempt to justify it.

Education of Minorities

Since one of the original eight communities of women religious was a community of black women it is clear that some account was being taken of the members of the black community. The efforts of the Oblate Sisters and the clergy and laity who supported them were not alone. In Georgetown the Visitation Sisters helped in the education of black girls, at least indirectly. The convent tradition has been that the poor school had its origins in the instruction given to their slaves. It is thought that there may have been some black girls among the early students at the academy but the scanty records that survive give no indication of this. The chief source for documenting the work of the sisters in this regard is the report of the Commissioner of Education, 1871.

In this report, first presented to the Senate in 1868, it is stated:

> The free colored people were taught in the Sunday schools and evening schools occasionally, and respectable mulatto families were in many cases allowed to attend, with white children, the private schools and academies. There are scores of colored men and women still living in this District who are decently educated, and who never went to any but white schools.[67]

This statement then, would indicate that there was a very good possibility that free colored girls did attend the academy at some time.

---

[67] Special Report, 1871, p. 195.

Later in the report, moreover, the Commissioner clearly credits the

Visitation Sisters with cooperation in the establishment of the first

seminary for colored girls in the District of Columbia. This school

was under the care of Maria Becraft, the daughter of a highly re-

spected and honored man, William Becraft. At the age of fifteen

she opened her first school for colored girls on Dunbarton Street in

Georgetown.

> In 1827, when she was twenty-two years of age, her remarkable beauty
> and elevation of character so much impressed Father Vanlomen, the
> good priest, that he took it in hand to giver her a higher style of
> school in which to work for her sex and race, to the education of
> which she had now fully consecrated herself. Her school was
> accordingly transferred to a larger building, which still stands
> on Fayette Street, opposite the convent, and there she opened a
> boarding and day school for colored girls, . . . The sisters of the
> Georgetown convent were the admirers of Miss Becraft, gave her in-
> struction, and extended to her the most heartfelt aid and approbation
> in all her noble work, as they were in those days wont to do in behalf
> of the aspiring colored girls, who sought for education, witholding
> themselves from such work only when a depraved and degenerate public
> sentiment upon the subject of educating the colored people had com-
> pelled them to a more rigid line of demarcation between the races.[68]

Beyond the fact that the Visitation Sisters helped Maria Becraft, who

entered the Oblate Sisters of Providence in 1831 (their records have

her name spelled Becroft), there is no indication of any unified effort

to help the free black women.

The third community that definitely was involved in instructing

negroes, other than slaves attached to the community, was the Sisters of

Our Lady of Mercy in Charleston, South Carolina.[69] Bishop England

specifically stated that one purpose of this community was "to have a

---

[68]Ibid., p. 205.

[69]ALM. Mss. 11, "Early Academies . . ." quotes Father Nerinckx's
plan for a Negro Sisterhood as given in Minogue, Loretto: Annals of a
Century, pp. 95-96. Since this was apparently never actualized it did
not seem necessary to include the matter in this study.

chool for free colored girls, and to give religious instruction to
emale slaves."[70] The Rule, as composed by Bishop Reynolds in 1844,
ontains no such specific statement.[71] During the summer of 1835 Bishop
ngland opened a school for free negroes in which two seminarians and
wo sisters formed the teaching staff. This school had to be closed
y the end of the summer. (Cf. Appendix 3). Abolitionists had
tirred up trouble and the leading citizens of Charleston requested that
he school be closed. Bishop England agreed only on the condition that
he other denominations also close theirs. A meeting was held at City
all, 10 August 1835, at which the clergy who had closed their schools
ere publicly thanked.[72] The sisters again began conducting a school
or free colored children in January 1841. This school was located in
 building across the street from the motherhouse. During the uncer-
ain times after Bishop England's death the school was moved to the
otherhouse. At the first council meeting presided over by Bishop
eynolds (1844) he ordered the sisters to remove the colored school from
he motherhouse grounds. The decision to close the school was made "for
he present" by the council, 12 May 1848.[73] There is no reference made
o the increasing debate over slavery, and consequently a greater fear of
ducated free colored persons. One can only surmise that this was a
actor. The 1849 Catholic Almanac stated that the sisters "give reli-
ious instructions to colored persons four evenings during the week."[74]

---

[70]ASCLM. "Historical Extracts."

[71]ASCLM. Constitution, 1844.   [72]Cf. Campbell, pp. 27-28.

[73]Ibid., pp. 40-42. Also ASCLM. Council Minutes: 20 May 1844;
2 May 1848.

[74]Catholic Almanac, 1849, p. 104.

The other communities, from what is known, provided for the religious education of their slaves, and possibly some other black people. On the whole, the records are silent.

A frequently forgotten sector of the American population was the Indian population. Early missionaries in Kentucky and areas to the west did mention them from time to time. They were concerned about the and wished to provide for them but filling immediate needs closer to the motherhouses of the various communities, added to the problems of support for the sisters and communication with them if they went to som what remote settlements, prevented any of these sisters from working with the Indians. This changed in 1847 when four sisters of Loretto responded to the request of the Jesuits to work with them in the Osage Indian Mission. The report by the Osage Sub-Agent and the Superintendent of Indian Affairs, St. Louis, Missouri in 1850 has appended to it a report signed by John Schoenmakers (no title given) and dated "Cathol Mission, Osage Nation,/ October 1, 1850." This report probably contain the best summary of barely three years' work.

> With regard to the female department, nothing has been left undo to insure permanent success, being well aware that the progress of civilization and the welfare of a rising nation greatly depend upon the female members of society; for they are to instil the first principles of virtue and morals, the fountains of a future happy generation. The pupils [29] are educated under the careful guidance of six religious ladies, who devote all their attention to the mental and moral improvement of their pupils; they are taught spelling, reading, writing, arithmetic, and geography; and besides, certain hours are set apart for knitting, sewing, marking, embroidering, &c. Between school hours they are engaged in the occupations of domestic economy. As the building for this female school was intended to accommodate only 20 children, it follows that it is much too small.[75]

---

[75]United States Government. Serial 587. Executive Documents Printed by Order of the Senate of the United States during the Second Session of the Thirty-First Congress, began and held at the City of

Teacher Training

In order to conduct the schools on any level the sisters needed to be trained. In the early years of each community the training was provided by some of the first members who were qualified by a better-than-average education and experience. In lieu of such qualified members, or in addition to them, the sisters were instructed by the priests connected with their foundations or by priests from nearby colleges and seminaries. Many of these priests had fine European educations themselves. High standards of teacher-training became the norm from the earliest years. In addition, it was common for the sisters to hire professional for art, music and dancing. When talented sisters were available they, too, were instructed and, in time, became the principal instructors. At Loretto, for example: "A portrait painter came from the East in 1831 or thereabouts. Pianos were procured and teachers engaged; a Mrs. Peterson, a Swede pianist, later a French lady, Miss Herminie Gruit, a pupil of Henri Herz, gave lessons on the piano, harp, guitar, etc."[76] The Clark sisters, Sisters Isabella and Eleanora, had reputations as artists and skilled teachers through much of the nineteenth century. "Thus we read that in 1846 the Sisters of Holy Cross, then in their formative period, sent their talented members to Loretto Convent, Kentucky, to perfect themselves in art and music. (Catholic Educational Review, September, 1911)."[77]

Sister Mary Ann Yeakel in her study of nineteenth century educa-

---

Washington, December 2, 1850. In 5 Volumes. Vol. I containing Document No. 1 (Washington: Printed at the Union Office, 1851), p. 70.

[76] ASL. Memoirs - Sister Theodosia Kelly.

[77] Brother Bede, p. 47.

tional work by the Sisters of Charity from Emmitsburg refers to an
archival record of provisions "for normal instructions of those Sisters
who were destined for teaching" as early as 1818.[78] The Sisters of
Loretto refer to teacher training becoming a thoroughly conducted department by 1820,[79] and available evidence indicates that the Visitation
sisters began to receive advanced training soon after Father Cloriviére's
arrival in 1819. Since Joseph Emerson began his formal preparation of
teachers about 1818 (cf. p.185) and the first state normal school in
the United States was opened in Lexington, Massachusetts, 3 July 1839,
it is clear that the Catholic sisters were at least as well prepared to
undertake the work of education as anyone else. Their organization made
the staffing of schools easier and resulted in more uniform standards
and continuity, a decided value in an age with little or no provision
for an educational system.

While the foregoing is only a sketch of the educational work of
the members of these eight religious communities, it is enough to indicate that women religious were neither narrow in their approach to
education nor ill-prepared for the tasks they undertook. These first
years certainly show there was a truly Catholic approach to the educational needs of the young nation. Lyman Beecher would not have been
able to fire the emotions of many anti-Papists in 1835, had not Catholic
schools been so competent and willing to accept non-Catholics as student.
The leadership of the Catholic Church in the United States was still

---

[78]Sister Mary Agnes Yeakel, The Nineteenth Century Educational
Contribution of the Sisters of Charity of Saint Vincent de Paul in
Virginia (Baltimore: The John Hopkins Press, 1939), p. 87.

[79]Cf. ASL. Memoirs - Sister Theodosia Kelly.

mphasizing the need to establish schools as a practical response to

he needs of the Church in the middle of the nineteenth century, but a

hift in emphasis was becoming apparent. It was no longer so much a

uestion of simply making an education available for Catholics so

ducation in the teachings of the Church and the practical aspects of

Christian life could be supplied by the clergy and by means of the

atholic press. The stress on a Catholic education in order to pro-

ect young people from the dangers of heretical thought was beginning

o take precedence by the middle of the century.

A few years earlier the Loretto Sisters had also pioneered in

nother field of education in Loretto, Kentucky. 1840 marked the

pening of a Deaf and Dumb Asylum. This apparently was the special con-

ern of Bishop Flaget. In 1835 he was traveling to France and took with

im his niece, Sister Eulalia from the Nazareth Convent.[80] After she

as in Europe the Bishop sent her a companion to learn sign language

nd a method of teaching the deaf. Sister Eulalia and her companion

ho later became Sister Philmene (Bernier) at Loretto were sent to the

eaf school at La Chartreuse, conducted by the Daughters of Wisdom.[81]

ery little is known about this school; it was probably closed in 1843.

he Catholic Almanac for 1841 contains the announcement of this school

stablished "for the mental and moral improvement of female children

ho are deaf and dumb, . . . All the branches taught in similar in-

titutions in France, or in the United States, will be taught in this

nstitution." The terms were $100. per annum, i.e. almost as expensive

---

[80]ASCN. The biographical data quote the Minute Book, 1836,
s stating the community would not take Sr. Eulalia back if she
eturned to Kentucky.

[81]ALM. Mss. 11, "Early Academies."

as the academies.[82] Maes said it was closed because Bishop Chabrat con

vinced Bishop Flaget that the needs of the seminary were greater. The

funds being expended on the asylum went to the seminary after the

asylum was closed.[83]

---

[82]The Metropolitan Catholic Almanac, 1841, pp. 185-186.

[83]Cf. Rev. Camillus P. Maes, The Life of Rev. Charles Nerinckx:
with a Chapter on the Early Catholic Missions of Kentucky; Copious Note
on the Progress of Catholicity in the United States of America, from 18
to 1825; An Account of the Establishment of the Society of Jesus in
Missouri; and An Historical Sketch of the Sisterhood of Loretto in Kent
Missouri, New Mexico, etc. (Cincinnati: Robert Clarke & Co., 1880), p.

CHAPTER V

"CHARITABLE EXERCISES"

Care of the Sick

When John Carroll penned his familiar prophecy to Elizabeth Seton: "A century at least will pass before the exigencies & habits of this Country will require & hardly admit the charitable exercises towards the sick . . ."[1] he probably thought the western expansion would decline rather than increase. He certainly did not envision the industrial revolution and the mass immigrations that would have such dramatic effects on the United States before the century closed. In 1811 when he wrote this letter to Mother Seton foreign immigration was not a major problem, but within a decade cities such as Boston and New York were having difficulties coping with large numbers of immigrants who arrived without money, without a trade, and often at the point of death from conditions aboard ship. The various aid societies that had satisfactorily cared for the needy in the past were no longer able to do so. Private and public institutions alike began seeking help from women religious in order to provide competent and economic care for the needy. And, on occasion, sisters became involved as an almost spontaneous response to severe need.

Except for temporary services, only two of the eight original

---

[1]John Carroll Papers, p. 157. John Carroll to Elizabeth Seton, Baltimore, 18 September 1811.

communities were staffing hospitals on a permanent basis before 1850.
The Sisters of Charity from Emmitsburg were the first to become involved
in the institutional care of the sick. The Sisters of Charity from
Nazareth were the only other community to become permanently involved
in the hospitals during this period. The Sisters of Our Lady of Mercy
staffed a small hospital founded by Bishop England for a society of
laborers (which he also founded) between 1838 and 1841.[2] The data on
the individual sisters for whom we have information about the type of
work they did (cf. Ch. III, Table 5) indicates that over one-fourth of
the sisters were engaged in nursing for at least a portion of their active years.

The pessimistic prediction of Bishop Carroll concerning the possibility of sisters caring for the sick must not be interpreted with a
background of twentieth century experience. In the early nineteenth
century there were very few hospitals anywhere in the United States.
Those which did exist served few persons other than the indigent. Anyone who could afford to pay for professional medical care usually remained at home. The medical profession, itself, was just emerging
from education through an apprenticeship to the development of medical
schools. The medical schools became the dominant mode of medical education only in the second quarter of the nineteenth century.[3] The most
accepted therapies in the first half of the nineteenth century usually
had no real relationship to the cause of the disease. The causes of

---

[2]Cf. Campbell, pp. 35-36.

[3]Cf. William G. Rothstein, American Physicians in the Nineteenth
Century: from Sects to Science (Baltimore: The Johns Hopkins University
Press, 1972), p. 85.

..sease were virtually unknown; therefore, only symptoms could be

·eated. Rothstein says:

> Active therapy was the hallmark of medical practice of the
> period; the patient was dosed, bled, and blistered by phy-
> sicians who adhered tenaciously to the belief that the best
> therapy produced the most rapid and observable symptomatic
> changes in the patient.[4]

; late as 1839 when Sister Ann McAleer was assigned to the Baltimore

ifirmary she said it was "the only Hospital for the Sick" in that area.

ie workmen on the Baltimore and Ohio Railroad, then being built, were

·ought in when they were sick "or hurt by Blasting of rocks to be

:tended by Dr. Smith at the Balt Infirmary."[5]

The general state of nursing was even less professional than

·dicine before 1850. Armiger's study of the hospitals conducted by

ie Daughters of Charity in the Eastern United States, 1823-1860, noted

iat the 1850 census did not even list nursing among professions, oc-

·pations, and trades. Formal nursing education in the United States

·gan only in 1873 with the training schools at Bellevue Hospital, New

·rk; Massachusetts General Hospital, Boston; and New Haven Hospital,

·w Haven, Connecticut.[6] Nursing was a woman's job and it seems most

·ople thought no special training or talent was required. Though there

·s no professional training and very little scientific basis for the

·erapy then in general use by the best doctors, patients in a hos-

.tal staffed by Sisters of Charity were probably among the best cared

·r in the nation. The majority of sisters working with the patients

----

[4]Ibid., p. 41.

[5]ASJCH. Sister Ann McAleer's Notes, p. 11.

[6]Cf. Armiger, p. 102.

remained in the work long enough to accumulate a store of wisdom as a result of their experience. What is more, as new sisters were assigned to the work they were given the benefit of the experience of the sisters who were already there. When one adds the dedication of the sisters and their concern for the patient it is not too difficult to understand the confidence that both doctors and patients placed in them

Four types of hospitals figure in the records of this period: general hospitals, marine hospitals, mental hospitals, and emergency hospitals, usually established hurriedly to meet the needs of an epidem such as yellow fever or cholera. The general hospitals were, of course the most prevalent. Sometimes these are referred to as infirmaries; while there may have been a technical distinction between an infirmary and a hospital, the records do not make it clear. The work of the sisters was not affected by the title given the institution. The sisters from Emmitsburg worked in the Baltimore Marine Hospital only two months (October-November) in 1827. During most of the period (1823-1876) in which these same sisters worked at the Baltimore Infirmary there was a marine department, or as Sister Ann McAleer calls it, a "Sailors Ward These hospitals also served as a quarantine area if there were cases of fever aboard ship. Whatever the specific type of hospital, it is only as one approaches the middle of the nineteenth century that the records indicate that persons of some means begin to accept hospitaliza This was due, in part, to the development of medical schools and the growing reputation of certain doctors as surgeons. Judging from the requests for sisters to staff new hospitals the doctors also recognized the value of having experienced dedicated nurses to staff a hospital.

No attempt was made to search for every request for sisters to taff hospitals before 1850. The Sisters of Charity from Emmitsburg id actually staff, at least for a short period, twelve hospitals in ifferent parts of the United States by that date. Some of these intitutions were established by municipalities, some by groups of octors--usually in connection with their medical school, some by local hurch authorities, and one was set up by the sisters themselves. The isters of Charity from Nazareth staffed the Infirmary in Louisville which developed in connection with St. Vincent's Orphanage; Bishop Miles was responsible for establishing the hospital in Nashville. The principal reasons for withdrawing from hospitals, at this time, were dificulties with the governing board and/or lack of sufficient finances o keep the hospital in operation.

Appendix 4 contains a letter from Rev. A. J. Elder in Baltimore o Bishop Flaget at Bardstown, Kentucky. Flaget had requested information about the Baltimore Infirmary which the Sisters of Charity staffed ecause an infirmary had been built in Louisville about this time and t was rumored that the Sisters of Charity might be asked to staff it. othing came of this. In 1836 the sisters opened an infirmary of their wn in Louisville. Elder's letter is important for the glimpse it gives s of the workings of what certainly was one of the better hospitals f the day. The Baltimore Infirmary was, after all, a teaching hospital connected with the University. The Sisters of Charity had provided the ursing staff for six years (since 1823) at the time this letter was written. Sister Ann McAleer, a zealous young sister, arrived at the altimore Infirmary in 1839. When she wrote the recollections of her experiences years later she gave us a more personal glimpse of the workings of the same hospital. At first she was appointed housekeeper in Sister

Sarah Ann's place "for two months only as I could not get along in this

Department, Sr. Sarah Ann returned & I was to be with the dear Sick."

The marine department, St. John's Ward, had been closed for over two

years due to some "Political business." Sister Ann's first responsibili

was to clean the ward and prepare it for the sailors' return. When all

was in readiness "some citizens" occupied the ward for a time. Her

account of receiving her first patient tells much about early nineteenth

century nursing.

> Well I was well pleased & was all anxiety until I would See Some
> dear poor Sick enter. Well as anxious as I was to receive patients
> my first gave me a terrible fright. I realy thought I never would
> get over. It was a Gentleman from Balt, a Merchant Who had been
> drinking & had Delirium Tremens and poor man cut his throat & was
> carried to the Infirmary. he was placed in my ward, dear Sister
> Ambrosia sent for me. tolde me that I had just received a Patient
> who had his throat cut, o dear me Who cut it, Sister said he cut
> it himself. Well said I, dear Sister if he cut his own throat what
> will he not do to me? he will cut mine too. Dear Sister saw I was
> frightened but told me not to be frightened as he would not hurt me
> & at the same time saying he is out of his mind. Should he say
> anything not to mind it. I said oh, dear Sister Ambrosia this is
> terrible and he is in that large ward & no one but himself in it. As
> sister & myself was on our way to see the poor unfortunate man we
> met one of the Professors. he wished to see Sister. I kept on to
> the ward, on my way I took my crucifix. I had my beads around my
> neck having on the black habit. . . . I held the crucifix in my
> hand & asked our blessed & dear Lord to take charge of me & I
> promised Him then I would do all in my power to please Him in every
> way I could until my death. I went in & up in the farthest corner
> of this large room, oh dear the sight of the poor dear creature
> all covered with blood runing from the cut. I bid him good morning
> or something of the kind & the poor man wished to answer & made an
> effort to speak. I thought the effert he made was to get out of
> the bed after me. now it took but a moment to get to the Passage &
> then to the steps & I fell down the steps. Sister heard the
> noise, met me & said what is the matter? oh here he is behind me.
> Sister ran up & found him in bed. yes the poor man scared me & I
> scared him. it brought him to his mind & he said I am not
> astonished that Sister ran from me for I am a disgusting sight. Oh
> God is it possible I wished to take my own life? oh dreadful! oh
> my poor dear Family what a disgrace I have brought!
>
> dear Sister Ambrosia spoke to the poor man of the goodness of God

in his behalf in not allowing him although your own will was to
put an end to yourself . . . So dear Sister said it was what you
took mad[e] or deprived you of your mind. well he said, suredly
it was. I will never drink any more Liquor as it was this fault
drove me to all this <u>disgrace</u> and shame. The Good Gentleman remained three weeks in a very critical way, fed on Beef tea,
Chicken water, cream. oh he would say, I am well humbled, the
poor man was very grateful to the Sisters, & often said he never
would forget the Sisters of Charity. They sold out & left the
city, as he said he could never meet his friends again in Balt. I
tell you a good fright in the beginning prepares you for all that
comes after. I remained in this same Ward, called St. Johns Ward,
18 years having charge of the good kind Sailors after their return.[7]

Sister Ann served as superior of the Baltimore Infirmary for three

ears prior to 1862, when she was transferred to St. Joseph's Hospital

renamed St. Agnes in 1863), Baltimore. Her initial fear of a patient

ertainly was due to lack of experience. Her long years in nursing and

he positions entrusted to her in later years testify to a true ability

o serve the sick. Her commentary on the relationship of the sisters

ith the doctors in the management of the hospital are, therefore,

aluable. Her account seems natural and it reflects a true mutual re-

pect for one another. The articles of agreement (cf. Appendix 5, pp.

80-2) and Rev. A.J. Elder's letter to Bishop Flaget (Appendix 4, pp.

78-9) are too formal to convey this, but the articles of agreement may

ell have provided the basis for the development of this professional

tmosphere.

. . . never was there a House whare [sic] the Srs of Charity had a
mission whare more real Charity was done then was done at the
Balt Infirmary, & no one knew better than our dear Sister Ann
de Sales [fifth Sr. Servant] this. As everything was put in
the Sister Servant hands although the Drs were all Protestants.
They never interfeared [sic] never asked a question one way, nor the
other, the Sister Servant was handed the money twice a week.
She bought & paid the Bills. I was at the Infirmary 24 years.
I am certain the Sisters Books were never opened by the Drs
during my time, no one could be more respectful to the Sisters

[7]ASJCH. Sister Ann McAleer's Notes, pp. 12-16.

then the Drs was to all the Sisters. The Drs all respected our
dear Sister Ann de Sales much, & many very nice remarks of her
we were all very sorry to part with dear Sister Ann de Sales . . .[8]

Conditions were not always as favorable as at the Baltimore In-

firmary. Five years after the sisters began to work in the infirmary

they were invited to go west and open a hospital in St. Louis. The

account found in the annals (written about 1873) says:

> A good gentleman [John Mullanphy] had given a lot, on which there
> was some kind of old building, as a beginning. Accordingly four
> Sisters were chosen; . . .
> Sisters Francis Xavier Love, Rebecca Deline [Delone], Martina
> Butcher and Francis Regis Barry. These four armed with the panoply
> of God, set out on their weary journey at four o'clock, October 15t
> 1828--Traveling at that period was not what it is at present . . .
> Their dwelling in St. Louis was not much more comfortable--The snow
> and rain found easy access, and often-times the small kitchen, when
> they ate their humble meal was so full of water, that they had to
> climb on benches to take their food on an old chest, that served fo
> a table. Every thing in the house was pretty much the same--It
> seems the people thought because they were Sisters of Charity, any
> thing was good enough for them--for as yet they scarcely knew what
> the title meant--Those dear Sisters often declared, that never in
> their lives had they felt such perfect happiness, such joyful
> cheerfulness.[9]

And as late as 1845, when the sisters in Detroit opened St. Mary's Hos-

pital there, conditions were still primitive.

> The good Bishop [Peter Paul Lefevre] could hardly wait until
> Sunday to publish in the Church that the Sisters would open a
> hospital. He tried to impress on the minds of the people, that
> their duty was to help us, by bringing bedding and articles to
> furnish the wards. - They brought us a few bedticks, somewhat
> longer than pillow-ticks, with a little straw in them. However,
> we fixed up some half-dozen beds ourselves on the lower floor
> for men, and the same number on the second floor for females.
> The stairway leading to the female department, started in the
> yard, and had no communication with the men's department.[10]

---

[8]Ibid., p. 29

[9]ASJCH. Annals, Vol. III, 253a-254.

[10]ASJCH. Sister Rosaline Brown, Mss. Account of Founding of St.
Mary's, Detroit as quoted in Armiger, p. 72.

he hospital was soon too small; the property for the new hospital was
onated in 1846 and the sisters soon began a subscription for building
urposes. The new hospital, "St Mary's House for Invalids," was
pened 6 November 1850 with accommodations for over one hundred patients.[11]

Little was found in the archives at Nazareth in relation to their
ursing activity at this time. They opened the Louisville infirmary in
836; it seems to have evolved somewhat from the orphan asylum. At
irst it, like the asylum, was called St. Vincent's. Later the infir-
ary was known as St. Joseph Infirmary. The references in the archives
how a concern for the increasing number of immigrants arriving in Louis-
ille on the river boats. Like many other immigrants they were sick and
mpoverished on their arrival. They needed care and the Sisters of
harity did all they could for them; in doing so they developed a hos-
ital which in time attracted other patients. The second hospital un-
er the care of the Sisters of Charity of Nazareth was St. John Hospital
n Nashville, Tennessee. Bishop Miles turned the old church which the
athedral replaced over to the sisters for a hospital. It was opened
n April 1848. The orphan girls lived there as well. The sisters were
ithdrawn from Nashville (both academy and hospital) in July 1851 rather
an "comply with requirements contrary to the Rule."[12]

Both the Sisters of Charity from Emmitsburg and those from
azareth were involved in the care of the mentally sick as well. All
hat is known about the Sisters of Charity of Nazareth is what is con-
ained in the series of letters from Mr. H. H. Gray of St. Louis to

---

[11]Cf. Armiger, pp. 72-73.

[12]ASCN. Sketches of Branch Houses now closed.

Mother Catherine Spalding, March to May 1845 (cf. Ch. I, p. 39). Somehow Mother Catherine's reputation had traveled to St. Louis. The distance that made correspondence necessary resulted in a record that would otherwise be lacking. Emmitsburg has more abundant records on this subject. These sisters began work at the Maryland Hospital (Baltimore), a hospital serving the mentally sick. The Articles of Agreement here, as in most institutions staffed by sisters from Emmitsbu: were much like those written for St. Joseph's Asylum, Philadelphia. Modifications were made at the time the sisters began work at the Baltimore Infirmary to meet the different needs. (Cf. Appendix 5 for the Articles of Agreement for St. Joseph's Asylum, Philadelphia and the modifications as found in the Agreement for the Baltimore Infirmary.) The only real difference in the agreement for the Maryland Hospital is that the Head Sister is to have control of mail to or from patients.[13]

The correspondence in reference to the Maryland Hospital in 1840 shows that the agreement of previous years, when interpreted differently by the doctors and the sisters, along with their superiors, could lead to serious difficulty. What correspondence is available implies that the original agreement had been an oral one, or at least the regulations to be in effect in the hospital were not put in writing at the beginning. The correspondence, some of it undated, that relates to the conditions that led to the sisters' withdrawal went on throughout the summer of 1840. The clearest statement of the difficulty is found in a letter of Sister Olympia McTaggert to Father Deluol, the ecclesiastical superio:

My dear Father,
    I have read your letter & do not see anything to add or retrench

---

[13]ASJCH. Letters, II:49. "Foundations."

I do not know when the Board will meet, but am very anxious to have
the agreement written, we are subjected to much inconvenience from
the Patients, without having the Doctor to contend with & if Drunk-
ards can go in & out without the Sisters permission I think it a
very improper place for us to be - . . . [14]

Following this letter is a set of regulations "observed in the Maryland

Hospital from January 7th 1834 to June 8th 1840." On 9 September 1840

Dr. Steuart notified Father Deluol that he was sending a copy of the

rules adopted by the board. An undated letter was sent that contained

the information that the rules were not approved and, therefore, regret-

fully "the connection of the Sisters of Charity with the Maryland Hos-

pital must now cease- . . ." This letter was acknowledged 16 September

1840.[15] The move of the sisters to a hospital of their own, St. Vin-

cent's, must have been very quickly accomplished because there is a

letter of 2 October 1840, signed by R. S. Steuart, Jos. Townsend, and

Jno. W. B. Latrobe and addressed to Rev. L. R. Deluol.

Dear Sir
    We have understood with much surprise, that there have been
removed within the last few days from Maryland Hospital, without
the knowledge of the President, the standing Committee, or the
members of the Board of Visitors, and through the agency of the
Sisters of Charity, some fifteen or twenty patients. As you
have, in the correspondence heretofore had in relation to the
Sisters, claimed to control these proceedings, we have to ask
of you respectfully the authority for the step now referred to,
in order that the matter may be laid before the Board of
Visitors--
                                Very respectfully
                                Your obedient servants

The reply contains no names, date, or place but is certainly a draft, or

summary, by Father Deluol of his reply.

---

[14]ASJCH. Letters, II, "Foundations," p. 56. Sister Mary Olympia
to Father [Deluol]; Maryland Hospital, 27 July [1840]. The letter, as it
appears in this volume seems to read 1846, six years after the sisters
were withdrawn from Maryland Hospital.

[15]Cf. Ibid., pp. 57-64.

. . . I believe you will find upon examination that these
patients have been removed by their Time, themselves or
by their directors, in the same manner as Patients have been
removed from the Hospital since the Sisters of charity entered
the Institution.[16]

These letters, admittedly, tell us almost nothing about the care
of the mentally sick during the 1830's except that the Sisters of Charity
were involved in the care. By the end of the decade disagreements had
arisen between the sisters and the doctors over at least some particulars in the care of the mentally sick, and this disagreement led
to a private hospital for the mentally ill, St. Vincent's, in which the
Sisters were responsible for both the management and the policies. The
fact that a number of patients followed the sisters shows that they,
or their families, placed a great deal of confidence in them. By 1844
St. Vincent's was too small and the sisters sought more adequate quarters
They purchased the former Mt. Hope College in 1844. Within a year these
facilities were also inadequate and additional wings had to be built.
In 1846 there were twenty-two Sisters of Charity and one hundred
patients at Mt. Hope.[17] Among the patients at Mt. Hope there were also
a few women religious. The records of both the Carmelites and the
Visitandines note that over the years several sisters from each community
were patients there. The Sisters of Charity graciously provided this
service for the sisters of these communities, and probably for other
communities whose records were not part of this study. One of the
patients who followed the Sisters from the Maryland Hospital to St.
Vincent's in 1840 was Sister Isabella (Olivia Neale) who had caused so

---

[16]Ibid., pp. 65-66.

[17]Cf. Armiger, pp. 55, 59-62.

much excitement the year before when she ran away from the Carmelite

Convent. In 1844 Mother Xavier, Emmitsburg, wrote to Rev. Mother

Angela in Baltimore, assuring her that they were

> too happy to have it in their power to render that small
> service to your holy Community. No charge will be made for
> Sister Isabella. The only return we ask is your fervent
> prayers for our dear Community.[18]

The sisters were meeting a very important need in the local com-

munity. Armiger quotes a long report of the methods used at St. Vin-

cent's in 1841 to Dr. N. Devereux of the Committee of the Trustees of

the New York State Lunatic Asylum. This report not only shows concern

for th individual patient, but a therapy that is much more in con-

formity with twentieth-century practices than the therapeutic measures

used by most physicians for physical ailments. The author of the report,

W. F. Read (commissioned to visit the institution under an act of the

New York Legislature), wrote that the sisters "never permit the inflic-

tion of blows." When some form of restraint was absolutely necessary

they did everything possible to disguise it because the patients were

"excessively sensitive." Neither did the sisters approve of isolating

the patient since "they find that the mind of the maniac, when deserted,

preys upon itself." The sisters tried to "elevate their patients in

their own self-esteem," and, therefore, tried to treat them as normal

persons as much as possible. They made use of occupational therapy,

outdoor activities, and social activities as well as encouraging par-

ticipation in religious exercises.[19]

---

[18]ACM-B. Cf. "Transcriptions by Sr. Stanislaus," pp. 34-35 and
S. M. Xavier, St. Joseph's, Emmitsburg to Rev. Mother Angela, Carmelite Convent, Baltimore, 19 November 1844.

[19]Cf. Armiger, pp. 55-58.

White, in his biography of Mrs. E. A. Seton, refers to the importance of having persons care for the "female lunatic" who is "familiar with the habits and manners of respectable life." He also noted that the indigent were cared for, and that the report of 1851 informs the reader that there were twenty charity patients. Unlike the general hospital, at least, this private mental hospital drew a large portion of its patients from classes of people who were able to pay for their care. The nature of the disease, no doubt, had some bearing on this. The treatment, however, provided under the care of Dr. William Hughes Stokes (after 1842) and the sisters offered help to many for the majority of patients were discharged after a period of time.[20]   The move from the Maryland Hospital to St. Vincent's appears as something of a milestone in the care of the sick by women religious in the United States. Almost two decades of experience apparently led the Sisters of Charity to the conclusion that despite financial difficulties their goals could be met more easily if they not only staffed the hospital, but were also responsible for setting policy as well. The sisters, as in the academies, made good provisions for the inmates while going without many things themselves. Armiger quotes from the recollections of Sister Matilda Coskery who related that in the late 1840's very few sisters at Mt. Hope had a bedstead. Most of them had only a husk

---

[20]Cf. White, pp. 449-451. There is no indication of a revision o this portion of the work for the later editions. See also MHR. Bound volume of the Annual Reports of Mount Hope from the seventeenth annual report, 1859-1895. The fly leaf is stamped: "The Lunacy Commission, Baltimore/Maryland." The 1892 report gives a retrospective view of the last fifty years. No new information relative to the period before 1850 was found in this report.

mattress that was placed anywhere at night and hidden early in the morning.[21]

Cholera

There is a considerable body of information about the activity of the sisters as nurses during the cholera epidemics. The method of care for the patients, however, was not found. Rosenberg's study, The Cholera Years, shows first, that the therapeutic measures used by physicians almost certainly did more harm than good; and, second, only the poor went to cholera hospitals, and then usually only in the advanced stages.[22] In most cases, therefore, the sisters working in the emergency hospitals could do no more than try to bring comfort and compassion to the patient. The first cholera epidemic in the United States was 1832, and a second epidemic struck in 1849. An increasing number of immigrants, advances in transportation, and the California gold rush all worked together to make the epidemic of 1849 even more widespread and devastating than the one in 1832. Charleston, South Carolina was not affected by the epidemics of 1832 and 1849, but was struck in 1836 and 1853. Other than the differences in years there seems little to distinguish the epidemics. Cholera had never appeared in the United States before 1832 and, in most areas, did not appear again until

---

[21]Armiger, p. 62. The quotation is from Sister Thecla Murphy, "Notes drawn from Sister Matilda Coskery's Account of the Beginning of Mt. Hope." Mss. archives of Seton Institute, p. 52f.

[22]Charles E. Rosenberg, The Cholera Years: The United States in 1832, 1849, and 1866 (Chicago: The University of Chicago Press, 1962). Most of the background for this portion of my study is dependent on this work. Rothstein's study of physicians in nineteenth century America, referred to above, p. 213, is also dependent on Rosenberg for his treatment of cholera.

1849. Medical science made almost no progress between these two dates. Rosenberg tells us that the second epidemic did leave some practical evidence of how to prevent it. Louisville, for example, had cleaned and properly ventilated some sections of the city which had suffered severely during the first epidemic. The epidemic did not affect these sections at all in 1849.[23]

The medical profession, with very few exceptions, did not believe that cholera was contagious. Their belief was that its cause lay in the atmosphere. Disease was not a specific entity. It "was a protean and dynamic condition. . . . mental, moral, climatic, and hygiene factors all interacted continuously to vary the manifestations of disease."[24] The most serious efforts at prevention were directed toward cleaning the streets; it seemed to be of little consequence where the refuse was deposited. Quarantine was an unnecessary interference with business since the disease was not contagious. Common belief among the people did consider the disease contagious and public opinion demanded at least some measure of quarantine. The great problem in meeting this demand for quarantine came when civic authorities attempted to rent buildings as hospitals for the sick passengers of ships arriving in port, or later the sick from the tenement areas; the local residents sometimes violently protested the erection of such a hospital in their neighborhood. On one point most Americans, whether physicians or laymen, agreed: cholera was a punishment of God for sin, and the ungodly or immoral were most susceptible.

---

[23]Cf. Ibid., p. 145.

[24]Ibid., p. 73.

An account of the work of the Sisters of Charity from Emmitsburg
n the care of cholera victims (written late in the nineteenth century)
eveals that the sisters generally accepted the common view of the
auses of cholera. The account of the outbreak of cholera in Washing-
on, D.C., 1832, related that since it was vacation time

> the Sisters went out to nurse some very bad cases, and though
> much exposed, none of them took it.-- But, the air seemed im-
> pregnated from disease [italics mine]; and soon three of the
> Sisters became very ill with bilious fever.[25]

he influence of the commonly held belief in the connection between sin
nd this disease, at least, is revealed in the account of the work of
he Sisters at the Baltimore Almshouse. The almshouse was an old mansion
utside the city. The city authorities were unable to find others to
are for the sick and, therefore, requested help from the sisters. Four
ere sent.

> But Alas! what words could convey any idea of the misery and
> degradation of the inmates of that splendid looking mansion--
> The very dregs of society were congregated there-- But what
> was most deplorable was the insensibility and hardness of heart,
> shown by those poor creatures in the very presence of death.
> In vain, the Sisters tried to awaken some sentiment of religion
> in those benighted souls-- One poor woman, who had been apparently
> dying for three days replied thus to the Sister, who was endeavoring
> to turn her thoughts to God: "Oh don't bother me, there is time
> enough to think of that by and by--" Alas! the by and by never
> came -- and she died as she lived -- . . . Towards the last days
> of our painful sojourn in this place, about four o'clock in the
> afternoon, there was a fearful case brought into the "Ward" --
> A young girl, very beautiful, who had been notoriously wicked--
> Her agony was excruciating, her cries piercing, and there was a
> fiend-like look about her when she fixed her large dark eyes
> upon you, that made one of the Sisters, wholly unaccustomed to
> such scenes, tremble from head to foot-- However, the honor of the
> Company was at stake, and the Sister nerved herself for the
> occasion, received the Doctor's direction, and did all she
> could to alleviate the tortures of this poor creature. . . .
> One of the Sisters began to ask her, "if she were not sorry
> for having offended God. And if she were not sensible that

---

[25]ASJCH. Annals, III:260.

she had sinned very grievously? At these words, she cried
out with a stentorian voice, that thrilled every one through
the whole ward: "I'm rolling, rolling in my sins." -- After
doing what could be done in such emergency to prepare her,
the Sister baptized her, and she died about two hours afterwards, apparently more calm. -- Oh! it was a fearful night--
The fierce agony of that poor soul can never be forgotten--[26]

Most accounts of the work of the various communities of sisters d

not relate details that allow us to get a glimpse of what the sisters

thought of the disease itself. The common elements in all the accounts

are the willingness, and even eagerness, of the sisters to risk their

own lives to help the victims. It was a terrible and mysterious disease

People were suffering and the sisters considered it their duty to help.

The authorities in Philadelphia were the first to ask for help. The

account as found in the "Guardian of the Poor Records" in the Philadel-

phia City Archives gives the prelude to this request.

When the Cholera made its appearance in the different
Wards of the Almshouse and lead [sic] to the belief that the atmosphere of the whole institution was infected the nurses and
attendants became Clamorous for an increase of wages and even
after their demands were gratified such was the appaling
nature and extent of the disease that fear overcame every
other consideration and it was found impracticable to keep
the nurses to their duty, or to obtain at a reasonable price,
proper persons to attend to the Sick.

The report continues with a description of conditions in the wards when

the committee made its daily visits. The few good nurses were greatly

overburdened as most did nothing. In one ward the nurses were so

intoxicated they were "heedless of the groans of the patients." These

disgraceful conditions led the committee to solicit "the Sisters of

Charity at Emmitsburg to take charge of the wards - and for this purpose

they applied to Bishop Kendrick [sic]. . ." The sisters left Emmitsburg

---

[26]Ibid., pp. 263-264.

two hours after receiving the request from the Bishop and were quickly

engaged in their duties. "Nothing but a high sense of duty and a dis-

interested love of their fellow creatures could have induced the Sisters

to take charge of our Wards." The committee was so impressed with the

work of the sisters that they wished to have the sisters remain on a

permanent basis.[27] The sisters remained until sometime in the spring

of 1833. The minutes for 20 May 1833, are primarily a testimony to

the selfless, Christian service given by the sisters. Since the "rules

and habits of the order" prevented the Board from bestowing any other

rewards these resolutions were to be a permanent testimony of their

gratitude.[28]

The city of Baltimore engaged both the Sisters of Charity and the

Oblate Sisters. The published edition of the "Consulting Physician's

[Horatio G. Jameson] Report" to the Mayor of the City Council, 31 December

1832 was primarily a report on the cholera epidemic. Included in this

report was a reminder of the arduous duties carried out by all health

officers and "the highly important services rendered at the hospitals

by the Sisters of Charity, without prospect of pecuniary reward."[29]

A letter from Arch Hirling, Secretary, Trustees for the Poor, dated

Baltimore, 25 September 1832 to Rev. Mr. Joubert is in the French Diary

of the Oblate Sisters. The purpose of this letter was to convey the

---

[27]Philadelphia City Archives. "Guardian of the Poor Records—
Minutes, 1832-1833," Record Group 35.6 - GP 38. 13, 27 August 1832.

[28]Ibid., 13, 20 May 1833.

[29]Baltimore City Health Department. "Consulting Physician's
Report," Vol.: 1815-1849. 31 December 1832. Appendix. A report of
the Commissioners of Health of the same date is also found in this
volume. It gives more details of the actual work of the sisters and
notes the deaths of Sisters Mary Francis and Mary George.

gratitude of Board to the "Colored Sisters of Providence," through
Father Joubert, "for the assistance kindly and charitably rendered by
them in nursing the Cholera patients in the Alms House." The sisters
were not called on until the epidemic had been raging for some time and,
therefore, their term of service was not long.[30] No record came to
light of any published acknowledgement of their services. Many such
references were found in reference to the Sisters of Charity.

Kentucky was also ravaged by cholera, especially in 1832-1833.
Here, as elsewhere, the sisters looked for no monetary reward, although
when engaged by city authorities, they readily accepted payment for their
expenses. It was probably indifference which led the Mayor of Louisville
and his council to substitute the word "services" for "expenses" when
ordering the money from the city treasury to reimburse the sisters. Moth
Catherine Spalding noticed the change, reported her disapproval, and was
assured it would be corrected. On 10 February 1834 she wrote:

> I remained satisfied that it had been done, until a late asper-
> sion from one of the pulpits of the city leads me to believe
> that it stands uncorrected on your books, for the same books
> were referred to in proof of the aspersion.
> If so, Gentlemen, pardon the liberty I take in refunding
> you the amount paid for the above-named expenses, well con-
> vinced that our community, for whom I have acted in this
> case, would prefer the expense rather than submit to such an
> unjust odium.
> Gentlemen, be pleased to understand that we are not
> hirelings; if we are, in practice, the servants of the poor,
> the sick and the orphan, we are voluntarily so, but we look
> for our reward in another and better world.

After quoting this letter Sister Marie Menard added that to the honor of
the Mayor and his council, an apology was made, the record corrected,
and the money returned.[31]

---

[30]AOSP. French Diary, pp. 30-31.

[31]ASCN. "Biographical Sketch of Mother Catherine Spalding" by
Sister Marie Menard (1912), pp. 19-21.

Cholera was not limited to the largest urban centers in Kentucky, but struck smaller settlements as well. The annals of Nazareth recount the first case involving the sisters outside Louisville. The Roberts family lived on a farm about three miles from Loretto. Sisters came from both Loretto and Nazareth.[32] By the time the sisters arrived the two black men were dead or dying. A brother with a negro driver came from Loretto to help bury the dead. Both the Roberts' children also died of the disease. The response Mr. Roberts is reported to have given Sister Martha when she asked his permission to baptize the children before they died most likely summarizes what were, from other accounts, the feelings of many victims towards the sisters (of any community) who nursed them.

> Sister, . . . my life, like my children's is in your hands,
> I can grant you nothing because I can refuse you nothing;
> if I still have anything it is all yours. My friends have
> forsaken me, and you who were a stranger to me have come and
> stood by me in my distress, at the peril of your life.[33]

Newspapers of the day, official reports (municipal reports and reports sent by the bishops to Rome and the several Mission Aid Societies in Europe), motherhouse archives and certainly many other sources that may still be untouched by researchers attest to the work of the sisters.[34]

---

[32]ASL. Original Rule, Chapter 3, #8. The original rule of Father Nerinckx stated: "If there should be any sick family, so distressed, that nobody could be had for assistance, the Mother may send the most fitting, for the relief of the Sufferings, without distinction of religion or denomination. two ought to go together."

[33]ASCN. Annals by Sister Marie Menard. 1833, "Cholera in Bardstown," pp. 98-103.

[34]Rosenberg's study lists numerous sources. A study of the numerous newspapers and periodicals of the period, many of which are now available on microfilm, would certainly yield many more references. The limitations of this study made such a search impractical.

Not all the communities received equal praise for equal work. Baltimore

and Philadelphia were cities known and observed by many visitors. There

were citizens in both cities who thought it important to make the work of

the sisters public. --The tenor of the times apparently did not allow

them to overcome prejudice to the degree of including the Oblate Sisters

in Baltimore.--Visitors to these cities, or residents who came from

other sections of the country, publicized the work even more. An example

of publicizing the work of the sisters beyond the immediate area, and

its possible effect, is found in the following letter found in the

Emmitsburg archives.

> Boston, November 7, 1832
>
> Madame Superior:
> Although a stranger to you permit me to make a most re-
> spectful inquiry.
> A short time ago, I saw in the public papers of the day,
> a notice that while the awful pestilence was raging in
> Philadelphia, several of the ladies of your Institution, <u>volun-
> teered their kind personal assistance to the sick and dying
> strangers</u> in that city, while the stricken were deserted by
> their friends and neighbors. This, in my opinion is the
> <u>greatest marvel of charity ever manifested in America!</u>
> Many of my friends, as well as myself, are desirous to
> know more about these interesting individuals:--the name of
> each, her native place; by whom the plan was suggested, etc.;
> and we should be exceedingly gratified to have their several
> signatures inclosed to us; we feel that the influence of
> such examples of charity should extend to the end of time.
> By granting this request, you will confer the highest
> favor on
> > Your obedient servant: with sincere respect,
> > Levi Bartlett,
> > 35 India Street, Boston[35]

Since the epidemic in Charleston did not occur during the same

years as in the rest of the country it does not figure in general ac-

counts of the epidemic. Sister Benedicta Datty, the Superior of the

---

[35]<u>Mother Augustine and Mother Xavier</u>, pp. 19-20. Also ASJCH.
Letters, III:54. No indication was found that the request was granted.

Sisters of Our Lady of Mercy, died of cholera contracted while nursing
the sick. Other records and manuscripts examined in Charleston did not
refer to the sisters. There are more references to their work during
the frequent yellow-fever epidemics.[36] Although a few specific
references were found to the work of the Sisters of Loretto they apparently did not lack public gratitude at the time. When Bishop Flaget
wrote his report of the work of the sisters in the cholera epidemic
he said: "The Sisters of the Third Order of St. Dominic have as much
claim to recognition as the Sisters of Charity and the Sisters of Loretto."
He then recounted their ingenious method of multiplying forces by
inducing lay women to help them (cf. pp. 44-45, above) nurse the sick
in their homes.[37] When the 1849 epidemic struck the Sisters of Charity
from both Emmitsburg and Nazareth were staffing regular hospitals and
at least some of the hospitals became cholera hospitals for the duration
of the epidemic. The fact that the sisters engaged in nursing was accepted in most of the urban centers. There were also many more congregations of women religious staffing institutions throughout the United States.
During epidemics many persons who otherwise ignored, or even distrusted,
the sisters recognized their service and expressed their gratitude.
In spite of this recognition in time of crisis the sisters were not
entirely spared the force of bigotry that made itself felt during the
interval between epidemics, for example in Baltimore in 1839 following
Sister Isabella's escape from Carmel and in Philadelphia, 1844, over
the issue of the bible in the schools. Most of the time the work of

---

[36]Cf. Bibliographical Essay, Charleston sources. Also, Campbell,
pp. 30-31; 35-36.

[37]Cf. O'Daniel, The Father of the Church in Tennessee, pp. 238-239.

the sisters was ignored by the vast majority. Gradually, over years of service to the poor and in times of crisis, the public image of the Sister improved. The first time anything like general acclaim for the Catholic Sister was ever heard in the United States was a result of the cholera epidemic of 1832.

Care of Orphans

The care of orphans had been a special concern of most of the sisters from the foundation of their institutes. Wherever there were boarding schools there were probably orphans. Immigration, whether from Europe or from other areas of the United States, often resulted in further dislocation. The newly arrived immigrant in a port city or the pioneer on the frontier seldom had other family members to turn to for help in times of crisis. The first mission of the Sisters of Charity outside Emmitsburg was to staff St. Joseph's Orphan Asylum in Philadelphia, beginning in October 1814. The need to care for orphans continued to grow, but outside ports of entry for immigrants the problem seemed manageable for some years. The cholera epidemic of 1832 began to change the picture. Suddenly there were many orphans and neither places to house them nor persons ready to care for them. The sisters, in every area, began to step in quickly. The need was still increasing when the century was half-over.

The Visitation Sisters cared for orphans and poor children from the beginning. Not all the orphans entrusted to them were poor, but all needed loving care. The three McNantz girls were placed in the care of the Visitation Sisters by Father Matthews to whom the dying mother entrusted them. All three girls entered the convent and two of them died a short time later of tuberculosis. The account in the "Convent

Book" relates the fear of the sisters, in the midst of great poverty, that Sister Bernardina, the last of the three girls to die would die before she was of legal age to inherit her estate.[38] Several of the records of the early sisters at Georgetown indicate that their father had placed them in school after the wife's death. There were surely other real orphans, whether from well-to-do families or not, who were entrusted to the care of the sisters and for whom no record exists. We know of these few because one or more of the family became a Visitation Sister. A letter of Mother Teresa Lalor to Archbishop Maréchal in 1818 says:

> There is also one of our poor Children who has been brought up in our Poor School and who has often petition[ed] to be admitted as a Lay Sister, She again renews her petition, with the same persevering disposition-- her name is Margaret Connor. She is going on 9 years with us, . . .[39]

The Sisters of Loretto and the Oblate Sisters of Providence also cared for orphans to the extent they could with their limited resources. The care of orphans is not specifically mentioned in the articles in the original constitutions which state the aim of either of these religious communities. Both communities, however, are known to have provided for orphans from the earliest years. Both communities had superiors general, at a later time, who had been orphans in the care of the sisters. At Loretto, Lucy Downs was a favorite of Father Nerinckx according to biographical information. As Sister Berlindes, she became superior after the fire of 1858. The information about the early foundations from Loretto recounts that Gethsemani Boarding and

---

[38] AGVC. Biographical Sketches.

[39] AAB. A[lice] Lalor to Archbishop Maréchal, 12 January 1818 (18 A 11).

Day School, 1818-1848 (at the site of the present Trappist monastery), was "founded as a preparatory school, but mothered so many orphans it has sometimes been designated as an orphanage."[40] The first historian of the Oblate Sisters wrote that "it was the expressed wish of Rev. Father Joubert that there should always be a number of children who were either orphans, or whose parents were unable to pay for them called 'the Children of the house' to be under the care of the Sisters." The author herself, Mother Theresa Catherine Willigman (Sarah Elizabeth), was one of these "children of the house." She and her sister, Charity Grant Willigman, had been "placed there by request of a dying mother, a converted Catholic"[41] about 1839. Other records of early members of the Oblate Sisters also carry the notation, "child of the house." No record was found at St. Catharine's Convent to indicate that they cared for orphans. The boys' school was conducted at the request of a widower and the conditions of the times make it almost certain that there were girls in the academy who had lost at least one parent. The care of orphans, during this period, was never a major concern for the Dominican Sisters. The other two communities were serving people who lived under poorer conditions. In the three communities--Visitandines, Sisters of Loretto, and Oblate Sisters of Providence--for whom records exist of the care of orphans in their boarding schools it is almost accidental. If a number of these orphans had not entered the three communities there might have been nothing but traditions to tell us of this work.

---

[40]ALM. Biographical series - Sister Berlindes Downs. Mss. 7, a compilation by Sister M. Matilda.

[41]AOSP. Manuscript of Mother Theresa Catherine Willigman, p. 21, and the brief account of Mother Theresa Catherine's life by her sister, Charity Grant.

The Sisters of Charity from both the Emmitsburg and Nazareth motherhouses and the Sisters of Our Lady of Mercy in Charleston cared for orphans in institutional settings. The institutions staffed by the sisters from Emmitsburg were designated by various titles; orphan asylum was the most common, of course, but there was also a "Half-Orphan Asylum" opened in New York in 1833. Many of these asylums were originally organized by a lay board, a parish, or representatives of a particular group such as the German Catholics. In some cases the sisters did not remain long due to differences of opinion about the management of the institutions. Unless the sisters were able to direct the total program too many difficulties arose to permit the smooth-running of the institution and the sisters were withdrawn. The superiors always had more requests for sisters than they could accept. Sisters were sent where there were possibilities of doing the most good. There was too much that needed attention to waste efforts on differences of opinion. The Articles of Agreement made between Father John Dubois, representing the Sisters from Emmitsburg and the managers of St. Joseph's Society in Philadelphia, as found in Appendix 5, formed the basis for subsequent agreements by this community before 1850. It appears quite specific but human beings can often find the means to interpret even carefully written documents in various ways. The people of the early nineteenth century were no exception when seen in the light of the archival records of the care of orphans by the Sisters of Charity from Emmitsburg. The best remembered and highly publicized disagreement was that between Bishop Hughes of New York and the superiors at Emmitsburg, but there are instances of the sisters remaining in an institution only a short time because of interference by a benefactor or the managers.[42]

The conditions were present that might have led to similar experiences for the other two communities, but serious differences of opinion were avoided. Bishop Chabrat, Coadjutor, wrote from Bardstown to Bishop Blanc in New Orleans, 1838:

> . . . you have an Orphan Asylum under the care of the Sisters of Charity. You would oblige me very much if you could send me their regulations and whatever the powers of the lay managers if there be any. Of late I have had some troubles with the ladies managers [sic] of Louisville, the Revd Mr Reynolds being at their head-- The Sisters of Charity there would have had about 16 female lay superiors, had I not interfered-- please oblige me in this if you can.[43]

The Rev. Mr. Reynolds seems to have learned from this experience. As Bishop of Charleston in 1845 he organized a ladies' society for the support of orphans. Their sole purpose was "to obtain donations in money, provisions, etc. and to devise means for the comfortable support and christian education of destitute Female Orphans in the Asylum erected in this City . . ."[44]

The best description of life in a Catholic orphanage during this period is found in a letter of Sister Margaret George to Mother Catherine Spalding.

---

[42]For example, the sisters opened an asylum in Georgetown in June 1831 at the request of Mme. Augustin Iturbide, the widow of the former Emperor of Mexico. They withdrew in September because Mme. Iturbide interfered too much. Cf. 1809-1959, pp. 20-23.

[43]UNDA, Archdiocese of New Orleans Collection. Chabrat, Guy Ignatius, Bardstown (Coadjutor) to Bishop Blanc, New Orleans. 23 December 1838. The sisters' own records indicate that when the sisters were given sufficient authority they were very effective managers.

[44]ASCLM. Catholic Orphan Society - Secretary's Book. Constitution and General Rules of the Society, #1.

Cincinnati, Ohio
St. Peter's Asylum
August 26, 1849

Mother Catherine Spalding
St. Vincent's Orphan Asylum
Louisville, Kentucky

Dear Sister Superior,

Yours of the 16th should have been answered ere this, urgent duties interfered with my intention; this will plead my excuse. You have been more favored than we, 5 of our little ones, all under 7 left us for our Father's Home-- happy little innocents secure of their immortal bliss. I trust they will not be unmindful of us, yet sojourning in this land of exile.

Usually our number through the year was generally one hundred fifty-six[.] have since been added to that by the cholera which deprived some of one parent and some others of both, some few have been adopted and some placed out since, which brings our number down to 137 at present. Many of these, say 60, are under 6 years of age. All at present in good health, not one in the Infirmary. As you have heard, the epidemic has left our city, thanks be to the Almighty giver of all good gifts, and we have reason to be grateful, dear Sister, that the goodness of God has spared us the more advanced in age and took a few of His <u>little children</u> for such is His Kingdom, "suffer such to come to Me." He has them and can provide for them in His own Sweet Mercy and yet such is poor human nature, we could not give them up without a sigh, nor without a tear.

Our orphans rise at 5, wash and comb during the hour

5½ - Morning prayers in common, after morning prayers the larger ones go to the Dormitories, presided by one of the Sisters in each dormitory, make the beds, sweep, dust, and put everything in order.

6½ - Mass 7 - Breakfast

8½ - School commences Three different class rooms, the ABC children and the little ones in one room, our rule is three years of age, not younger unless some particular circumstances require a dispensation.

11 3/4 - Dinner prayers - same as the ones, which of course you know.

12   Dinner - Silence, of course (reading when we are altogether). At this moment we cannot take our meals in the refectory on account of being crowded.

1½ - School opens- at four o'clock those that are able to study employ this hour in studying lessons for the next day- the little ones continue their lessons with one Sister and one Sister can keep all the studies of the other, thus three [?] Sisters are engaged[.] during the hour the Sisters keep the studies the two class Sisters can make their spiritual exercises. After meals, 10 or 12 of the larger children assist in washing the dishes and cleaning the refectory, etc. but must not stay longer

240

than the commencement of school without special per--
mission each time from myself- which I rarely grant-
the only chance these poor children have for education
is while they are with us, therefore, we should do all
we can for them.
We form them into band for fine combing; this is done every day,
say twenty for each Sister, in recreation or in the morning,
at the convenience of the Sister.
    The Externs never mix with the orphans neither in or out of
school- separate rooms and separate teachers- sore eyes have
been our torment and the only remedy I find is separate towels
and basins for each one and we have to be particular to see that
this is observed. Each child is numbered, clothes, box, and
everything belonging to her marked in her number. No school
on Saturdays. A general reviewing of the dormitories, etc.-
bathing the children in summer, etc. in the afternoon, they
have sewing classes and read. I mean during the week.

Dear Sister,
    I have hastily sketched the above. At any time I shall
feel happy to communicate any little information in my power.
We are somewhat older than yours and each one's experience may
add a little to the general good. Our children--such as are
able--go to the Cathedral twice every Sunday. This keeps them
before the public who love to see them and encourages them
to contribute to their support. It is getting too dark and
I must finish abruptly, so dear Sister, please excuse this--
my time is not my own just now-- opening of schools, work
new, mechanics and all the etceteras of our Martha life for
Sister Servants, or as yours, Sister Superiors, you know and
can feel for us-- pray in union with us all for the accomp-
lishing the will of our one Supreme and only good.
                    Yours in the adorable Heart,
                                    Sister Margaret
. . . .
I had forgotten to say all our bedsteads now are five feet
high and have mosquito bars on them - $3.50 a piece, very good
and cheap.[45]

    The details in this letter are probably quite representative o
every orphanage conducted by the Sisters of Charity from Emmitsburg
during this period. Reading the archival records one becomes aware of
a practical approach to any new work. Thus, for example, in the care
of orphans schedules were gradually worked out and systematized. It is
also very probable that this letter of Sister Margaret George to Mother

[45]ASCN. OLB- I:72.

Catherine Spalding was not unique. If the sisters themselves did not share knowledge of their experiences with sisters of the many other communities of women religious that began to staff orphanages during the 1830's and 1840's the bishops or priests overseeing the establishment of such institutions probably did. Two things stand out in this letter: (1) The schedule and way of life seems to be at least as much determined by the sisters' way of life as the needs of the children. (2) Doctors may not have known about the germ-theory (cf. pp. 226-227, above) but Sister Margaret's practical experience found an effective means of combating contagious diseases.

The Nazareth Archives also contain letters that reflect another side of this problem. The priests of the diocese often turned to Mother Catherine of whom Father John Quinn said in one letter "[e]very orphan in the city claims you as their mother." Several of the letters refer to fathers bringing their motherless children.[46] One letter speaks of a need that closely resembles a twentieth-century need.

[no location given]
June 25, 1846

Mother Catherine,
  Mrs. Clementine Allen, who will present you this, was some eight months ago divorced from her husband. I prosecuted the trial for her- all the developments in the case were greatly to her credit. She is very poor, has two children, a girl and boy, which she has thus far by the most laborious labor supported. She desires now to place her daughter under the charge of the excellent Sisters of Charity, of whom you are the principal. I advised her by all means to do so,- if it be practical. Mrs. Allen, is, I doubt not in all things, a correct woman, and is much to be relied on.

---

[46] ASCN. OLB-I:11, 44 (DLB-I:180-183). Rev. John Quinn to Mother Catherine, Louisville, 9, 10 April 1849; 11 June 1849.

Be assured, Madam, of my high regard,
Thos. M. Thruston[47]

There is also a document, the "Surrender of children to Mother Catharine

by Cerilla Cag." In this a widow with two girls gives "all rights and

powers over said children, which by law, I can give and surrender."

She wishes the girls to be baptized and raised as Catholics. She her-

self was apparently illiterate since her name is followed by a mark (X);

she said she was unable to give her children the proper care.[48] There

were many destitute people and those children were fortunate that found

love and security as well as a basic education and training in an or-

phanage of the kind described here.

The large, and increasing, number of orphans made it necessary

to find employment for them as soon as possible. An unfinished and un-

dated letter to Father Aud, probably from Mother Catherine, gives an

example.

> . . . I was waiting to place out some of our large or-
> phans in order to make room for the numerous applications
> that I receive every day from different parts of the state.
> The house is overcrowded; if, nevertheless, the one you
> are writing about is five years of age and can take care of
> himself, you may send him by the first opportunity.[49]

There seems to be little concern in the extant documents about the

need for institutions to care for infants during the first half of the

nineteenth century. The clue to this is probably the notation of 1816

found on the reverse of the Articles of Agreement for St. Joseph's Or-

---

[47]ASCN. OLB-I:82 (DLB-I, 159). Thos. M. Thruston to Mother
Catherine, 25 June 1846.

[48]ASCN. DLB-I:162 (The location of the original is not given.)

[49]ASCN. OLB-I:62 (DLB-I:51). [Probably] Mother Catherine
Spalding to Rev. Athanasius A. Aud, n.d.

phanage in Philadelphia (cf. Appendix 5). The managers of St. Joseph's Society were responsible for __all__ orphans, but infants would be placed in the care of a nurse until age three. This very likely was the general practice--allowing for a variation in the minimum age at which different institutions accepted a child. There was concern for the young people who were "placed out." The task of finding good families for the young people to live with and a suitable job or apprenticeship so that they could begin to support themselves was certainly no easy task. One problem that always entered in was how to ensure not only the freedom, but also the encouragement, of the young person to practice the Catholic religion. One document gives a plan set forth by the Sisters of Charity from Emmitsburg. It shows how carefully the sisters assessed their own work, as well as their concern for those for whom they cared, and a sensitivity to public opinion.

It is believed by those who have considered the subject well that the Sisters of Charity do comparatively little good in their Orphan Asylums. The reason of this is that the children are sent when too young from the Institutions. The good impressions made upon their tender minds are quickly effaced by the contagion of bad example and the force of temptation to which they are exposed; their virtue being yet too weak to keep them in the path of rectitude.

Scarcely have they time to acquire the first rudiments of a plain English education: - and their knowledge of domestic concerns is equally limited. The consequence is that being of little service to their employers, who are frequently unreasonable in their exactions they become discouraged, and either throw themselves away for a livelihood, to the disgrace of religion and the ruin of their immortal souls, or at best, remain useless members of society.

The remedy of these frightful evils is within the reach of friends of humanity and religion, and may, we believe, be applied with fewer difficulties, than might at first be imagined.

Let there be two institutions for female orphans in each large city: the first of which will be preparatory to the second. In the preparatory Asylum they will remain until the age of 10 or 12, and be taught Spelling, Reading, Writing, Arithmetic and Catechism, Sewing and domestic duties,

as far as their strength and age will permit. The children
of said asylum will seldom be able to learn much being for
the most part so small as to require constant care and attention.

At 12 years of age let them be removed to the second
Asylum in which they will receive a plain English education
comprising Orthography, Reading, Writing, Arithmetic, English
Grammar, Geography and History; and, above all, Sacred History
and a thorough knowledge of the tenets of our holy religion.
They will also have the advantage of learning every description of useful needle work, as well as all kinds of domestic
duties, such as cooking, washing, ironing, house-cleaning, &c.
The hours shall be regulated as to afford a sufficient time
for each occupation.

The children shall remain in this second Institution until the age of 18, by which time they will have had leisure
and opportunity to be so well grounded in piety, and to have
acquired such habits of virtue and industry as will enable
them to go forth armed with the means of support and strength
to resist the crafty wiles of the enemy: --in a word,--as honorable and useful members of society.

This second Institution will, by taking in work, be enabled,
in a great measure, to maintain itself: --and the public, seeing
the beneficial effects of such a system, will no doubt be induced
to contribute to its support.

Should any among the orphans give evidence of extraordin-
ary capacity, they may be sent to the Orphan Asylum attached to
the Mother-house at St. Joseph's, near Emmitsburgh, where they
will receive a liberal education, so as to fit them for gover-
nesses, teachers in Public Schools, &c.--

St. Joseph's November 1844[50]

There is no indication that such a plan was put into effect befor

1850. The pace at which the Church was growing at that period, largely

due to increasing immigration, would have made it difficult for almost

any bishop to encourage the establishment of anything beyond the most

necessary institutions--schools, hospitals, or orphan asylums for the

very young. It is quite certain from accounts of St. Joseph's Academy

in Emmitsburg that occasionally a gifted orphan girl was sent there for

advanced education. The same is true in Nazareth. The question of

---

[50]UNDA. Archdiocese of New Orleans Collection. Sister Xavier
[Mother Xavier Clark], St. Joseph's Emmitsburg, to Bishop Blanc, New
Orleans. Enclosure with a letter, November 1844.

placing orphans was a matter for the Sisters' Council to decide in Charleston. The minutes of the Council take this matter up from time to time. Sometimes the question is whether to place an orphan with the boarders at the academy at the community's expense. An informative account is found in the minutes for 26 October 1849. The council was informed that the Bishop wanted three orphan girls (Margaret Davy, Margaret ONeill and Sophia Reddet) placed in the academy to get a good education with an eye to training them for the Sisterhood should they appear to have a vocation. The council concluded:

> After some considerations the proposition was unanimously objected to —as it was thought more adviseable [sic], to act in accordance with a former resolution of the Council regarding these children Viz --to put them to business, and give them an opportunity of trying their vocation (if they had any) by living in the world a few years.

The council was partially overruled. The Bishop conceded that Sophia Reddet may be put to business, but the other two girls were to be kept another six months in the institution.[51] That he did not completely overrule the sisters might be attributed to a grudging confirmation of the wisdom gained by the sisters from past experience. Young girls who knew no home but with the sisters could easily think they had a vocation when given special considerations. Such examples of decisions made by the sisters on the basis of the wisdom which came from their practical experience can be found in every motherhouse archives. Institutions were closed, or sisters withdrawn, when this wisdom was not recognized and the sisters were not directly subject to the person or board who had the final responsibility for the institution. There was little that could be done when the person giving

---

[51] ASCLM. Council Minutes, 26 October 1849.

the directive was the bishop of the diocese in which the central house was located. But the little that could be done was apparently done since there are frequent indications that compromises were reached. Deference and wise decisions based on experience were carefully balanced.

CONCLUSIONS

Before the Irish began emigrating to the United States in large numbers in the 1820's the center of the Catholic community was in Maryland, and the leadership was to be found among the descendants of early colonists. The majority of Catholics were southern and Anglo-American. If the Catholics of Pennsylvania did not fit this description they had certainly adopted many of the characteristics of the Anglo-Americans. Perhaps one of the most important characteristics of the American Catholic Church that this study underlines is this southern, Anglo-American dominance in the early nineteenth century. All of the first eight permanent communities were founded in the south—the two latest foundations (1829) being the only two without a solid core of members descended from the old Maryland families. The listing of "Female Religious Societies" in the 1850 Almanac, as inexact as it is, indicates that most of the communities founded after 1829 were serving newly developed areas in the west and north.[1] By 1850 most of the large numbers of immigrants who had entered the United States had settled in the ports of entrance or moved to the newly developing urban centers in the interior of the continent. A great deal of leadership was still exerted by the old Anglo-Americans, but the most prominent leadership had shifted to the Irish-born.

The only one of these eight communities which had moved out of the original southern, Anglo-American culture on a relatively large scale

---

[1] Almanac, 1850, pp. 228-230.

was the Sisters of Charity of St. Joseph in Emmitsburg. This may be why there are so few references to slavery at Emmitsburg. It is also of interest that the two divisions in the community (New York and Cincinnati) occurred in cities where Irish-born bishops resided. Surely this was only one factor in the divisions, and possibly a very minor one. Whatever the causes for the divisions from the viewpoint of the leadership, or the trend they may suggest to a modern historian, at the time the divisions took place each sister had to make her decision in the light of her own understanding of the situation. For the women religious of our own time who face similar situations, it is encouraging to recall that other women religious have faced them as well. The convictions of the sisters, on both sides, that their decisions were the correct ones under the circumstances led to the formation of new communit that have enriched the life of the church.

The growing consciousness of American "nationalism" was probably experienced in all the communities, but documentation for it was not found in all of them. It is related that Father Nerinckx suggested inviting sisters to come from Europe to train the original members of the Sisters of Loretto; but they objected, saying they preferred Father Nerinckx's guidance.[2] There are definite reactions to the idea of being part of a French community recorded in the archives of the Daughters of Charity in Emmitsburg and the Sisters of Charity in Cincinnati (cf. Chapter III, pp. 162ff), as well as in the archives of the Sisters of Charity of Nazareth (cf. Chapter 1, p. 38). At the Visitation Convent the absence of references to an important influence on the community by

---

[2]Cf. Sr. M. Matilda Barrett, S.L., Courage American: Mother Mary Rhodes, Foundress of the Sisters of Loretto (Louisville, Ky.: Printed by Schuhmann Printing Co., 1962), p. 11.

the Sisters Father Wheeler brought from Europe implies that the American sisters considered their American interpretation of needs in the light of their constitutions satisfactory.   The experience of having the French sisters live with them and direct them for a short time apparently increased the American sisters' confidence in their own judgement.   Certainly the growing strength of nativism and the emphasis on the "Americanization" of the immigrants encouraged the sisters to think of themselves as Americans whether they were born in the United States or not.   On the other hand, the paucity of references to frequent tensions between the sisters and the nativists may be due to the predominantly American membership in most of the communities.   Since the American members often held positions of leadership and those who were immigrants could not be classed among the ignorant and the destitute, these sisters did not pose a clear threat to American society.   The popular literature pictured Catholic nuns as ignorant women who became pawns of corrupt clergymen.   The real picture was very different.   These women were intelligent and competent teachers and nurses.   One suspects that the nativists simply ignored these sisters and their institutions on most occasions.

These women, as it has been said earlier, were women of their times.   Women were looked upon by men in both the Church and the State as weak and ill-prepared to make important decisions.   In the early nineteenth century an unmarried woman was the exception.   Women in the colonial period had an important role in the total community, but as men moved out of the home in pursuit of business women were relegated to an exalted position in the home but denied many legal rights.   In this situation women, in general, looked to sisterhood with other women

as a means of companionship and of exercising some influence on society.
Many mission societies with various purposes such as the distribution
of bibles, help for the indigent and the care of orphans, were formed
during this period. Sisterhood, as practiced in religious communities,
however, was otherwise unknown in the United States. In some ways it
embodied the ideal preached by many non-Catholic women, while at the
same time it bypassed the primary calling of a woman to marriage and
a family.

Before 1850, professionalism for women was an exception. Even
the teacher-training institutions that were being founded did not expect
most of the women who attended them to devote their lives to teaching.
The sisters were again exceptions; they were well trained and most of
the teaching sisters were teachers until illness or old age made it necessary for them to stop. Every community except the Carmelites initiated
some type of teacher-training, almost from the beginning. Mother Seton
directed the training and supervision of new teachers in the early years
at Emmitsburg. At the Visitation Convent, the three convents in Kentucky
and the Oblate Sisters' convent in Baltimore, well-educated and experienc
priests directed the earliest training, but gradually the experienced
sisters took over the responsibility with occasional help from priests
and lay people for advanced instruction in philosophical subjects or
music and art.

By the mid-nineteenth century the work of the sisters had achieve
the general outlines that it would retain until after the Second Vatican
Council. The first schools of the sisters were usually academies for
girls from the more affluent families. This was a practical matter.
It was the most acceptable and effective means of support. Such academi

were not the exclusive work of any community. In most communities other works soon outnumbered the academies and where they were retained it was because the income was a necessary means of support and because of the need upper classes had for Catholic education. Parish schools were increasing in number, especially in urban centers, in response to the Protestant domination of the public schools, where these existed. The ever-increasing number of immigrants, added to repeated epidemics of such diseases as cholera and yellow-fever, made the establishment of orphanages necessary. These same factors, plus the growing congestion in the cities, also provided the impetus for the establishment of hospitals. A few of these sisters were still managing the domestic work and caring for the infirmaries in seminaries; but the proportion, while never great, was even less by 1850. In the early part of the century all the schools were open to non-Catholics, as long as they were willing to be present at all the classes and religious exercises (a requirement made for purposes of supervision of the pupils rather than a means of proselytizing). By the middle of the century this openness, at least in the day schools, seems to have decreased. Again it was more the result of practical concerns than a conscious change in policy. Public schools were being established, the ever-increasing number of Catholic children often seemed like too many for the available space, and the teachers were overburdened.

Through all the years the sisters were quite dependent on the approval of bishops and priests. Nineteenth century American society did not expect women to act independently and neither did the Catholic Church. Since the American Catholic Church, however, was constantly struggling just to meet the most basic need of its members as a result of the westward movement and the growing number of immigrants, many of whom were Catholic, the women religious had to shoulder most of the responsibility for their own finances and the day-to-day management of their institutions. Major decisions usually required at least the approval of the bishop or his representative. But nineteenth century society, especially in the south, was also deferential and so what may appear as unwarranted dependence to someone in the late twentieth century was considered quite normal in the early nineteenth century. Studying the records of all eight communities, however, leaves the very strong impression that it was societal norms, not the ability of the sisters, that required this dependence. The women were quite capable of managing their own affairs; repeatedly, in the conduct of their work, they gave evidence of their wisdom and ability.

The years 1790 to 1850 were years of changes and growth not only in the character of the American Catholic Church, but also among women religious. From 1830 to 1850 many additional communities of women religious made permanent foundations in the United States. Some were founded here while others were established by communities already existing in Europe. Bishops and priests, as well as the women themselves, had learned that adaptations were essential. The most difficult lesson at that time, perhaps, was the recognition that American women religious could depend on no government support or foundations from wealthy people to support their work. Their support, and that of their charitable works, depended almost entirely on their ability to meet the needs of a pluralistic, and often pioneering, society.

Sixty years after the first Carmelites arrived in the United States there were hundreds of women religious teaching, nursing, and caring for the poor throughout the country. Even the Carmelites were teaching school but this had never been accepted by them as anything but a temporary aberration. Once this school was closed in 1851 the Carmelite nuns of Baltimore lived the same life as Carmelite nuns in any other part of the world.

The question of the authority of the community versus that of a local bishop was, perhaps, the single most important factor in the difficulties that arose as the sisters within each religious community gradually moved from what Wach termed the "circle of brotherhood" to the institutional stage.[3] This question did not arise when Visitation Sisters from Georgetown founded a new monastery in a different diocese, since they followed an old, accepted Rule and Constitution which provided that each monastery would be an independent community. Among the six communities founded between 1809 and 1829, the intensity of the crisis seems to be proportional to the intensity of the move to stabilize institutional norms. The superiors at Emmitsburg were faced with guiding the life and work of the largest number of sisters, spread over the greatest geographic expanse, and involved in the most varied types of work. The task required clearly defined responsibilities and the effort to establish these led to severe crises. The Dominican Sisters, on the other hand, had overcome their serious financial difficulties and had arrived at a _modus vivendi_ with the priests of the Dominican Order. The relatively small number of sisters in both Kentucky and Ohio precluded multiple establishments. Nothing seemed to demand further definition of the existing constitution. Some foundresses were still alive in 1850,

---

[3] Cf. Wach, p. 141.

but in every community there were members who had personal experience of its beginnings. In the smaller communities the oral transmission of this experience was still very powerful. It had become apparent in the larger communities that there was a need for written documents to insure the unity of the common goals and the way in which these goals were met. The standards of the written document were beginning to take precedence over oral tradition in the on-going development of the particular religious community. These standards, however, never quite overshadowed the pragmatism, or utility, first enunciated by Bishop Carroll. The question of what was the most practical means to attain specific goals has always been in the background of any undertaking.

In the late eighteenth century and the first half of the nineteenth century women religious came together to serve God by serving the needs of a minority Church in a pluralistic society. If there is one set of experiences of the early nineteenth century that should be highlighted today it would seem to be that during periods of rapid change and development a readiness to be flexible, along with loyalty to ideals, can be more important than fulfilling specific regulations of a written constitution in assuring a continued existence. These eight communities exhibited such qualities. Flexibility and readiness to change in order to meet changing conditions were not always interpreted in the same manner, even by members of the same community. Various opinions sometimes led to painful decisions by an individual who left one community for another, or a group who formed the core of a new community, or for the sisters and their superiors when a decision led to withdrawing sisters from an institution or diocese.

American women religious have been from the beginning, dependent

n the goodwill of the general populace. Very few institutions have ever
een supported by the government or adequate endowments. Women reli-
ious in the United States have almost always been responsible for their
wn support. This required good management as well as educated, capable
ersonnel. The public have expected this high quality among the person-
el in schools and other institutions and, therefore, also looked to
omen religious for leadership in education, health care, and social
ervice. This self-support by the sisters has also given the women re-
igious a degree of independence they might not have otherwise enjoyed.
he superiors could withdraw sisters from a given place if conditions
arranted it, for example if bishops (outside the diocese in which the
otherhouse was located), priests, or lay managers interfered too much
n the lives of the sisters. Sometimes the sisters were withdrawn be-
ause the sisters were not being adequately supported. None of the com-
unities hesitated to send sisters to serve where there was real poverty,
ut they did object to indifference to their needs by the people or
ocal church authorities.

The very qualities that made American women religious so important to the growth and development of a vital Catholic Church in the
democratic and pluralistic society of the United States--for example,
their understanding of and openness to American society in general, their
capability, and their training--also led to the conditions in which there
were always sisters who asserted their right to make their own decisions
about their life-style and the conduct of their institutions. In places
or times where there was relative stability these qualities were often
muted, but changing conditions could also change that. Nevertheless,
these sisters did come from a deferential society in which respect for

authority was very pronounced. A sense of commitment and obligation was also stronger in this society where the interdependence on one another was realized much more strongly than today. The early nineteenth century and the late twentieth century are both characterized by rapid tech nological development and a changing social scene. There is much less stability in either period than was apparent in the late nineteenth and early twentieth centuries. Yet in spite of the instability the commun- ities of women religious in the nineteenth century not only remained healthy, but also grew stronger.

Some things remain a mystery even to those on the "inside." The early nineteenth century of American Catholic Church history is not only a period of some mystery to the Catholic in the post-Vatican II era, it is also a period that becomes more fascinating the more one looks at it. In many ways it seems to have more in common with our own times than doe the history of the century from approximately 1850 to 1950. Undoubtedly it was a pioneering age, but with the pioneering came the questioning of directions to be taken and the air of instability. The woman religiou of today can find much that speaks to her own experience, despite the vast changes in the externals of life, as she compares the religious life of largely pre-industrial America to that of the post-industrial ag

APPENDIX I

CHRONOLOGICAL OUTLINES

Carmelites, Port Tobacco and Baltimore

Prior to 1790 - Americans of special note in Belgian convents

Antwerp - Miss Mary Brent, daughter of Robert Brent and Mary Wharton
entered sometime before 1773 (perhaps even before 1760)
Mother Margaret Brent was apparently a second cousin of
Father Charles Neale.

Hoogstraeten - Ann Mathews, Sr. Bernardina Teresa Xavier of St.
Joseph, professed Nov. 24, 1755, age 23.
Susanna Mathews, Sr. Mary Eleanora of St. Francis Xavier,
and Ann Teresa Mathews, Sr. Mary Aloysia of the Blessed
Trinity, sisters of Fr. William Mathews of Washington,D.C.
- they were professed in 1784.

Sr. Teresa of Jesus Coudray at Antwerp was greatly responsible for interesting Mr. de Villegas d'Estainbourg in making the
American foundation possible.
Currier, p. 57: "This sister informed him that there was in
the Convent of Hoogstraeten a nun called Mother Bernardina
Mathews an American, and Prioress of the Monastery, whose
two nieces had come from the New World and entered the
Monastery of Hoogstraeten, to imbibe the true spirit of the
Carmelite Rule, with the intention of returning to their
native country, to establish a Convent of the Order." He
began to devise ways to raise money to make the foundation
possible, and advanced some himself."

1790 - the three Mathews women, with Sr. Clare Joseph Dickenson, chosen
by Fr. Charles Neale from the Antwerp community, prepared
to leave for America in the company of Frs. Charles Neale
and Robert Plunkett.

July 2.   They arrived in New York, where they stayed in the home of
a Mrs. White.

July 10. In the evening they arrived at the landing place of Mr.
Robert Brent's property. They stayed in the home of Mr.
Ignatius Mathews for about 8 days before going to Mr.
Neale's home in Port Tobacco.
Fr. Charles Neale spent his entire patrimony for the
Carmelites. Finding that his property was not the most
suitable he exchanged it for the property of Mr. Baker
Brooke. In order to acquire the entire 800 acres he also
paid 1370 pounds to Mr. Brooke. The house on the property
was a gift.

257

October 15. The Carmelites took possession of their new property.
Both Bishop Carroll and Mr. de Villegas approached wealthy
persons in Europe and were able to acquire substantial gif
from them for the Sisters.

1793 - Bishop Carroll informed the Sisters of the dispensation he receiv
for them from the Cardinal Prefect of the Propaganda to
teach. The sisters did not use this dispensation at the
time.
-----The sisters supported themselves by spinning and the farm. Fr.
Charles Neale directed the farming.

1800 - Mother Bernardina, the first Prioress, died. She was succeeded b
Mother Clare Joseph Dickenson who was appointed by Bishop
Carroll and empowered to appoint the sub-prioress and the
discreets.

1808 - Disputes had begun to arise over the title to the land. These
first ones involved boundaries which Fr. Charles Neale was
able to settle by means of arbitration, but it still cost
the community money.

1809 - Mother Clare Joseph Dickenson wrote to the Archbishop requesting
him to preside at an election of a prioress in conformity
with the rule. Bishop Neale presided on April 14, and
Mother Clare Joseph was duly elected.

1817 - Mr. Baker Brooke died and his heirs brought suit against the sisters over the property.

1824 - Archbishop Maréchal informed the Community he had secured the ser
vices of Roger B. Taney to defend their cause in the
property struggle.

1829 - The lawsuit was finally settled in favor of the Carmelites throug
the efforts of Roger B. Taney.

1830 - March 27. Mother Clare Joseph Dickenson died; she had been
superior for 30 years.

April 14. Sr. Angela of St. Teresa (Mary Ann Mudd) was elected
prioress.
---About this time the temporal reverses of the community
had increased to the point where the sisters found it
necessary to observe an even stricter life style than
the rule required. Archbishop Whitfield thought it advisable for them to move either to Washington or Baltimore
where they could support themselves through the instructio
of children.

September 29. The cornerstone of the new convent in Baltimore wa
laid by Archbishop Whitfield. (Aisquith Street)

1831 – February 24. The Archbishop informed the Sisters that the rescript permitting them to teach had been re-activated
by the Cardinal Prefect of the Propaganda.

August 10. The Archbishop authorized the nuns to quit their enclosure in Charles Co. and move to Baltimore.

September 13. The sisters left Mt. Carmel, accompanied by Fr.
O'Brien and Mr. Washington Young, the brother-in-law of
Sr. Stanislaus. They spent the night at the home of the
Young family.

September 15. The Archbishop said Mass in their chapel. This was
followed by the Te Deum.

October 3. The school was opened with Sisters Delphina, Teresa
and Gertrude as teachers; Sister Stanislaus began teaching the following September.

1832 – The Sisters were granted an Act of Incorporation by the General
Assembly of Maryland.

1833 – November 12. Sr. Mary Aloysia Mathews, the last of the foundresses, died.

1836 – July 16. The cornerstone of a new chapel was laid. Fr. Herard,
the chaplain gave $3,000. and interested some ladies of
the city who opened a fair which netted $3,500.

1837 – The new chapel was blessed with Bishop Benedict J. Fenwick cele-
brating the Mass at the request of the Archbishop and
the discourse was delivered by Bishop England.

1839 – August 18. Sr. Isabella Neale fled the convent and almost caused
a riot which necessitated the intervention of the Mayor
along with other men of prominence. The military dis-
persed the mob after 3 days, but the convent was guarded
for 3 weeks. She was judged to be "not of sane mind" by
a panel of Protestant doctors at the request of her
brother-in-law, Col. Wm. Brent of Georgetown. Until
her death in 1867, she was cared for by the Sisters of
Charity in their hospital.

1850 – Sr. Anastasia, the portress, gave a woman a basket of food;
the woman had typhoid and Sr. Anastasia caught it and
it was passed on to others. Three died (Srs. Ursula
Mudd, Joseph Hammersly and Sr. Austin Bradford).

1851 – Francis Patrick Kenrick became Archbishop of Baltimore. He was
instrumental in effecting the close of the school on
Friday, December 20th.

Georgetown Visitation

1798 - The Poor Clares opened the George Town Academy for Young Ladies.
Fr. Leonard Neale was assigned to Georgetown; he replaced Fr.
DuBourg as President of the College.

1799 - The Poor Clares rented the house on the corner of the present
35th and P Streets from John Threlkeld.
Neale asked Alice Lalor, Mrs. Maria McDermott & Mrs. Sharpe to
come to Georgetown from Philadelphia.

1800 - The Poor Clares purchased the Threlkeld house.
Neale purchased a Threlkeld house on the lot adjoining the Poor
Clares for the "Three Pious Ladies."

1802 - death of Sister Ignatia (Mrs. Sharpe)

1804 - death of Mother de la Marche of the Poor Clares

1805 - Leonard Neale purchased the Poor Clare property from the remaining two Poor Clares before they returned to France.

Bishop Leonard Neale translated the copy of the Rule of the Order
of the Visitation that had been in the library of the
Poor Clares which they had sold to Fr. Francis Neale.

1808 - Bishop Neale deeded all the property previously acquired by him
to the "Sisters of the Visitation of the Virgin Mary"
for the consideration of one dollar (cf. Sullivan, p. 51).
- - - Bishop Carroll continued his efforts to regularize the community
in the eyes of the Church, but his suggestions were not
favorably received.

1814 - At Archbishop Carroll's suggestion the members of the community
took simple vows.

1815 - Archbishop Carroll died. Leonard Neale became Archbishop of
Baltimore.
He requested Papal approval of the community as a convent of the
Order of the Visitation.

1816 - A Papal Indult of July 14, 1816, granting the request of Archbishop Neale was received in Georgetown, November 10.

1817 - During January most of the remaining nineteen "novices" made
solemn vows.

June - Archbishop Neale died. He was succeeded as Archbishop by
Ambrose Maréchal.

1818 - Father Kohlman, President of Georgetown College, was appointed
spiritual director for the Visitation Convent.

1819 - Father Clorivière assigned as spiritual director of the
Visitation Convent.
A new building for the Benevolent School was erected.

1821 - The chapel was erected.

1822 - The first "Prospectus" for the school was published.

1823 - The Monastery was threatened with dissolution due to a financial
crisis, but was saved by the payment in advance by
Mr. Lasalla for his two daughters and also because
Fr. Clorivière received his money from France.

1824 - The new academy building was erected.

1826 - Death of Father Clorivière.
Father Michael Wheeler, S.S. was appointed the new spiritual
director. He was responsible for many advances in the
school curriculum.

1828 - The Sisters of the Visitation were incorporated, along with the
Sisters of Charity of Saint Joseph, by an act of
Congress.
President John Quincy Adams presided at the closing ceremonies
for the school year.
Father Wheeler sailed for Europe.

1829 - August. Father Wheeler returned from Europe with three
Visitation nuns (two French and one Swiss).
A new addition to the dormitory building was erected.

1831 - Father Wheeler was relieved of his duties due to ill health.

1832 - The first establishment from Georgetown was made at Mobile, Ala.,
led by Mother Madeleine Augustine d'Arreger (Swiss);
four sisters went with her and five more were sent the
following year when Mother Madeleine returned to
Fribourg.

1833 - A monastery and school were established at Kaskaskia, Illinois,
at the suggestion of Bishop Rosati of St. Louis. Eight
sisters, including Mother Mary Agnes Brent and Sister
Mary Austin Barber, and one postulant, the daughter of
Sister Mary Austin, began this foundation.

1844 - At the time of the erection of the diocese of Chicago, six sisters, including Mother Mary Agnes Brent, went to St.
Louis, at the request of Bishop Peter R. Kenrick, the co-
adjutor of St. Louis. In June, the Kaskaskia building
was washed out by the flood. The sisters and students
were rescued; the sisters joined the earlier group who
had gone to St. Louis and began the Academy in that city.

262

1837 - The monastery at Baltimore was founded.

1846 - The monastery at Frederick was founded. The school had previously been under the direction of the Sisters of Charity.

1848 - A monastery at Philadelphia was founded, but it was found necessary to close it again in 1852.

1850 - Sisters from Baltimore, Frederick and Georgetown, began the foundation in Washington. They took the flourishing Academy of the Sisters of Charity which they relinquished in order to comply with the practice of the French Daughters of Charity.

Emmitsburg, Sisters of Charity

This chronology lists only the most important items - usually only the first establishment in an area or the first establishment involving a new type of work. A few other establishments are included because they also involve other communities at a later date.

1805 - Elizabeth Ann Seton made her profession of faith in St. Peter's Church, Barclay Street, New York.

1808 - Mrs. Seton and her family moved to Baltimore where she established a school on Paca Street.

1809 - The Sisters of Charity began the foundation of the community and St. Joseph's School in Emmitsburg.

1810 - February. St. Joseph's Free Elementary School was begun - the forerunner of the parochial school system.

May. St. Joseph's Boarding Academy was begun.

1814 - Philadelphia. The first mission of the American Sisters of Charity was established with the opening of St. Joseph's Orphan Asylum under the direction of the Sisters.

1815 - The Sisters took responsibility for the Domestic Department and the Infirmary at Mt. St. Mary's College, Emmitsburg.
(This was transferred to the Sisters of Charity of Nazareth in 1851.)

1817 - Direction of the New York Orphan Asylum (St. Patrick's) was assumed. This was the first mission of the Sisters of Charity in the state of New York.

1821 - January 4. Death of Mother Seton.

July. The Sisters opened St. Mary's Free School and Asylum in Baltimore.

1823 - The Sisters began their first hospital work at the Baltimore Infirmary.

1824 - December. The Sisters arrived to begin St. John's Free School and Asylum in Frederick.

1825 - At the request of Father William Mathews the Sisters opened St. Vincent's Free School and Asylum in Washington.

1828 - Albany. The Sisters opened St. Mary's School and Asylum.

St. Louis. Mullanphy Hospital was opened. This was the first Catholic Hospital in the United States, and the first west of the Mississippi River.

1829 - At the request of Bishop Edward Fenwick, Sisters were sent to take charge of St. Peter's Asylum. (Transferred to the Cincinnati Sisters in 1852).

1830 - St. Peter's School and Asylum was founded in Wilmington, Delaware, the oldest such institution in the state.

October. The first Sisters went to New Orleans at the request of the Lady Managers-Poydras Female Orphan Asylum.

1832 - Alexandria, Va. St. Francis School was opened. (The academy was discontinued in 1837, the free school was retained two years.)

Boston. The Sisters opened St. Aloysius School and Asylum at the request of Bishop Benedict Fenwick.

1832-1833 - Cholera Epidemic. The Sisters gave heroic service, especially in Baltimore, Philadelphia, New York, Albany, Washington and St. Louis.

1834 - The Sisters took over the care of Charity Hospital in New Orleans.

Baltimore. The Sisters began work at the Maryland Hospital (for the insane).

1835 - The Sisters began work at St. Paul's Asylum and School (both Pay and Free School) in Pittsburgh. (In 1845, these were transferred to the Sisters of Mercy whom Bishop O'Connor had introduced into the Pay School.)

1838 - The Sisters began work at St. Mary's School in Vincennes, Indiana, which was transferred from the Sisters of Charity of Nazareth. In 1843, it was transferred to the Sisters of Providence.

1840 - Baltimore. The Sisters withdrew from the Maryland Hospital and
            opened Mt. St. Vincent which was later called Mt. Hope.

1841 - May. Motherhouse Chapel consecrated.

        December. The Sisters took over the direction of St. Mary's Asyl
            and School in Mobile, Alabama.

1845 - January 1. Opened St. Vincent's Asylum and School in
            Donaldsville, La. A Novitiate was connected with
            this institution between 1845 and 1850.

1846 - About 30 Sisters elected to remain in New York with Bishop Hughes
            and form the nucleus of a new community when the de-
            mands of Bishop Hughes and those of the superiors at
            Emmitsburg became irreconcilable.

1848 - The Sisters opened St. John's Infirmary (changed to St. Mary's
            Hospital in 1858) at the request of Bishop John M.
            Henni, Milwaukee, Wisconsin.

1849 - The Sisters opened a school for free colored girls in Mobile, Ala

1850 - The union with the original foundation of the Daughters of Charit
            of St. Vincent de Paul, Paris, was formally consummated.

Loretto, Kentucky

1805 - Father Charles Nerinckx, a Belgian refugee, arrived in Kentucky.

1812 - April 25. The first three postulants were received as novices
            by Fr. Nerinckx.

        June. The sixth member became a novice. They held their first
            regular election; Sr. Ann Rhodes, the youngest member,
            was elected superior. The community was given the Rule
            written by Fr. Nerinckx.

        December 11. Mother Ann Rhodes died of consumption. She was the
            first to make perpetual vows, doing so three days before
            her death.
            Shortly after Mother Ann's death, Mother Mary Rhodes, the
            real foundress, was chosen superior and remained such for
            ten years.

1813 - August 15. The five sisters made perpetual vows (no temporary vo
            were made before 1829.)

1815 - Fr. Nerinckx left for Europe. There were 14 members at the time a
            shortly afterwards ten more were added.

1816 - The first foundation was established by Bishop Flaget at Calvary,

Ky. It was a boarding and day school.
The Rule written by Fr. Nerinckx was commended by the Holy See.

.818 - A school was established at Gethsemani (the present site of the
Cistercian Monastery).

.820 - Fr. Nerinckx had the Rule printed in London.
Teacher training had become well established at the Motherhouse.

.823 - The first foundation outside Kentucky, at Bethlehem, Perry Co.,
Missouri, was established.

.824 - Bishop Flaget gave the sisters St. Stephen Farm in exchange for
their property of Mt. St. Mary's where a school for boys
had been begun.
Fr. Nerinckx left Kentucky for Missouri because of differences
with Bishop Flaget.

August 12. Fr. Nerinckx died in Missouri.
Rev. Guy I. Chabrat was appointed superior of the Sisters
by Bishop Flaget.

November. The motherhouse was moved to St. Stephens.

1825 - Three sisters were sent from Missouri to Lafourche, Louisiana.

1826 - The new convent and chapel of Loretto were blessed.
The changes in the Rule required by Rome were made (e.g. the adoption of the Rule of St. Augustine)

1827 - Bishop Rosati visited Lafourche and recognized the difficulties due
to the language problem. He would have the sisters join
the Society of the Sacred Heart.

1829 - Act of Incorporation by Kentucky Legislature.

1834 - Chabrat was consecrated as coadjutor Bishop of Bardstown.

1835 - A new Academy building was erected. In less than three years 98
pupils were studying there.

1840 - The Rule was revised by Father Timon, C.M. at the direction of
Bishop Flaget.

1841 - The sisters founded a mission at Little Rock, Arkansas (closed
about 1843).
Father Fouche, S.J. wrote a Rule at the request of Mother Isabella
Clarke. (There was only one election under this Rule.)

1844 - The new Rule was promulgated to the community. The novitiate in
Missouri was abolished.

1847 - Four sisters left St. Louis for the Osage Indian mission in Kansas.

Loretto Academy in Florissant, Missouri was opened.

1849 - Bishop Martin J. Spalding changed the Government, Part II of the
       Constitution. This remained in force until 1896.
       There was no printed Rule between 1820 and 1896.

Nazareth, Kentucky

1812 - November. The first two members placed themselves under the dire
       tion of Father David at St. Thomas, Kentucky.

1813 - June 2. The community chose the name of Sisters of Charity of
       Nazareth. They elected their first officers - a Mother
       Superior, an assistant, and a Procurator.

1814 - The sisters, now seven, adopted a distinctive habit.

1816 - February 2. The first four sisters were allowed to make first vo

1819 - The first establishment, Bethlehem Academy in Bardstown, was
       founded.

1822 - The sisters purchased their own property and moved the entire
       community and students.

1824 - The first chapel was built at Nazareth.
       The first sisters were sent out of the diocese to Vincennes,
       Indiana (closed 1838). Sisters of Charity from
       Emmitsburg took over the school.

1826 - The sisters nursed victims of a malignant fever in Vincennes and
       Sr. Harriet Gardiner became a victim.

1829 - An Act of Incorporation of the Sisters of Charity of Nazareth and
       the Sisters of Loretto was passed by the Kentucky
       Legislature.

1832 - St. Vincent Orphanage was founded in Louisville.
       The sisters nursed cholera victims in Kentucky.

1833 - The sisters again nursed victims of the cholera epidemic. This
       year three sisters and two pupils died of the disease.
       Many sisters were weakened for months afterwards as a
       result of the epidemic.

1834 - The sisters were withdrawn for the first time from Indiana; they
       returned in 1835.

1836 - St. Joseph's Infirmary was opened in Louisville.

1841 - The Sisters respectfully, but firmly, opposed Bishop Flaget's
       suggestions for change in their community.

1842 - The sisters founded St. Mary's Academy in Nashville, Tennessee.

1845 - The first record of a mental patient being cared for at the Infirmary in Louisville, is found under this date.

1846 - The sisters nursed the victims of the smallpox epidemic in Nashville.

1848 - St. John's Hospital in Nashville, was founded.
---The Sisters of Charity of Nazareth withdrew their sisters from the two establishments in Nashville, in 1851. Several remained and formed the nucleus from which the Sisters of Charity of Leavenworth, Kansas developed.

Dominicans, St. Catharine, Kentucky

1805 - Father Edward Fenwick and two companions established the Dominican Order in the United States at St. Rose, Washington Co., Kentucky.

1822 - February 28. Father Thomas Wilson, O.P. appealed to the young ladies of the congregation to form a religious community and promote Catholic education.

April 8. The community was established in Washington Co., Ky. The permanent site of St. Magdalen's Convent was land on Cartwright's Creek with a cabin and a still-house which was given to the community by Mr. Sansbury who had three daughters in the new community.

1823 - St. Magdalen's School was opened.

1825 - By this time a few "colored servants" had been brought by those entering the novitiate, thus relieving the sisters of the hard labor.

1828 - The new building was completed and opened with increased patronage.

1829 - Father Raphael Muños, O.P., a Spanish Dominican, was named prior at St. Rose. From the beginning he was opposed to the existence of the sisters community. He was determined they should disband and liquidate their debt by selling the property. The sisters refused; their community had been approved by the Holy See.

1830 - The Sisters were experiencing great poverty. Rev. Stephen Montgomery was appointed prior of St. Rose. He had faith in the Sisters and convinced their creditors that the debt would be paid.
The first foundation was made at St. Mary, Somerset, Ohio.

1833 - Conditions had improved and the Sisters were able to bring the

Academy standard of living up to that required of
Academies of that time.

A school for boys under the age of 12 was opened with about 25
pupils.

The Sisters themselves not only nursed the cholera victims in the
area, but induced other women to associate themselves
with the sisters for this work.

1839 - December 19. The Institution was chartered as the "Literary
Institution of St. Magdalen."

1847 - June. The cornerstone of the new Gothic chapel was laid. It's
design was based on that of the chapels of Dominican
nuns in Europe and, therefore, had an enclosed choir
area for the sisters.

1848 - The Sisters petitioned Pope Pius IX for the favor of making solemn
profession, but without the obligations of reciting the
Divine Office and the enclosure.

1851 - The name of the Academy was changed from St. Magdalen to St.
Catharine and the Act of Incorporation was amended to
read the "Literary Society of St. Catherine of Sienna."

Oblates of Providence, Baltimore

ca. 1817 - Elizabeth Lange, the Cuban born daughter of San Domingan refugees, came to the United States and eventually
settled in Baltimore.

Elizabeth and a friend, Marie Balas, offered a free education to
black children in Elizabeth's home for about ten years.
The project was supported by money left to Elizabeth by
her father.

1828 - Father Joubert, S.S. received the approval of Archbishop Whitfield
to found a congregation of colored women to provide for
the education of the black children.

June 13. The first four postulants went to live in a rented house
and began their work of teaching.

1829 - June 5. Archbishop Whitfield approved the Constitution of the
Oblate Sisters of Providence which had been drawn up by
Fr. Joubert.

July 2. The four novices pronounced their vows. Sister Mary
Lange, Mary Frances Balas, Mary Rose Boegue, and Marie
Therese Duchemin.

1831 - October 2. The community was officially approved by Pope Gregory
XVI. The news was received in Baltimore in March, 1832.

269

1832 - Cholera Epidemic. Trustees of the Baltimore Bureau of the Poor
       requested the aid of the sisters in the almshouse hospital.
       Sr. Anthony Duchemin nursed the Archbishop and his
       housekeeper and then succumbed herself.

1839 - The Oblates were threatened by the mob that assembled after hearing
       of Sister Isabella's "escape" from the Carmelites.

1841 - June 24. Sr. Marie Therese Duchemin was elected Superior.

1843 - November 5. Death of Father Joubert.

1844 - Mother Marie Therese Duchemin proposed a new constitution. It was
       presented to the community in December by Father Deluol.

       December. Archbishop Eccleston presided over a general election.
       Sister Louise Noel was elected Superior and Sr. Marie
       Therese became the assistant.

1845 - September 9. Mother Marie Therese departed from the community.
       She and Sister Ann Constance went to Monroe, Michigan,
       where they founded the Immaculate Heart Sisters under
       the direction of Father Gillet, C.SS.R.

       Father John Neuman, C.SS.R. sent Father Smulders, C.SS.R. to
       preach a retreat to the Sisters, the first time in
       three years.

1847 - October. The situation was desparate. Father Anwander, C.SS.R.
       went to Archbishop Eccleston with the full support of
       his superior, Fr. Neuman, and begged permission to
       attend the Oblates. After the permission was given
       he begged from door to door and encouraged parents to
       send their children to the school.

1849 - The first new members since 1844 joined the Oblates of Providence.

1850 - Archbishop Eccleston confirmed a large class of children and con-
       verts. He expressed his approval of the work of the
       Sisters and his friendship for Father Anwander.

Our Lady of Mercy, Charleston

1829 - November. The first four young women arrived in Charleston, with
       Bishop England, who met them in Baltimore.

       December. The young women were established in a house on Friend
       Street, and became known as Sisters of Our Lady of Mercy.

1830 - January. They opened a school with six pupils. Sister Martha was
       assigned to supervise the household concerns of the
       diocese.

1831 - January 9. The first four sisters pronounced annual vows for the
       first time.

      Spring. A larger house was rented for the sisters which permitted
       them to accept more boarders and orphans.

1832 - Five additional members pronounced vows, including Julia Datty -
       Sister Benedicta - who was a refugee from the West Indies
       and an experienced teacher.

1833 - Father Byrne, the ecclesiastical superior, appointed Sr. Benedicta
       Datty as superior in compliance with the unanimous wishes
       of the community. The character of the school changed and
       became more refined thus leading to the possibility of
       supporting more orphans.

1834 - Bishop England returned from a trip to Europe and found a general
       state of deterioration in the diocese which had also
       affected the sisters.

1835 - February to March. Bishop England interviewed everyone in the
       convent. He drew up a new code of rules and promised a
       constitution at a later date.

      Summer. Bishop England opened a school for free colored children.
       Two sisters taught the girls. The school was closed by
       August due to community pressures.

      Autumn. The Sisters of Our Lady of Mercy, as well as the Ursulines
       were incorporated by the State for a period of 14 years.

1836 - August to November. The sisters nursed victims of the cholera
       epidemic. Sr. Benedicta Datty, the superior, was a
       victim.

1837 - Bishop England turned over the Cathedral choir to the Ursulines and
       forbade the Sisters of Our Lady of Mercy to teach French
       and Music.

1838 - Bishop England founded the Brotherhood of San Marino (a Catholic
       Benevolent Society) and then rented and converted a
       house on Queen Street as a hospital for the Society.
       He appointed Sr. Aloysius McKenna as superior of the
       hospital and two other sisters assisted her.
       (Closed 1841)

1839 - Three sisters were sent to Augusta, Georgia, to nurse the victims
       of the yellow fever epidemic.

1841 - The school for free colored children opened with 70 pupils. This
       time there was no popular protest.

1842 - Bishop England died. The See of Charleston remained vacant for two years. During 1842 and 1843, the Sisters had neither a retreat nor the privilege of renewing vows.

1843 - Ignatius Reynolds was appointed Bishop of Charleston, December 15.

1844 - Ascension Thursday. Those previously professed renewed their vows and five new sisters made first vows.
Bishop Reynolds called the Sisters together to <u>elect</u> their own community officers according to the rules and constitution he had drawn up.

May 20. Bishop Reynolds directed the Sisters to discontinue the boy's school and remove the colored school from the Motherhouse grounds.

1845 - Bishop Reynolds informed the Sisters they were well enough organized to send six Sisters to open a branch establishment in Savannah, Georgia.

1846 - December. Mother Vincent wrote from Savannah about a proposed separation. Such a move was provided for in the constitutions so arrangements were made.

1847 - The Ursuline Sisters closed their Academy and withdrew from the diocese in June.
Bishop Reynolds and the clergy had, therefore, voted in May to give further support to the Sisters of Our Lady of Mercy to fill the vacancy, i.e. broaden the curriculum at their Academy.

1848 - May. The decision was made to close the colored school.

November. The orphans were separated from the Free School.

APPENDIX 2

COURSES OF STUDY

Carmelite Sisters' Academy

The course of study for this day school for girls that was opened in
October 1831 in Baltimore is given as it appeared on the Academy's
Prospectus as found in the archives of the Baltimore Carmel. The entries
in the various Catholic Almanacs published during the ten years of the
school's existence indicate no significant change was inaugurated during that period.

The Sisters having charge of this institution propose a course
of instruction which will comprise Orthography, Reading, Writing,
Arithmetic, Book-Keeping, Grammar, English Composition, Geography,
the use of Maps and Globes, Sacred History, Ancient and Modern
History, Chronology, Mythology, Botany, Rhetoric, Natural Philosophy, Astronomy, French, Vocal and Instrumental Music, Drawing
and Painting in water colors, Painting on Velvet in oil colors,
Plain and Ornamental Needle Work, Embroidery in gold and silver,
Tapestry, Lace Work, Bead Work, &c.

Young Ladies' Academy

at

The Convent of the Visitation

The oldest extant prospectus, about 1822, (found in the convent archives
and also reprinted in the limited edition, 1895, of A Story of Courage
by George Parson Lathrop and Rose Hawthorne Lathrop) gives the following
information.

The common branches of Education taught in this institution, are
READING, WRITING, ARITHMETIC, ENGLISH GRAMMAR and COMPOSITION,
GEOGRAPHY, with the use of Maps and Globes, ELEMENTS OF HISTORY,
plain and ornamental NEEDLE WORK.

. . . .

The FRENCH LANGUAGE, DRAWING, and MUSIC, form separate charges:
. . .

The 1827 Prospectus adds the following subjects which had been taught
during the last term:

Sacred History, Profane History, ancient and modern; Chronology,
Mythology and Rhetoric--French, Music on the Piano Forte and Harp;

272

Dancing, Drawing and Painting; . . . Tapestry, Lace-work, or Figuring on Bobinet, and Bead-work, &c.

To this course of study was to be gradually added:

Algebra, Versification and Poetic Composition, Female Elocution, Popular Astronomy, with the assistance of the newly invented Geocyclic of Delamarche, Logic, Ethics, Metaphysics, Natural Philosophy in its various branches, Anthology, the Spanish, Italian and Latin Languages, if required, Vocal Music, the Guitar, and Painting on Velvet.

As parents have frequently expressed a wish that their daughters should be acquainted with mantua-work, to compose dress in its various forms, the knowledge and practice of this useful branch of female economy, will, if required, be taught by persons of experience.

Domestic Economy, comprising the various exercises in Pastry and the Culinary art, Laundry, Pantry, and Dairy Inspection, &c. as conducted at the Academy of St. Denis Banlieue de Paris, will be an article which will occupy considerable attention in the enlarged system of education now laid before the public.

St. Joseph's Academy

Emmitsburg

The prospectus as printed in the 1822 Laity's Directory (pp. 99-100) gives the following course of study.

The English, and if required, the French language, reading, orthography, writing, history, geography, arithmetic, music, drawing, painting, embroidery, plain and fancy work.
. . . .

The prospectus published in the 1833 Catholic Almanac (pp. 87-89) has the following, expanded course.

The course of instruction embraces the English, French, and Spanish languages, Orthography, Grammar, Composition, Writing, Practical and Rational Arithmetic, Book-keeping, Geography, History, Moral and Natural Philosophy, Astronomy, Chemistry, Music, Drawing, Painting on Velvet, Embroidery, Plain and Fancy Needle-Work. . . .

Female School of Loretto (Kentucky)

According to a compilation of information about Lorettine Academies before 1850 by Sister M. Matilda, and filed as Mss. 1 in the Loretto Motherhouse Archives, the sisters conducted only primary schools before 1826. In these schools only reading, writing, orthography and arithmetic were taught.

"In 1826, the school was opened on a new basis. Not only grammar,

geography, astronomy, drawing, painting, every kind of needlework were taught, but other studies were added as called for."
The prospectus as it appeared in the United States Catholic Miscellany, January 12, 1828, and several weeks thereafter gave the following courses of study:
3. The branches actually taught in this Institution are, Reading, Writing, Arithmetic; English, Grammar, Geography, with the use of Maps and Globes; plain Sewing, Marking, Needle-work, Embroidery, Drawing and Painting: Rhetorick; including composition and Natural Philosophy.
By 1836 the prospectus that was published in the Catholic Almanac (p. 138) gave the following course of study.
Reading, Writing, Arithmetic, English Grammar, Geography with the use of Maps and Globes, History, Ancient and Modern, with Chronology and Mythology, Rhetoric and Composition, Botany, Optics and the Elements of Mechanics, Hydrostatics and Astronomy. Chemistry and Natural Philosophy, the French Language, Needle work, plain and fancy, Marking, Lace and Bead work, Drawing and Painting in water colors, Crayon Drawing, Painting on Satin and Velvet. Music, Vocal and on the Piano Forte.
On page 140 the following paragraph concludes the prospectus:
The conductors of the academy have from M. Peterson, Professor of Music, certificates of the ability of their professors of Music, and of the proficiency of their pupils which may be seen in the Bardstown and Louisville papers.
The 1849 Catholic Almanac has information concerning instruction on the guitar and the harp as well as the piano forte; by that time the academy was also offering instruction in the Spanish language and dancing

Female School of Nazareth (Kentucky)

The prospectus for this academy first appeared in the United States Catholic Miscellany, 13 October 1827. The same prospectus was reprinted several times in October 1828 as well. The following information is given regarding the course of study:
. . . The school is conducted on principles similar to those of St. Joseph's College [whose prospectus is on the same page] . . . .
. . . .
The branches taught are:
Reading, Writing, Arithmetic, English Grammar, Geography (with the use of Globes), History, Rhetoric, Botany, Natural Philosophy, including the principles of Astronomy; Opticks, Chemistry, &c.; Plain Sewing, Marking, Needle Work, Drawing, Painting, Music, and the French Language. The last branch, to-wit, (the French Language) is taught with the greatest correctness, both as to grammar and pronunciation; there being actually in the institution several French sisters, besides others, who understand and speak the language very correctly. A course of lectures on Rhetoric and Philosophy (Natural and Moral,) shall be annually given by the Professor of St. Joseph's College. Lessons and exercises in polite English Literature will also be occasionally given.

In noting the various charges the prospectus states that there is an extra charge for Music and the use of Pianos ($24. per annum). There is no change in the prospectus as it is printed in the Catholic Almanac in 1833. The Motherhouse archives, however, contain two articles of agreement between Mrs. Blaique and Frances Gardiner, Mother Superior of Nazareth. The first is undated, but the second--with some variations--bears the date 7 March 1835 (cf. OLB-I:65-66 or DLB-I:44-45). In the first agreement it states: ". . . said Mrs. Blaique binds herself to teach the art of dancing, as also elegance of carriage and deportment to the young ladies of Nazareth at the rate of $10.00 per quarter for each pupil; . . ."

Female Academy of St. Magdalen's

Near Springfield, Kentucky

The name of this academy was changed to St. Catharine's in 1851. The first prospectus for this academy that was printed in a directory was found in 1838, The Metropolitan Catholic Almanac, and Laity's Directory, pp. 126-27. (It is dated: "St. Magdalen's Convent, Oct. 1835.") The course of study was given as:
   . . . Orthography, Reading, Writing, Arithmetick, English Grammar, Geography, with Maps and Globes--Philosophy, Rhetoric and English Composition--Music, Drawing and Painting, Plain and Ornamental Needlework--Embroidery, Beadwork, &c.
. . . .
The charges included a special charge for "Music and the use of Piano" ($20. per annum).

In 1834 the sisters who had left Kentucky for Somerset, Ohio as a result, at least partially, of the financial crisis of the sisters in Kentucky included French Language as part of their prospectus. They probably had taught it prior to this time in Kentucky. By 1849 the academy in Kentucky was offering instruction in French as well as the following additions to the 1838 entry: Astronomy, Chemistry, Botany, Fancy Chenelle Work and Wax Work and Music on the Guitar (cf. Catholic Almanac, p. 204).

School for Coloured Girls (Baltimore)

The Catholic Almanac, 1834, has the following entry in reference to the course of study:
   Besides the care bestowed in their religious education, girls of colour are taught English, French, Cyphering and Writing, Sewing in all its branches, Embroidery, Washing and Ironing.
Later entries have only a minimum entry. Some of the other well established academies did little more so it is difficult to assess what effect the growing fear of rebellion being incited by free, and educated, blacks may have had. In consideration of all the negative forces that the sisters had to face during the 1830's and 1840's it seems remarkable that the school continued to be listed in the annual almanacs.

<u>Female Academy of the</u>

<u>Sisters of Our Lady of Mercy</u>

<u>Charleston, South Carolina</u>

The first entry for this academy was found in the 1834 edition of the <u>Catholic Almanac</u> (pp. 118-119). The course of studies included the following subjects: Spelling, Reading, Writing, Arithmetic, English Grammar, Geography with the use of Maps and Globes, History, Plain Sewing Marking and Needle Work. French was available as an additional course.

By 1848 the academy offered the following courses: Orthography, Reading, Writing, Arithmetic, Grammar, Geography, History, Rhetoric, Composition, &c. &c. For additional charges the following courses were available: music on the piano and guitar, the French language "(taught at this time by a French gentleman,)" Painting and Drawing, Ornamental Needlework and Embroidery and Dancing which was taught only during the winter season. Plain sewing and Marking were taught to all students boarding at the institution if their parents wished it.

APPENDIX 3

SCHOOL FOR FREE NEGROES

CHARLESTON, 1835

Campbell's "Bishop England's Sisterhood: 1829-1929," gives an account of this brief attempt to educate free negroes in 1835. She names
the two sisters who taught in the school: Sister M. Martha (O'Gorman)
and Sister M. Vincent (Mahony). Because this history gave every evidence
of careful research and this work was one specifically named by Bishop
England for these sisters I did not look for further verification when
doing research in Charleston (1977). I was surprised, however, when
in order to clarify some details for the historical sketch of the community I checked histories of the Ursuline Sisters and found an Ursuline
history that claimed the Ursuline Sisters had been the teachers for the
free negro girls in this school. The book was old, and definitely meant
for edification; the information did not seem worth noting at the time.
A short time later, however, I found that Ewens in her work, The Role of
the Nun in Nineteenth Century America, (p. 101) wrote: "A few communities, the Josephites of St. Louis and the Charleston Ursulines for
example, taught Negroes in a separate school or after school hours. . . .
The Ursulines of Charleston had to stop their instruction of Negro
children because it was against the law." The exact source for including the Ursuline sisters in this group is not clear from the footnote.
This seemed to indicate that further verification of the matter was
needed. I found that Guilday, The Life and Times of John England, Vol. II,
also says that the Ursuline Sisters taught the free negroes in 1835.
The only reference applicable to this information is Guilday's quotation
of Bishop England's address to the Fourteenth South Carolina Convention
in which he says that the Ursulines have given religious instruction to
females of every colour (cf. pp. 151-156; 159).

Failing to find adequate documentation to clarify the point, I
contacted the archivist for the Sisters of Charity of Our Lady of Mercy
in Charleston. The sister-archivist replied by telephone, 28 April 1980.
She had contacted Sister M. Anne Francis Campbell, the author of the
history of the first one hundred years. She said the principal source
for the history of the school was the Charleston Courier, 11 August 1835.
Other information was gleaned from informal accounts that have survived.
It would seem that Campbell's study is correct in the matter of the school
for free negroes. Both the Ursulines and the Sisters of Our Lady of
Mercy undoubtedly gave religious instructions to negro girls whether
slave or free.

There is no question about which community, the Ursulines or the
Sisters of Our Lady of Mercy, conducted the school for free negroes when
it was reopened in 1841 and continued until 1848. There are sufficient
references to this school in the council minutes of the Sisters of Our
Lady of Mercy to verify responsibility for staffing this school.

APPENDIX 4

Government of the Baltimore Infirmary

Re: Sisters of Charity

Source: Archives of the Sisters of Charity of Nazareth. OLB-II:11
(DLB-I:21-22).

Letter of Rev. A. J. Elder, Baltimore to Bishop Flaget, Bardstown, Kentuck

St. Mary's College, Baltimore
October 29th, 1829

Rt. Rev^d & Dr. Sir:

Agreeably to promise I have to inform you that I have sent all your
boxes to Wheeling, and that inclosed in one of your boxes is a small one
for Mr. Morehieser's daughter, who is at Nazareth.

The hurry of business prevented me from giving you the information
you asked for with regard to the Infirmary of the City. I will give you a
hasty account of its government, etc.

The Legislature placed it under the direction of a Committee of
twelve persons (or fifteen, who are called trustees of the University).
The Governor of the State for the time being is President--Ex Officio,
the other members are taken principally from the city, yet one or two
have been taken from Frederick Town. The same Board of Trustees manage
the affairs of the University, appoint the Professors, etc. and have
power to fill their own board, when any one resigns or dies. They are
not elected but have been appointed by the Legislature and to the Legislature they have to render an annual account of their proceedings, the
Board of Trustees appointed a special Committee, out of their own body,
to attend to the affairs of the Infirmary. Mr. Etting, a Jew, is at the
head and Chairman of the committee. He purchases all the provisions and
pays all the expenses of the house- to the Sisters they pay $42 per year
for each- the Sisters pay all their own traveling expenses, etc. this
money is sent to the Mother House from whence the Sisters receive all
their clothes, etc. This is the case with all the branch houses established by the Community, except they do not receive so much for services,
as in the different schools. They do not wear and tear half as much
clothes as laboring amongst the sick.

In the Infirmary there are 3 medical students, always one who is
nearly done his studies, these young men board in the neighboring house,
but they study and lodge in the Infirmary, and must be in at nine o'clock
unless absent, attending a lecture, etc. and in this case, the Sister at
the head of the establishment must be informed thereof, and then she sees

that they have entered before ten o'clock, at which hour the house is locked up; should they not be in at that hour and come later they would have to look out for a night's lodging elsewhere, and in the morning Mr. Etting gives them a lecture; but I assure you the young gentlemen do not expose themselves to be dealt with thus, as they know the advantages to be derived in the Institution; and convinced that nothing disorderly will be tolerated, they are always home from the Lecture in good time. These young gentlemen attend with the attending physician and surgeon every morning, and take down the prescriptions on a slate, and prepare them, they also dress all the sores and attend entirely the men who may have any secret disease, or a sore on any private part of the body. The Sisters dress sore legs and blisters, but they, the Sisters, dress all the wounds of the women, unless it may be from an operation in which case the surgeon dresses the wound himself, attended by one of the students. The Sisters administer all the medicine. They have two hired men to attend to taking the men up, etc. The young gentlemen received nothing for their attention in the house, their instruction is of more importance. They have two rooms and a fine library, and it is very difficult to get there to study, as Mr. Etting is very choice in his selections. The Professors of the University attend daily by turn, one surgeon and one physician attend for three months and then change. They receive nothing <u>directly</u> for their attendance, but the Infirmary draws many students here to attend lectures, and in this way the professors are paid by selling their tickets to more students. Any student who is attending the lectures in the university, by paying $5.00 receives a card of admittance to all operations, etc. that takes place in the infirmary during the session, every year Mr. Etting sells from $150 to $250 worth of tickets, the others, who do not take the tickets, are not admitted, excepting always the three resident students who buy no ticket, but attend all operations, etc. Sometimes the resident student asks leave of absence from Mr. Etting and proposes a friend to take his place in the infirmary. This is always done in writing; the request and the granting, both recorded in the minutes, kept in the infirmary. Sometimes such students have conducted themselves in so very becoming a manner that to them Mr. Etting sends a free card.

The Sisters chose their own physician and he alone attends them when sick, unless another be invited to attend. The resident students never enter the parlour of the Sisters, they call the Sister out to tell her anything, that the professor wants, standing in the passage. The Sisters do not enter their rooms except when they are gone to take breakfast, their beds are made and their rooms cleaned. Mr. Etting receives all the money. The house more than supports itself and has lately enlarged its walks.

Yours Afftly,
A. J. Elder

P.S. Such sick persons pay $3.00 per week--everything is included--washing also. And for private rooms, $5.00 per week. Two women are hired to wash and one to cook.

APPENDIX 5

Articles of Agreement

Sisters of Charity of St. Joseph

Emmitsburg, Maryland

An Agreement between Rev. John Dubois and the Managers of St. Joseph's
Society, Philadelphia, [This is the prototype of all Articles of
Agreement during this period.]

Source: Archives of St. Joseph Central House. Letter Book II, "Foundation

An Agreement entered into between the Superior General of the Sisters of
St. Joseph of Emmitsburg Maryland, in their name and in their behalf. And
the Managers of the Roman Catholic Society of St. Joseph's for Educating a
Maintaining poor Orphan Children in Phila.

1st   The Revd John DuBois Superior General of the Sisters of Charity of St
Joseph's Engages to Supply four Sisters, who shall undertake the managemen
of the Orphan House in Phila to attend to the economy of the house, the
care of the children, their schooling and Religious instructions.

2nd   All donations received by the Sisters, to be accounted for by them to
the Managers of St. Joseph's Society, who have the exclusive direction of
the funds belonging to that Institution.

3rd   No children to be admitted into the Asylum, other than by the Manager
whose duty it shall be from time to time to consult the head Sister thereu

4th   The Managers hereby engage to support the house, Supplying from time
to time, any monies that may be wanted, should the donations prove insufficient for that purpose.

5th   Flour and wood will be provided for by the managers, all articles of
Clothing by the Ladies Society, established for that purpose. Groceries
generally to be purchased by the Sisters, at the same time leaving it
optional with the head Sister to purchase those articles themselves or
to have them bought by the managers.

6th   No other duties or charges shall be imposed on the Sisters without
the consent of the Central government, the managers being desirous that
they shall attend to the orphans exclusively.

7th   The Regulations and management of the house to be left to the dis-
cretion of the Sisters, in whom the managers repose intire [sic] confidence and with whose rules and customs they will not interfere.

8th The managers by their appointment feel themselves in duty bound to attend to the wants of the Children and of course reserve to themselves, the right to visit the house at proper hours and season, it being understood that they are not to interfere or interrupt the Sisters in their religious exercises, these visits to be confined to the school and lower part of the house.

9th The Ladies who have undertaken to provide for and furnish the Asylum with clothing and other necessaries are to have the privilege of visiting every part of the house. It being nevertheless understood that they shall appoint monthly or quarterly Committees for that purpose—consisting of at least two members, the visits to be at such hours as not to interfere with the Sisters in their religious duties. The Ladies at their quarterly meetings are to examine the children when small premiums will be distributed by them to the most deserving.

10th Strangers visiting the Asylum may be introduced to all parts of the house, for the first time, either by one or more of the managers, or by the Sisters if those visits are repeated they can only be received in the parlour, the same privilege is allowed also to the person or persons who may introduce said managers for the first time, altho' themselves may have repeated the visits frequently.

11th The Sisters are to board at the Asylum conformable to the Simplicity of their rules.

12th The Ladies will pay to the head Sister thirty six dollars per annum for each Sister employed in the Asylum, for their clothing and furnish them with shoes, but in case of their not so doing - the managers hereby engage to do the same.

13th The travelling expenses of the Sisters, coming to or going from Phila, shall be paid by the managers when the health of any one of the Sisters or any reasonable cause, may be such as to require her removal to Emmitsburg and of course another will have to supply her place, whose expenses will also be borne. In case of the decease of any one of the Sisters at the Asylum - the managers are to pay the funeral expences. All removals of the Sisters other than the foregoing to be paid for by the Central Government.

        In confirmation whereof the said parties have hereunto set their hands and Seals this twenty eighth day of July one Thousand Eight-hundred and twenty.

                            John Dubois, Superior of the Sisters of
                                    Charity of St. Joseph's
Signed   Joseph Synder Secretary to the Board of
                                    Managers of St. Joseph's Society

On the reverse side of the Articles of Agreement

      At a meeting of the managers of St. Joseph's Society on the 18th of April 1816. The following Resolution passes unanimously. That no child be admitted into the Orphan house, under three years of age. Nor more than Seven years old, nor that any child wanting mental intellects or one who is a cripple shall be admitted into said house. Provided nevertheless, it be understood that children under three years of age be still objects of the care of the Society.

    Madam
                        I have been requested to furnish you with the above resolution.

                        with sentiments of due respect
                        I remain yours
                        Joseph Synder
                        Secty to the Managers

                        Mr. Ashley told me - when they would be obliged to take infants - they would be placed under nurses for us to overlook - until they would be three years old.

The Articles of Agreement with the New York Asylum, 1821 (Letter Book, II:) provides for the separation of girls and boys except in classes as it would be too inconvenient to teach them separately. It also contains articles relative to the sisters living at the Asylum but teaching in a pay school on adjoining property.

The Articles of Agreement with St. Mary's, Philadelphia, 9 February 1833, provides for an annual stipend of $50. per sister.

The Articles of Agreement with the governing boards of hospital facilities are also based on those made with St. Joseph's Society in Philadelphia but do have important modifications to fit the specific needs of a hospital. The following are the most important changes as found in the Articles of Agreement with the managers of the <u>Infirmary</u> in Baltim Letter Book, II:40.

2dly as for the management of the temporalities relating to the Infirmary the Said Sisters will be altogether under the authority and controul of the managers of Said Institution, and of the Physicians who attend it, to whom they will pay implicit odebience for the same objects, so that they will be ready to interrupt their religious Exercises, anticipate or put off the time thereof or even omitt them altogether, if necessary - that being their main and 1st obligation.

3dly the Said Sisters shall have alone the care and management of the interior concerns and Labours of the Said Infirmary, without having any Woman or Girl associated with or employed under them - being ready and willing to fulfill the most menial or disgusting offices for the sake of

him who did not disdain to annihilate himself for us poor Sinners; so
that the service of the Infirmary may be performed with more propriety,
regularity and union, but they will have under them as many servant men,
or hired men as the Service of the Infirmary may require, appointed by
themselves & whom they will be at Liberty to dismiss if they think proper
- the object of those men is to render to the Infirmary such services as
cannot be expected from Women.

6thly if the Sisters should become infirm or sick, in consequence of the
services they should render to the house, they will not be sent way, unless recalled home by the aforesaid Superior General, but they will be
maintained and kept in Said Infirmary with their other Sisters, nursed
and furnished with the necessary medicine, as members of the house: . . .

8thly whereas many of the sick brought to the infirmary, particularly
the blacks, may have ragged, dirty clothes, even full of Vernim, . . .
provision is made for a type of hospital gowns during their stay as well
as the clearning and mending of their own clothes.

12thly ---doors are to be locked at 10:00 p.m.

14thly the Head Sister will render monthly a detailed account of the
money left in her hands for market or other expenses . . .

BIBLIOGRAPHICAL ESSAY

Two important ends towards which this study was directed were to further our knowledge and understanding of the lives of the many women who formed the original communities of women religious in the United States and to enhance or correct the tradition about American women religious as it has come to us in the present generation. Much of the published, secondary material was written before World War II and consists largely of biographies of founders and foundresses or strictly institutional histories of a particular religious community. In order to accomplish my purpose it was necessary to use archival material as much as possible. I found that while there are many regrettable gaps in the records due to such factors as poverty and fatigue in a common situation that did not encourage chronicling events as they happened, fires, and sometimes a lack of appreciation of the value and importance of documents not considered essential, the richness of archival material made it impractical to extend either the research time or the length of this study by examining extant newspapers of the era.

The archives of the various motherhouses (here used to denote the principal house of each of the religious communities before 1850) vary in the number and kind of documents available. This is due, in part, to the manner in which the community grew before 1850. The Sisters of Charity from Emmitsburg who were to be found in almost every area of the United States and were engaged in conducting schools, hospitals, and the care of orphans had need for extensive correspondence not only

284

ith bishop and priests, but with the sisters as well. At the other

nd of the scale were the Carmelites who moved their monastery but did

ot send sisters out to found a new monastery before 1850. Both archives

ave good collections for their early years. The archives of the Arch-

iocese of Baltimore, the collections housed at the University of Notre

ame archives, including the microfilms of the material from the archives

f the Propaganda Fide proved valuable in supplementing motherhouse

rchives. The seven volumes, United States Documents in the Propaganda

ide Archives: A Calendar, compiled by Finbar Kenneally, O.F.M. proved

elpful not only as a guide to the microfilms, but also as a source

hrough which one could gauge whether a particular question or difficulty

as unique to a particular group or time or whether it was common to

any communities and/or for a long period of time. Other archival sources

ere the archives of the archdiocese of Cincinnati and the diocese of

harleston, the National Archives, the Hall of Records in Annapolis,

aryland and the archives of the city of Philadelphia. Secondary sources

ere used to supplement the material gleaned from the archives and as a

ource of comparison.

Some of the religious communities, particularly the three in

entucky, have begun to do some genealogical research concerning the

arly members. In searching beyond the information available within

otherhouse archives I found Ben J. Webb's Centenary of Catholicism in

entucky (1884) the most helpful. I was introduced to the work in the

entucky motherhouses; a librarian at the Maryland Historical Society

ecommended it to me as the best starting point in looking for genea-

ogical information about Maryland Catholic families. Webb researched

he families as carefully as he could. He indicates some of his procedures within his text and a letter--Ben J. Webb, Louisville, Ken-

tucky to Rt. Rev. W. H. Elder, 9 June 1879--which is among the Elder

Pre-Cincinnati Papers in the archives of the Archdiocese of Cincinnati

confirms his efforts. The letter itself is a request for clarification

and additional information regarding the genealogy of the Elder family.

The other genealogical studies of Maryland Catholic families added littl

to the information I had already found in Webb. An important source for

information about all eight communities, their work, and sometimes obit-

uary notices, were the various Catholic Directories or Almanacs publishe

in 1817, 1822, and annually beginning with 1833. At least once, some

information was given about the community itself, and the prospectuses

for the academies were published each year in the later editions.

The most valuable studies in preparation for my own work were

Sister Mary Christina Sullivan's "Some Non-Permanent Foundations of Reli

gious Orders and Congregations of Women in the United States (1739-1850)

published in Historical Records and Studies, Volume XXXI (1940), Ewens'

"The Role of the Nun in Nineteenth-Century America" (1971), and Porter-

field's "Maidens, Missionaries, and Mothers" (1975). Sullivan's article

accounts for the communities omitted here as well as other non-permanent

foundations such as the Visitation convent and academy at Kaskaskia,

Illinois which was abandoned after the property was destroyed by a floo

Ewens' work is a valuable overview based largely on published sources

and concerned with all women religious in nineteenth century America.

There are some misinterpretations of her sources since community archive

were not consulted. Several points where I disagree with her interpre-

tation have been pointed out in the text. These differences are not of

major importance, but they do point out the importance of more studies being made from different viewpoints. There are too many sources and too many communities of women religious to be thoroughly covered in any one study. Porterfield's work underscored the change that took place in the position of women in America from the relative equality in Puritan New England--which was mirrored again and again on the frontier--to the ideal of the woman who remained in her own sphere, nurturing goodness and peace in the home in contrast to the man who dealt with reason and economic competition in the factory or market place. Other recent works in women's studies added further clarification and detail. They all confirm the conclusion that the American woman religious was not an anomaly in the early nineteenth century even though she appeared as such to many of her contemporaries. Because of her Roman Catholicism and the different manner in which she expressed her ideals of womanhood she was suspect to those who did not know her.

Religious history from 1790 to 1850 has many different aspects. General studies such as Wach's Sociology of Religion and Griffin's "Religious Benevolence as Social Control, 1815-1860" (1957) and Banner's critique of his interpretation (1973) helped to keep the larger picture in focus so that my findings were not viewed in isolation. Specific works were consulted as they related to persons or events of importance. One of the best publicized (and probably over publicized) difficulties that Roman Catholics were faced with was Nativism. Contemporary works such as Lyman Beecher's Plea for the West were often inflammatory and much has been made of them by authors such as Billington and Ray while others, for example Duesner, Lannie and Diethorn, and Stritch recounted specific riots. The writings of contemporary European visitors, even Mrs. Trollope and Harriet Martineau of England, were often very favorable toward the growing Catholic Church and its various institutions.

The Catholic Church was not only growing numerically during this period, but it was also beginning to assume the character of a predominantly urban church. Only the Visitandines, the Oblate Sisters, and the Sisters of Our Lady of Mercy were founded in an important city, but by 1850 the Dominican Sisters were the only community which had no sisters in an important urban center. Wade's The Urban Frontier was particularly helpful in evaluating doubtful or apparently contradictory information in the annals of the three religious communities in Kentucky. The Catholic community in Kentucky retained a large proportion of its membership in the rural areas where they prospered by supplying needed agricultural products to the growing cities of Louisville and Lexington. The development of the city and society of Washington, D.C. is most satisfactorily covered by Constance Green's Washington: Village and Capital, 1800-1878 and The Secret City: A History of Race Relations in the Nation' Capital. Together these two works are important for supplying details not accounted for in the sisters' records. This background is essential for an interpretation of data that were found elsewhere. Young's The Washington Community, 1800-1828 was concerned with the relationship of politicians and the local constituency and was, therefore, of little value to me. The three port cities which attracted so many immigrants and in which the Catholic Church was probably the most important institution that commanded their loyalty were Boston, New York and Philadelphi Handlin's Boston's Immigrants, 1790-1865 and Knight's The Plain People of Boston, 1830-1860 were most helpful when taken together since Knight's work is so predominantly quantitative that the social issues, with which the sisters were directly concerned can easily be overlooked. The day-

to-day life of immigrants in New York is portrayed in Robert Ernst's
Immigrant Life in New York City, 1825-1865 while Jay Dolan, The Immigrant Church: New York's Irish and German Catholics, 1815-1865, deline-
ates the development of the Church and its importance in the life of the
immigrants during approximately the same period. Sam Bass Warner, Jr.
in The Private City, Part Two, "The Big City 1830-1860" shows why the
"City of Brotherly Love" could be the scene of such violence as took place
during the Bible riots of 1844. Michael Feldberg's monograph, The Philadelphia Riots of 1844: A Study of Ethnic Conflict, goes even further in
explaining the conditions under which the Irish were living and working
in Philadelphia which made violence there more likely than in New York.
Each of these works point out the poverty, congestion and lack of sani-
tation in the urban areas occupied by recent immigrants. Feldberg points
out, however, that in Philadelphia the Irish had the added disability
of being in several smaller areas and, therefore, were unable to use
political power as the Irish in New York could do. A worthwhile general
study is David Ward's Cities and Immigrants. This is a largely quantitative study but it does not lose sight of social realities. It is not
limited to one city, and therefore, the generalizations may not fit any
city. On the other hand it does provide background for the many urban
centers for which there is no specific study.

Education in the United States is the subject of many books and
articles. The Library of Congress has enough volumes written by the
mid-nineteenth century to warrant a detailed study of that field alone.
One that was of special interest was American Education, Its Principles
and Elements by Edward D. Mansfield. The chapter entitled "The Education of Women" served as a basis for comparing the work of the sisters

with that of Protestants in this field. Three works often referred to by twentieth-century commentators on the first Catholic schools in the United States are Sister Maria Alma's Standard Bearers: The Place of the Catholic Sisterhoods in the Early History of Education . . . until 1850, Burn's The Catholic School System in the United States, and Burns, Kohlbrenner and Peterson's A History of Catholic Education in the United States. These works were published between 1908 and 1937. There is a real need for new studies using sources not available earlier and modern methodology. The Nineteenth Century Education Contribution of the Sister of Charity of Saint Vincent de Paul in Virginia by Sister Mary Agnes Yeakel was most valuable for its presentation of the teacher-training provided to the Sisters of Charity at Emmitsburg.

Social works of the sisters, outside the schools, have very little written about them. Government documents sometimes refer to the works, especially if some subsidy was granted or taxes were exempted. The two most helpful studies were Sister Bernadette Armiger's "The History of the Hospital Work of the Daughters of Charity of Saint Vincent de Paul in the Eastern Province of the United States, 1823-1860" and Rosenberg's The Cholera Years. The latter work was based not only on medical reports but also on a thorough use of contemporary newspapers. Together these two works covered the nursing activities of the sisters that were the first steps in the extensive, present-day involvement of women religious in the health care fields.

Carmelite Monastery

The principal sources for the history of the Carmelite nuns were the records in the monastery archives: Annals, Vow Book, Death

Book, various lists, letters, "Various Items Transcribed from Papers
[newspapers] written out by Sister Stanislaus of the Infant Jesus,"
and several items from the school. In addition, Charles Warren Currier's
Carmel in America: A Centennial History of the Discalced Carmelites in
the United States (1890) is thoroughly done; all the letters that were
printed from the Carmelite archives were printed without alteration,
therefore, it is assumed that letters printed from European archives or
private sources were also faithfully reproduced. At the time the work
was published there were still sisters alive who had known some of the
earliest members. Another important source was The John Carroll Papers,
3 volumes, edited by Thomas O'Brien Hanley, S.J. This collection was
most helpful for the letters Bishop Carroll wrote to persons outside
the community and in which he commented on the life and work of the
Carmelite nuns in America.

Georgetown Visitation

The monastery archives of the Visitation Sisters in Georgetown
have more information than one might suspect from the paucity of pre-
1850 documents. Information on individual members was obtained from
biographical essays recently compiled by several sisters from official
books which have been added to from the beginning and are by now un-
wieldy and never leave the strictly enclosed area where they are kept.
An indispensable source of the earliest history is Archbishop Neale's
letter to the Superior of the Visitation Monastery at Annecy, 6 March
1816. There are no annals from the early years, but there are the lists
requested by Archbishop Maréchal. The archives of the Archdiocese of
Baltimore contain a collection of very informative letters. These are

letters of the sisters, usually the superior, to the Archbishop of Baltimore beginning with the accession of Archbishop Maréchal. Other letters were found among the letters in the collections at the Carmelite Monastery in Baltimore and in the University of Notre Dame Archives.

The principal secondary sources were A Story of Courage: Annals of the Georgetown Convent of the Visitation of the Blessed Virgin Mary from the Manuscript Records by George Parsons Lathrop and Rose Hawthorne Lathrop, and Georgetown Visitation Since 1799 by Eleanore C. Sullivan. The first work was published in 1894. At the present time there are very few primary sources to substantiate this work, but while recognizing that some events may well have been romanticized the Visitation Sisters at Georgetown have also recognized this work as an important source of information for many years. In 1975 the sisters welcomed the appearance of Sullivan's history which was researched with great care. Ms. Sullivan was given all possible help by the sisters at the Georgetown monastery. One of the more interesting early records about the convent and academy is found in Sketches of History, Life and Manners, in the United States by a Traveller (Mrs. Ann Royall) which was published in 1826. The frontspiece is a picture of the Georgetown academy; pages 178-181 are an account of Mrs. Royall's visit. While the work was not used directly for this study it is an indication of the visibility of the academy and the favorable impression the sisters had on non-Catholics. Contemporary newspapers, the Georgetown Directory for the Year 1830, and government documents were also valuable sources of information, particularly about the Young Ladies' Academy.

Sisters of Charity - Emmitsburg

The archives at St. Joseph's Provincial House (Daughters of

harity), Emmitsburg, Maryland, have rich holdings regarding the initial
ears of the community's existence. The sisters have published, for
heir own use, the lives of the early superiors which are chiefly
hronological narratives that utilized the chronicles and letters of the
articular superior's years in office. I found that the major distinc-
ion between the printed form and the originals was that modern spelling,
rammar, and custom were imposed. An example of the latter is that prior
o 1850 the common manner of addressing or speaking about priests was
imply "Mr. N." (addresses and some formal references use "Rev. Mr. N.");
hese references were all changed to "Father N." in the printed form.
n general the printed letters have a more formal quality than the orig-
nal, but the meaning was not changed. When the identity of the recipi-
nt of the letter was too vague to locate the original in a reasonable
ime I used the printed form. Another valuable source for an overview
f the development of these sisters was another privately published work,
809-1959. This is a documented account of the development of Emmits-
urg Province from the time of Mother Seton to 1959. It is arranged
ccording to the terms of office of the highest superior in Emmitsburg,
nd a chronological listing of major events follows each chapter. Again
nformation was found in the John Carroll Papers, the archives of the
arious motherhouses of the other communities in this study, and the
niversity of Notre Dame.

Three biographies of Saint Elizabeth Seton were consulted: Charles
. White, D.D., Life of Mrs. Eliza A. Seton, Foundress and First Superior
f the Sisters or Daughters of Charity in the United States of America:
ith Copious Extracts from Her Writings, and an Historical Sketch of the
isterhood from Its Foundation to the Time of Her Death (first edition,

1852). It is of interest that long quotations from the Rule of St. Vincent de Paul, as modified in Baltimore with the approval of Bishop Carro
are included in the text, but there is no indication that they are quotations.

Joseph I. Dirvin's Mrs. Seton: Foundress of the American Sisters
of Charity (1962) was clearly written more for the general reader than
the scholar, but it is based on thorough research. Sources are found
at the end of the book and are given according to the page number on
which the information was given—there are no footnotes, as such. Dirvi
treats the question of the later union with France very directly and
clearly states that there is no way to determine what Elizabeth Seton
would have done in 1850 concerning the union with the Daughters of Charity in France.

Annabelle M. Melville's Elizabeth Bayley Seton, 1774-1821 was
originally published in 1951. This is the most highly documented work
on the life of Elizabeth Seton. It is a valuable source for the early
history and the documentation can lead one to other sources of interest
in the development of the total community. As a guide to the interpretation of later events such as the union with France it gives so much
evidence without comment that one can easily read into it the interpretation that is already most familiar.

Sisters of Loretto

The Sisters of Loretto also have an extensive and well organized
archives at the motherhouse. Fires in the early history of the community, particularly the devastating fire at the motherhouse in 1858, grea
ly limit the primary sources prior to that time. An effort has been ma

in recent years to secure copies of original documents, such as letters
written by the sisters, that are located in other religious archives.
In addition to the archival sources, the principal secondary sources
were: Sister M. Matilda Barrett, S.L., Courage American: Mother Mary
Rhodes, Foundress of the Sisters of Loretto (1962); Sister M. Lilliana
Owens, S.L., Loretto on the Old Frontier, 1823-1864 (1965); and Augustin
C. Wand, S.J. and Sister M. Lilliana Owens, S.L., Documents: Nerinckx -
Kentucky - Loretto, 1804-1851, in Propaganda Fide, Rome (1972). This
latter work was particularly helpful since the related documents were
gathered together, translated and then printed. I found nothing in the
work to lead me to question the accuracy of the documents themselves;
I did not always agree with the editorial commentary.

Martin John Spalding's Sketches of the Life, Times, and Character of the Rt. Rev. Benedict Joseph Flaget, First Bishop of Louisville
(1852) was valuable since Spalding was a contemporary of the early members of the three religious communities founded in Kentucky between
1812 and 1822. There are factual errors, but the interpretation of one
who also played such an important role in the early days of the Catholic
Church in Kentucky is important. Webb's The Centenary of Catholicity in
Kentucky (1884) was a basic reference for the history of the Church in
Kentucky and because of Webb's careful research (see p. 285) it was more
reliable than Spalding's work for factual data.

Sisters of Charity of Nazareth

The Nazareth motherhouse archives are well organized; besides
the usual annals (those for the early years were written at a later date)
there are many letters. The originals of these letters as well as other

documents have been copied and placed in Duplicate Letter Books for ordinary research purposes. A card file has been made for each sister with all the known vital statistics and notations of the source of references to the individual sister in the various record groups in the archives. There is also a collection of newspaper clippings that has been kept from the earliest years.

The secondary sources include Martin J. Spalding's Life of Bishop Flaget and Webb's Centenary of Catholicity in Kentucky. Also consulted were: Anna Blanche McGill, The Sisters of Charity of Nazareth, Kentucky (1917); Sister Agnes Geraldine McGann, Sisters of Charity of Nazareth in the Apostolate: Education, Health Care, Social Services, 1812-1976 (1977), an excellent overview of the work of the sisters in chronological perspective; and Sister Columba Fox, The Life of the Right Reverend John Baptist Mary David (1761-1841), Bishop of Bardstown and Founder of the Sisters of Charity of Nazareth (1925).

Dominican Sisters - St. Catharine, Kentucky

The "Profession Book, 1822-1919" is the most complete original document. This book contains the "Brief History" written in 1846 and a copy of the rule and constitution as given to the sisters by Father Wilson, O.P. A fire at the motherhouse in 1904 consumed much of what otherwise might have been preserved, but even after this preservation of documents was not a priority until recent years and much was lost through lack of concern. In the first half of this century Sister Margaret Hamilton spent as much free time as was possible gathering documents and oral histories from the older sisters so that some of the most valuable sources in the archives today are a result of her work.

Among the secondary sources, in addition to Spalding's Life of

Bishop Flaget and Webb's Centenary of Catholicism in Kentucky, were:

Anna C. Minogue, Pages from a Hundred Years of Dominican History (1921),

for which Sister Margaret Hamilton did most of the research work; Sister

Monica Kiefer, O.P., Dominican Sisters, St. Mary of the Springs, a

History. Log Cabin Days - Kentucky, 1822-1830 (ca. 1972). The works of

Victor F. O'Daniel, O.P. were consulted but had a minimum of information

about the Dominican Sisters in Kentucky. In The Dominican Province of

St. Joseph: Historico-Biographical Studies O'Daniel refers the reader

to Minogue for information about the sisters.

Oblate Sisters of Providence

While the archives at the motherhouse have little in the way of

letters of the early members there are a few letters, the original rule

written by Father Joubert, S.S., and the French Diary he began and which

others continued into the 1840's. The first history was a manuscript his-

tory written by Sister Theresa Catherine Willigman toward the end of the

nineteenth century. She had been in the care of the sisters after the

death of her mother and had experienced with them the trying days in the

1840's after the death of Father Joubert. She served as Superior Gen-

eral from 1885 to 1897. In her introduction she wrote: "May its many

imperfections be overlooked, as the events are of the past, and memory

fails to recall accurately bygone days . . ." In spite of this warning,

the only clear mistake was a reference to Bishop Fenwick, rather than

Kenrick in Philadelphia. Where references can be checked with other

sources there is no discrepancy.

The most valuable secondary source concerning the apostolate of the sisters was the Special Report of the Commissioner of Education on

the Condition and Improvement of Public Schools in the District of

Columbia (1871) which is available at the National Archives.

Sisters of Our Lady of Mercy

The motherhouse archives have good records after the accession

of Bishop Reynolds in 1845. Most of what relates to the earlier periods,

as in the case of some of the other religious communities, was written

at a later date. Bishop England's statements were published in the

United States Catholic Miscellany so important information can be found

in its pages regarding the sisters and their work between 1830 and Bishop

England's death in 1842. This, the first of the American Catholic news-

papers, is available on microfilm. An additional source for Bishop

England's plan is to be found in "Letters from Right Rev. John England.

D.D. to the Honorable William Gaston, LL.D."

The most important secondary source was Sister M. Anne Francis

Campbell's dissertation, "Bishop England's Sisterhood, 1829-1929" (1968).

SOURCES CONSULTED

Archives

Archdiocese of Baltimore, Maryland

Archdiocese of Cincinnati, Ohio

Carmelite Monastery - Baltimore, Maryland

Daughters of Charity - St. Joseph's Provincial House (Central House)
    Emmitsburg, Maryland

Diocese of Charleston, South Carolina

Dominican Generalate - St. Catharine, Kentucky

Georgetown Visitation Convent, Washington, D.C.

Loretto Motherhouse, Loretto, Kentucky

Maryland Hall of Records, Annapolis, Maryland

National Archives, Washington, D.C.

Oblate Sisters of Providence, Baltimore, Maryland

Philadelphia City Archives, Philadelphia, Pennsylvania

Sisters of Charity - Mount Saint Joseph, Cincinnati, Ohio

Sisters of Charity of Nazareth, Kentucky

Sisters of Charity of Our Lady of Mercy, Charleston, South Carolina

University of Notre Dame, Notre Dame, Indiana

N.B. The archives of the archdiocese of Louisville, Kentucky "are practi-
    cally non-existent for [the] era" of this study (Rev. John Hanrahan,
    Chancellor, to the author; 2 November 1979).

Manuscript collections and files were also examined at:

Charleston Historical Society, Charleston, South Carolina

Charleston Room of the Charleston Public Library, Charleston, South Carolina

Georgetown Public Library, Peabody Room, Washington, D.C.

The Library Society of Charleston, Charleston, South Carolina

Library of the Maryland Historical Society.

Published Sources

Baltimore City Health Department: The First Thirty-Five Annual Reports, 1815-1849. Baltimore: 1953.

Bangart, William V., S.J. A History of the Society of Jesus. St. Louis: The Institute of Jesuit Sources, 1972.

Banner, Lois. "Religious Benevolence as Social Control: A Critique of an Interpretation." Journal of American History, Vol. 60 (1973), pp. 23-41.

Barrett, Sister M. Matilda, S.L. Courage, American: Mother Mary Rhodes, Foundress of the Sisters of Loretto. Louisville, Ky.: Printed by Schuhmann Printing Co., 1962. (Pamphlet)

Bede, Brother, C. F. X. A Study of the Past and Present Applications of Educational Psychology in the Catholic Schools of the Diocese of Louisville. Master's Dissertation, University of Louisville, 1923. Revised, 1926. Baltimore: St. Mary's Industrial School Press, 1926.

Beecher, Lyman. Plea for the West. Cincinnati: Truman and Smith, 1835. (Mechanic's Institute).

Bernstein, Marcelle. The Nuns. Philadelphia and New York: J. B. Lippincott Company, 1976.

Billington, Ray Allen. The Protestant Crusade, 1800-1860: A Study of the Origins of American Nativism. New York: The Macmillan Company, 1938.

Blandin, Mrs. I. M. E. History of Higher Education of Women in the South Prior to 1860. New York and Washington: The Neale Publishing Company, 1909.

Bogue, Donald J. The Population of the United States. New York: The Free Press of Glencoe: A Division of the Crowell-Collier Publishing Company, 1959.

Brewster, George. Lectures on Education. Columbus: Printed for the Author by John Bailhache, 1833.

Bridenbaugh, Carl. Myths and Realities: Societies of the Colonial South. Baton Rouge: Louisiana State University Press, 1952.

Burns, James A. The Catholic School System in the United States: Its Principles, Origins, and Establishment. New York: Benziger Brothers, 1908.

_____, Bernard J. Kohlbrenner and John B. Peterson. A History of Catholic Education in the United States. New York: Benziger Brothers, 1937.

Cassidy, Sister M. Stephana [from verbal accounts of Sister Rose Tenley]. The Foundation of the Pioneer Sisters of Saint Dominic in the United States, 1822. Privately Published. [Dominican Sisters of St. Catharine, Kentucky], 1924.

City of Charleston, South Carolina. Year Book - 1883. Charleston: The News and Courier Book Presses.

Clements, J. W. S. Origins of Clements-Spalding and Allied Families of Maryland and Kentucky. Louisville: Published by the author, 1928.

Code, Rev. Dr. Joseph B. Bishop John Hughes and the Sisters of Charity. Reprint of the Miscellanea Historica in honoran Leonis Van Der Essen. Universitatis Catholicae in Oppido Lovaniensi. Iam Annos XXXV Professoris. n.d. [ca. 1946 - one hundred years after the New York-Emmitsburg separation.]

Cott, Nancy F. The Bonds of Womanhood: "Woman's Sphere" in New England, 1780-1835. New Haven: Yale University Press, 1977.

Currier, Charles Warren. Carmel in America: A Centennial History of the Discalced Carmelites in the United States. Baltimore: John Murphy & Co., 1890.

[Daughters of Charity]. 1809-1959. Emmitsburg, Maryland: Saint Joseph's Central House, 31 July 1959.

_____. Mother Augustine Decount and Mother Xavier Clark. Emmitsburg, Maryland: Saint Joseph's, 1938.

_____. Mother Etienne Hall. Emmitsburg, Maryland: Saint Joseph's, 1939.

_____. Mother Rose White. Emmitsburg, Maryland: Saint Joseph's, 1936.

Deusner, Charles E. "The Know-Nothing Riots in Louisville." The Register of the Kentucky Historical Society, LXI (April 1963), pp. 122-147.

Dirvin, Joseph I., C.M. Mrs. Seton: Foundress of the American Sisters of Charity. New York: Farrar, Straus and Cudahy, 1962.

"Documents." Catholic Historical Review I (October 1915): 310-319.

Dolan, Jay P. The Immigrant Church: New York's Irish and German Catholics, 1815-1865. Baltimore: The Johns Hopkins University Press, 1975.

Donnelly, Sr. Mary Louise. Maryland Elder Family and Kin: William Elder 1707-1775; Emmitsburg, Maryland Pioneer. Privately published by Sr. Mary Louise Donnelly, 1975.

302

Dorchester, Daniel. The Problem of Religious Progress. New York:
    Phillips & Hunt, 1881.

Ellis, John Tracy. American Catholicism, second edition, revised.
    The Chicago History of American Civilization, Daniel J.
    Boorstin, editor. Chicago: The University of Chicago Press, 1969.

_____, ed. Documents of American Catholic History. Milwaukee: The
    Bruce Publishing Company, 1962.

Ernst, Robert. Immigrant Life in New York City, 1825-1863. New York:
    King's Crown Press, Columbia University, 1949.

Feldberg, Michael. The Philadelphia Riots of 1844: A Study of Ethnic
    Conflict. Contributions to American History, Number 43.
    Westport, Connecticut: Greenwood Press, 1975.

Fox, Sister Columba. The Life of the Right Reverend John Baptist Mary
    David (1761-1841), Bishop of Bardstown and Founder of the Sisters
    of Charity of Nazareth. New York: The United States Catholic
    Historical Society, 1925. United States Catholic Historical
    Society Monograph Series IX.

Garraghan, Gilbert J., S.J. The Jesuits of the Middle United States,
    Vol. II. New York: America Press, 1938.

George, Carol V. R., ed. "Remember the Ladies": New Perspectives on
    Women in American History. Essays in Honor of Nelson Manfred
    Blake. Syracuse, New York: Syracuse University Press, 1975.

The Georgetown Directory for the Year 1830: To Which Is Appended a Short
    Description of the Churches, Public Institutions, etc. The
    Original Charter of Georgetown and Extracts from Laws Relating
    to the Chesapeake and Ohio Canal Company. Georgetown, D.C.:
    Printed by Benjamin Homans, 1830.

Good, H. G. A History of American Education, second edition. New York:
    The Macmillan Company, 1962.

Green, Constance McLaughlin. The Secret City: A History of Race Rela-
    tions in the Nation's Capital. Princeton, New Jersey: Princeton
    University Press, 1967.

_____. Washington: Village and Capital, 1800-1878. Princeton, New
    Jersey: Princeton University Press, 1962.

Griffin, Clifford S. "Religious Benevolence as Social Control, 1815-
    1860." Mississippi Valley Historical Review, Vol. 44 (1957):
    423-444.

Guilday, Peter. The Catholic Church in Virginia (1815-1822). New York:
    The United States Catholic Historical Society, 1924. United
    States Catholic Historical Society Monograph Series VIII.

_____. A History of the Councils of Baltimore (1791-1884). New York: The Macmillan Company, 1932.

_____. Life and Times of John England, First Bishop of Charleston (1786-1842), 2 volumes. New York: The America Press, 1927.

_____. The National Pastorals of the American Hierarchy, 1792-1919. Washington, D.C.: National Catholic Welfare Council, 1923.

Hamilton, Mary Jane. "A History of Married Women's Rights," In Women & Men: The Consequences of Power. A Collection of Essays, pp. 168-183. Edited by Dana V. Hiller & Robin Ann Sheets. Cincinnati: Office of Women's Studies, University of Cincinnati, 1977.

Handlin, Oscar. Boston's Immigrants, 1790-1865: A Study in Acculturation. Cambridge: Harvard University Press, 1941.

Hanley, Thomas O'Brien, S.J., ed. The John Carroll Papers, 3 volumes. Notre Dame: University of Notre Dame Press, 1976.

Harney, Martin R. S.J. The Jesuits in History: The Society of Jesus through Four Centuries. New York: The America Press, 1941.

Herbermann, Charles George. "The Sulpicians in the United States." Historical Records and Studies, IX:9-100. New York: The United States Catholic Historical Society, 1916.

"Historical Studies and Notes: Letters from Bishop Benedict Joseph Flaget to Bishop Joseph Rosati, St. Louis, Mo." Social Justice Review 62-63 (September 1969 through July-August 1970): 169-172; 206-208; 241-244; 278-280; 314-318; 419-422; 28-30; 61-63; 97-99; 136-138.

Howlett, Rev. W. J. Life of Rev. Charles Nerinckx, Pioneer Missionary of Kentucky and Founder of the Sisters of Loretto at the Foot of the Cross. Techny, Illinois: Mission Press, S.V.D., 1940, second edition. (First edition, 1915).

_____. "The Very Rev. Stephen Theodore Badin." Historical Records and Studies, IX:101-146. New York: The United States Catholic Historical Society, 1916.

Husslein, Joseph, S.J. Social Wellsprings, Volume II: Eighteen Encyclicals of Social Reconstruction by Pope Pius XI. Milwaukee: The Bruce Publishing Company, 1942.

Kenneally, Finbar, O.F.M. United States Documents in the Propaganda Fide Archives: A Calendar, seven volumes. Washington, D.C.: Academy of American Franciscan History, 1966-1977.

Kiefer, Sr. Monica, O.P. Dominican Sisters, St. Mary of the Springs, A History. Log Cabin Days - Kentucky, 1822-1830. Columbus, Ohio: Springs Press, n.d. (ca. 1972).

Knight, Edgar W., ed. A Documentary History of Education in the South before 1860, Vol. IV. "Private and Denominational Efforts." Chapel Hill: The University of North Carolina Press, 1953. [This ignores Roman Catholic efforts.]

Knights, Peter R. The Plain People of Boston, 1830-1860: A Study in City Growth. New York: Oxford University Press, 1971.

Lathrop, George Parson and Rose Hawthorne Lathrop. A Story of Courage: Annals of the Georgetown Convent of the Visitation of the Blessed Virgin Mary from the Manuscript Records. Boston: Houghton, Mifflin and Company, 1894.

Lannie, Vincent P. and Bernard C. Diethorn. "For the Honor and Glory of God: The Philadelphia Bible Riots of 1840 [1844]." History of Education Quarterly, Vol. VIII (Spring 1968):44-106.

Lannon, Maria M. Mother Mary Elizabeth Lange, Life of Love and Service. Black Catholic Series, No. 2. Washington, D.C.: The Josephite Pastoral Center, 1976. (pamphlet)

McAvoy, Thomas T., C.S.C. A History of the Catholic Church in the United States. Notre Dame and London: University of Notre Dame Press, 1969.

McCann, Sister Mary Agnes. The History of Mother Seton's Daughters: The Sisters of Charity of Cincinnati, Ohio, 1809-1917, Vol. II. New York: Longmans, Green and Co., 1917.

McElroy's Philadelphia Directory, for 1850: Containing the Names of the Inhabitants, Their Occupations, Places of Business, and Dwelling Houses; Also a List of the Streets, Lanes, Alleys, the City Offices, Public Institutions, Banks, &c., thirteenth edition. Philadelphia: Edward C. & John Biddle, No. 6 South Fifth Street, 1850.

McGann, Sr. Agnes Geraldine. Sisters of Charity of Nazareth in the Apostolate: Education, Health Care, Social Services, 1812-1976. Privately printed [1977].

McGill, Anna Blanche. The Sisters of Charity of Nazareth, Kentucky. New York: The Encyclopedia Press, 1917.

Maes, Camillus P. The Life of Rev. Charles Nerinckx: with a Chapter on the Early Missions of Kentucky; Copious Notes on the Progress of Catholicity in the United States of America, from 1800 to 1825; an Account of the Establishment of the Society of Jesus in Missouri; and an Historical Sketch of the Sisterhood of Loretto in Kentucky, Missouri, New Mexico, etc. Cincinnati: Robert Clarke & Co., 1880.

Mansfield, Edward D. American Education, Its Principles and Elements. Dedicated to the Teachers of the United States. New York: A. S. Barnes & Co. Cincinnati: H. W. Derby & Co., 1851.

305

Maria Alma, Sister, I.H.M. Standard Bearers: The Place of the Catholic
Sisterhoods in the Early History of Education and Schools within
the Present Territory of the United States, as Seen by Contrast
and Comparison with the Education Provided for by Federal and
State Legislation from Earliest Sources until 1850. New York:
P. J. Kennedy & Sons, 1928.

Martin, Wendy, ed. The American Sisterhood: Writings of the Feminist
Movement from Colonial Times to the Present. New York: Harper
& Row, Publishers, 1972.

Martineau, Harriet. Society in America, in two volumes. New York:
Saunder and Otley, Ann Street and Conduit Street, London, 1837.

Melville, Annabelle M. Elizabeth Bayley Seton, 1774-1821. St. Paul,
Minnesota: Carrillon Books, 1976. Originally published by
Charles Scribner's Sons, 1951.

Meriwether, Colyer. History of Higher Education in South Carolina with
a Sketch of the Free School System. Circular of Information No.
3, 1888. Contributions to American Educational History edited
by Herbert B. Adams, No. 4. Washington: Government Printing
Office, 1889.

Miller, Randal M. and Thomas D. Marzik, ed. Immigrants and Religion
in Urban America. Philadelphia: Temple University Press, 1977.

Minogue, Ann C. Pages from a Hundred Years of Dominican History. New
York & Cincinnati: Frederick Pustet & Co., ca. 1921.

Nerinckx, Charles]. Rules of the Society and School of Loretto, Ken-
tucky. London: Printed by Keating and Brown, Printers to the
R. Rev. the Vicars Apostolic of England, 38 Duke Street,
Grosvenor-Square, 1820.

Newman, Harry Wright. The Maryland Semmes and Kindred Families.
Baltimore: The Maryland Historical Society, 1956.

Niebuhr, H. Richard. The Social Sources of Denominationalism. New
York: World Publishing - A Meridian Book, 1957. First published
by Henry Holt and Company, Inc., 1929.

Norton, Arthur O., ed. The First State Normal Schools in America: The
Journals of Cyrus Peirce and Mary Swift. Cambridge: Harvard
University Press, 1926.

"Notes and Comments." The Catholic Historical Review VI (October 1920):
381-386.

O'Daniel, Victor Francis, O.P. (Sermon preached by). Centenary of the
Death of the Very Reverend Samuel Thomas Wilson, O.P., S.T.M.,
The First American Provincial. -At St. Rose's Convent, in
Kentucky, May 1924. St. Dominic's Press.

_____. The Dominican Province of Saint Joseph: Historico-Biographical Studies. New York: National Headquarters of the Holy Name Society 1942.

_____. The Father of the Church in Tennessee, or the Life, Times, and Character of the Right Reverend Richard Pius Miles, O.P., the First Bishop of Nashville. Washington, D.C.: The Dominicana, 1926.

_____. A Light of the Church in Kentucky, or the Life, Labors, and Character of the Very Rev. Samuel Thomas Wilson, O.P., S.T.M., Pioneer Educator and the First Provincial of a Religious Order in the United States. Washington, D.C.: The Dominicana, 1932.

_____. and James Reginald Coffey, O.P. The First Two Dominican Priories in the United States. Saint Rose's Priory, near Springfield, Kentucky: Saint Joseph's Priory, near Somerset, Ohio. New York: National Headquarters of the Holy Name Society, 1947.

Owens, Sister M. Lilliana, S.L. Loretto on the Old Frontier, 1823-1864. Nerinx, Kentucky: Loretto Motherhouse. 1965.

Parente, Abbe. Life of Saint Angela Merici of Brescia, Foundress of the Order of Saint Ursula. With an Account of the Order in Ireland, Canada and the United States by John Gilmary Shea. New York: P. J. Kennedy & Sons, n.d.

Potter, J. "The Growth of Population in America." In Population in History: Essays in Historical Demography, pp. 631-688. Edited by D. V. Glass and D. E. C. Eversley. Chicago: Aldine Publishing Company, 1965.

Powell, Milton, ed. The Voluntary Church: American Religious Life (1740-1865) Seen through the Eyes of European Visitors. New York: The Macmillan Company, 1967.

Ray, Sister Mary Augustine, B.V.M. American Opinion of Roman Catholicism in the Eighteenth Century. New York: Columbia University Press, 1936.

Records of the American Catholic Historical Society of Philadelphia. "Correspondence between the Sees of Quebec and Baltimore, 1788-1847." Vol. XVIII (1917): 155-189; 282-305; 434-467.

"Diary of Archbishop Maréchal. 1818-1825." Vol. XI (1900):417-454

"Letters of Rt. Rev. John England, D.D. to the Honorable William Gaston, LL.D." Vol. XIX (1908): 147ff.

"The Remarkable Conversion of the Barber Family." Reprinted from the "Catholic Transcript." The Catholic Mind, 22 May 1924, pp. 89-93.

Rosenberg, Charles E. The Cholera Years: The United States in 1832, 1849, and 1866. Chicago: The University of Chicago Press, 1962.

Rothstein, William G. American Physicians in the Nineteenth Century, from Sects to Science. Baltimore: The Johns Hopkins University Press, 1972.

Rothsteiner, Rev. Joh. "Father Charles Nerinckx and His Relations to the Diocese of St. Louis." St. Louis Catholic Historical Review I (April 1919): 157-175.

Royall, Mrs. Anne]. Sketches of History, Life, and Manners, in the United States. By a Traveller. New Haven: Printed for the Author, 1826.

Rutherford, William Kenneth and Anna Clay (Zimmerman). Genealogical History of Our Ancestors. [Privately published by W. K. Rutherford], 1970.

Ryan, Mary P. Womanhood in America, from Colonial Times to the Present, second edition. New York/London: New Viewpoints, A Division of Franklin Watts, 1979. (First edition, 1975).

Schroeder, Sister Mary Carol, O.S.F. The Catholic Church in the Diocese of Vincennes, 1847-1877. Washington, D.C.: The Catholic University Press, 1946.

Semmes, Raphael Thomas. The Semmes and Allied Families. Baltimore: The Sun Book and Job Printing Office, Inc., 1918.

Sklar, Kathryn Kish, Catharine Beecher: A Study in American Domesticity. New Haven and London: Yale University Press, 1973.

Spalding, M. J., D.D. Sketches of the Life, Times, and Character of the Rt. Rev. Benedict Joseph Flaget, First Bishop of Louisville. Louisville, Kentucky: Webb & Levering, 1852.

Stritch, Rev. Alfred G. "Political Nativism in Cincinnati, 1830-1860." Records of the American Catholic Historical Society 48 (September 1937): 227-278.

Sullivan, Eleanore C. Georgetown Visitation Since 1799. Privately printed, 1975.

Sullivan, Sister Mary Christina, S.U.C.S. "Some Non-Permanent Foundations of Religious Orders and Congregations of Women in the United States (1739-1850)." Historical Records and Studies, Vol. XXXI. New York: The United States Catholic Historical Society, 1940, pp. 7-118.

Thompson, Warren S. and P. K. Whelpton. Population Trends in the United States. New York: McGraw-Hill Book Company, Inc., 1933.

U.S. Department of Commerce, Bureau of the Census. Historical Statistics of the United States: Colonial Times to 1970, Part I. Bicentennial edition. 93rd Congress, 1st Session; House Document No. 93-178. (Part 1), 1975.

U.S. Department of Education. Special Report of the Commissioner of Education on the Condition and Improvement of Public Schools in the District of Columbia. Submitted to the Senate, June, 1868, and to the House with Additions, June 13, 1870. Washington: Government Printing Office, 1871.

[U.S. Government] Charles Moore, compiler. Joint Select Committee to Investigate the Charities and Reformatory Institutions in the District of Columbia. 21 July 1897 - Presented by Mr. Faulkner, from the Joint Select Committee . . . , and ordered to be printed. Part I: Hearings; Statements; Reports from Cities; Suggestions for a Board of Charities. Washington: Government Printing Office, 1897.

[U.S. Government] Serial 587. Executive Documents Printed by Order of the Senate of the United States during the Second Session of the Thirty-First Congress, begun and held at the City of Washington, December 2, 1850, in 5 volumes. Vol. I containing Document No. 1. Washington: Printed at the Union Office, 1851, pp. 66-71.

U.S. Office of Education. Reports of the Commissioner of Education, 1870 to 1875. Washington: Government Printing Office, 1871-1876.

[Ursuline Sisters]. Half a Century's Records of the Springfield Ursulines. Springfield, Illinois: The H. W. Rokker Co., 1909.

Wach, Joachim. Sociology of Religion. Chicago: The University of Chicago Press, Phoenix Books, eleventh impression, 1967. (University of Chicago, 1944; first Phoenix edition, 1962).

Wachter, Kenneth W., Eugene A. Hammel, and Peter Laslett with the participation of Robert Laslett and Hervé LeBras. Statistical Studies of Historical Social Structure. New York: Harcourt Brace Jovanovich, Publishers, Academic Press, 1978.

Wade, Richard C. The Urban Frontier: Pioneer Life in Early Pittsburgh, Cincinnati, Lexington, Louisville, and St. Louis. Chicago: The University of Chicago Press, 1959.

Wand, Augustin C., S.J. and Sister M. Lilliana Owens, S.L. Documents: Nerinckx - Kentucky - Loretto, 1804-1851, in Propaganda Fide, Rome. Nerinx, Kentucky: Loretto Literary and Benevolent Institution, 1972.

Ward, David. Cities and Immigrants. New York: Oxford University Press, 1971.

309

Warner, Sam Bass, Jr. The Private City: Philadelphia in Three Periods
of Its Growth. Philadelphia: University of Pennsylvania Press,
1968.

Webb, Ben. J. The Centenary of Catholicity in Kentucky. Louisville:
Charles A. Rogers, 1884.

White, Charles I., D.D. Life of Mrs. Eliza A. Seton, Foundress and
First Superior of the Sisters or Daughters of Charity in the
United States of America; with Copious Extracts from Her Writings,
and an Historical Sketch of the Sisterhood from Its Foundation
to the time of Her Death, tenth edition. New York: P. J. Kenedy,
1901. (First edition, 1852).

Yeakel, Sister Mary Agnes. The Nineteenth Century Educational Contribution of the Sisters of Charity of Saint Vincent de Paul in
Virginia. Baltimore: The Johns Hopkins Press, 1939.

Young, James Sterling. The Washington Community, 1800-1828. New York:
Harcourt, Brace & World, Inc., 1966. A Harbinger Book.

Microfilm Reproductions

The American Catholic Directories, 1817-1879; a microfilm edition.
Washington, D.C.: Catholic University of America Press, n.d.

1817. The Laity's directory to the Church service, for the
year of our Lord, 1817. . . . with an Almanac. . . .
New York, published and sold by M. Field, 1817. Also
entitled: The Catholic laity's directory.

1822. The Laity's directory to the Church service, for the
year of our Lord, M, DCCC, XXII. . . . Revised and
corrected by the Rev. John Power, of St. Peter's
church. New York: William H. Creagh, 1822.

1833-1837. The United States Catholic almanac; or, Laity's
directory. . . . Baltimore: James Myres. The cover-
title of the 1833 volume is: The Catholic almanac; or,
Laity's directory. Late in 1833 an additional publication was issued: The Catholic calender and Laity's
directory. . . . Baltimore: Fielding Lucas, 1833.

1834. The Catholic calendar and laity's directory. Baltimore:
Fielding Lucas, 1833.

1838-1845. The Metropolitan Catholic almanac, and Laity's
directory. Baltimore: Fielding Lucas, Jr.

1846-1849. The Catholic Almanac. Baltimore: Fielding Lucas, Jr.
[Cover-title for 1846 and 1848 reads Metropolitan
Catholic Almanac].

1850-1857. The Metropolitan Catholic Almanac, and Laity's
directory. Baltimore: Fielding Lucas, Jr.

Archives of the Propaganda Fide. University of Notre Dame Archives.

National Intelligencer. Washington, D.C., 1824-1828. Library of Congress
microfilm.

The Truth Teller, New York. 1825-1830. Washington, D.C.: Catholic University of America, Photoduplication Service, The Library.

United States Catholic Miscellany. Charleston, South Carolina, 5 June
1822 - 13 December 1860. (none published January - December
1823 and January - June 1826). Washington, D.C.: Catholic
University of America, Photoduplication Service, The Library.

Unpublished Sources

Armiger, Sister Bernadette. "The History of the Hospital Work of the
Daughters of Charity of St. Vincent de Paul in the Eastern
Province of the United States, 1823-1860." Master's thesis,
The Catholic University of America, Washington, D.C., 1947.

Campbell, Sister M. Anne Francis. "Bishop England's Sisterhood, 1829-
1929." Ph.D. dissertation, St. Louis University, 1968.

Deye, Anthony H. "Archbishop John Baptist Purcell of Cincinnati: Pre-
Civil War Years." Ph.D. dissertation, University of Notre Dame, 19.

Ewens, Mary, O.P. "The Role of the Nun in Nineteenth-Century America:
Variations on an International Theme." Ph.D. dissertation,
University of Minnesota, 1971.

Flynn, Sister Mary Grace, V.H.M. "A Bibliography of the Works in English
by and about the Visitation Order, 1799-1963." Master's thesis,
The Catholic Univesity of America, Washington, D.C., 1964.

Labbé, Dolores Egger. "Women in Early Nineteenth-Century Louisiana."
Ph.D. dissertation, University of Delaware, 1975.

Lacey, Margaret Ethel. "Joseph Emerson as an Educator: A Study in the
Education of Women in the United States during the Early Part
of the Nineteenth Century." Ph.D. dissertation, New York
University, 1916.

Neal, Sister Marie Augusta. "Sisters' Survey, 1967."

Porterfield, E. Amanda. "Maidens, Missionaries, and Mothers: American
Women as Subjects and Objects of Religiousness." Ph.D. dissertation, Stanford University, 1975.

Price, Marian Gail. "A Study of Some of the Effects of Nineteenth Century Revivalism on the Status and Accomplishments of Women of the Evangelical Covenant Church of America." Ph.D. dissertation, Boston University, 1977.

U.S. Congress. Committee on the District of Columbia. "Petition of the Sisters of the Visitation of Georgetown, D.C. Praying that an Act of Incorporation May Be Passed in Their Favor, April 8, 1828." 20th Cong., 1st sess., 1828. (Georgetown Public Library, Peabody Room).

Verstynen, Sister M. Sariti, trans. (1962). Nagelaten Brief van den Weleerw. Heer Carolus Nerinckx in leven Missionaris in Kentucky aan zyne Bloedverwanten en Vrienden in Nederland. Te's Graven-hage Ter Drukkery van geb.S Langen huzzen Achter de Groote Kerk, no 23, 1825. The translation was made from the New York Public Library copy. Typescript.

ABBREVIATIONS USED IN THIS DISSERTATION

Archives of -

Archdiocese of Baltimore	AAB
Archdiocese of Cincinnati	AAC
Carmelite Monastery - Baltimore	ACM-B
Daughters of Charity - St. Joseph's Provincial House (Central House) Emmitsburg, Maryland	ASJCH
Diocese of Charleston (South Carolina)	ADC
Dominican Generalate - St. Catharine (Ky.)	AOPStC
Georgetown Visitation Convent (Washington, D.C.)	AGVC
Archives Sisters of Loretto	ASL
Maryland Hall of Records (Annapolis)	MHR
Oblate Sisters of Providence (Baltimore)	AOSP
Sisters of Charity - Mount Saint Joseph (Cincinnati, Ohio)	ASCMSJ
Sisters of Charity of Nazareth (Ky.)	ASCN
Sisters of Charity of Our Lady of Mercy (Charleston, S. Carolina)	ASCLM
University of Notre Dame	UNDA

From the holdings of the archives of the
   Sisters of Charity of Nazareth

Duplicate Letter Book	DLB
Original Letter Book	OLB
Catholic Historical Review	CHR
United States Catholic Miscellany	USCM

312

The Heritage of
American Catholicisim

1. EDWARD R. KANTOWICZ, EDITOR
   MODERN AMERICAN CATHOLICISM, 1900-1965:
   SELECTED HISTORICAL ESSAYS
   New York 1988

2. DOLORES LIPTAK, R.S.M., EDITOR
   A CHURCH OF MANY CULTURES:
   SELECTED HISTORICAL ESSAYS ON ETHNIC AMERICAN CATHOLICISIM
   New York 1988

3. TIMOTHY J. MEAGHER, EDITOR
   URBAN AMERICAN CATHOLICISM:
   THE CULTURE AND IDENTITY OF THE AMERICAN CATHOLIC PEOPLE
   New York 1988

4. BRIAN MITCHELL, EDITOR
   BUILDING THE AMERICAN CATHOLIC CITY:
   PARISHES AND INSTITUTIONS
   New York 1988

5. MICHAEL J. PERKO, S.J., EDITOR
   ENLIGHTENING THE NEXT GENERATION:
   CATHOLICS AND THEIR SCHOOLS, 1830-1980
   New York 1988

6. WILLIAM PORTIER, EDITOR
   THE ENCULTURATION OF AMERICAN CATHOLICISM, 1820-1900:
   SELECTED HISTORICAL ESSAYS
   New York 1988